Youth, Emerging Adults, Faith, and Giving

Special Issue Editor
Patricia Snell Herzog

MDPI • Basel • Beijing • Wuhan • Barcelona • Belgrade

MDPI

Special Issue Editor
Patricia Snell Herzog
University of Arkansas
USA

Editorial Office
MDPI
St. Alban-Anlage 66
Basel, Switzerland

This edition is a reprint of the Special Issue published online in the open access journal *Religions* (ISSN 2077-1444) from 2015–2017 (available at: http://www.mdpi.com/journal/religions/special issues/religions-youth).

For citation purposes, cite each article independently as indicated on the article page online and as indicated below:

Lastname, F.M.; Lastname, F.M. Article title. *Journal Name* **Year**, *Article number*, page range.

First Editon 2018

Cover photo courtesy of Patricia Snell Herzog.

ISBN 978-3-03842-478-9 (Pbk)
ISBN 978-3-03842-479-6 (PDF)

Table of Contents

About the Special Issue Editor

Patricia Snell Herzog, PhD is Assistant Professor of Sociology and Co-Director of the Center for Social Research at the University of Arkansas. Prior to this, Herzog was a Postdoctoral Fellow with Rice University Kinder Institute for Urban Research and before that was Assistant Director of the Center for the Study of Religion and Society at the University of Notre Dame, where she also completed her doctoral degree in sociology. Herzog's interests include social scientific investigations of youth and emerging adults, charitable giving, and religiosity, especially with attention to how social inequalities permeate, shape, and are shaped by organizational participation. With a commitment to outreach, Herzog has delivered numerous research-related talks to a variety of organizational audiences, and her research has received media attention in the New York Times, CNBC, ABC News, Seattle Times, The Atlantic, The Foundation Review, Philanthropy News Digest, The Chronicle of Philanthropy, The Nonprofit Times, and NPR.

Preface to "Youth, Emerging Adults, Faith, and Giving"

The impetus for this volume began years ago, when I was Assistant Director of the Center for the Study of Religion and Society (CSRS) at the University of Notre Dame. I had the opportunity to work with Christian Smith, Director of the CSRS, on a number of research projects related to youth and religion. This included the National Study of Youth and Religion (NSYR) and the Northern Indiana Congregations Study (NICS). It was then, more than a decade ago now, that I began to gain a greater awareness regarding the changing contexts of youth and emerging adults, especially as related to faith and giving.

In the years since then, I have been fortunate to work with hundreds of emerging adults who have helped to further inform my thinking on this topic. This book is dedicated to these outstanding students, truly as they are my greatest teachers. Anyone who spends enough time listening to young people should know just how tremendously they defy the stereotypes about youth, especially the many negative labels about the millennial generation.

Of all these students, who I have learned from in countless ways, I owe some of the greatest change in my thinking about the changing contexts of youth to Stephanie Collier. We were discussing the changes in technology with new media usage among youth, specifically responding to the works of Sherry Turkle and Susan Pinker on the losses resulting from shifting (at least some of) face-to-face contact online. I mentioned that many of my colleagues reference the loss to text-based communication, with younger students increasingly communicating with professors in a series of tweet-like statements, rather than elaborated essay paragraphs. Collier looks at me with wisdom in her eyes and says, "But perhaps those are not losses as much as they are changes. Maybe youth are learning to communicate in new mediums. If a 'picture says a thousand words,' then maybe youth can communicate deeper meaning visually and do not need as many words to explain."

While this volume is not specifically about changing technology or new media, the tone of that comment informs the special issue that lead to this volume. Perhaps we, as scholars studying religion, need to seek new ways of understanding social change. Along with a story of decline in various forms of institutional religiosity and diminishing forms of charitable giving and civic engagement is a possibility that the millennial generation ushers in changes that challenge are pre-conceived notions for how to study these topics. The contributors to this volume offer new, reinvigorated, re-theorized, and also traditional ways of understanding the faith and giving of youth and emerging adults.

I am also deeply indebted to David King, Director of the Lake Institute for Faith and Giving in the Lilly Family School of Philanthropy at IUPUI, for hosting an emerging scholar event that prompted my rekindling the idea of editing a volume on this topic. Also key at that event were Hilary Davidson, Jared Peifer, and Brandon Vaidyanathan, who have always shared, honored, and entertained my fascination with the changing contexts of youth and emerging adults. Moreover, the 22 scholars who contributed to this volume have breathed into life the vision for this volume. Their scholarship provides multiple, and also overlapping, ways forward in studying youth, emerging adults, faith, and giving. Though the primary audience for these works is scholars, we also aim to inform practitioners, pastors, youth ministers, and parents about how to better understand the young people they serve.

Patricia Snell Herzog
Special Issue Editor

religions

MDPI

Editorial

Youth and Emerging Adults: The Changing Contexts of Faith and Giving

Patricia Snell Herzog

Department of Sociology & Criminal Justice, University of Arkansas, 218 Old Main Building, Fayetteville, AR 72701, USA; herzog@uark.edu

Received: 28 June 2017; Accepted: 5 July 2017; Published: 7 July 2017

1. Introduction

This is a book about young people—youth and emerging adults. The contributors in this volume investigate the religious and spiritual lives of young people, especially as they relate to inclinations to do good for others. People are increasingly interested in, concerned about, and excited for the generational changes occurring to faith and giving, as young people become adults. Emerging adulthood and the millennial generation receive considerable scholarly and public press attention. Prior generations wonder: What will happen to the future of faith and giving, and how can we help the new generation emerge into adult leaders? Younger generations wonder: How can we reshape the future of faith and giving, and how can existing religious and civic organizations respond to younger generations?

This edited volume is the result of a special issue that invited social scientific insights on responses to these questions. The background for this volume, summarized below, is the evolving life course developmental processes, as well as the culmination of numerous social and cultural changes in recent decades and their implications for socialization of religiosity, spirituality, and generosity. The included chapters focus on the faith and giving of youth and emerging adults, in the United States and internationally. The emphasis is on research that contributes breadth to social scientific understandings of religion, charitable giving, volunteering, generosity, youth, and emerging adults. We are especially interested in trends related to participation in religious and civic organizations, including changing cultural structures, beliefs, and orientations to faith and giving in less formal or non-organizational contexts.

2. Changing Trends

Scholars identify certain adulthood transitions as critical moments in the life course. The series of events when emerging adults negotiate their own experiences with those instilled by their upbringing begin to firmly set their adulthood patterns (e.g., (Tanner 2006)). For individuals, this emerging adulthood life stage is characterized by exuberant hope and optimism for personal futures (e.g., (Arnett 2015)). However, a number of troubling social trends have developed in recent decades. Trends for the past 50 years indicate significant growth in relative income for those with the highest incomes, compared to stagnation across time for those with lowest incomes (Russell Sage Foundation 2012). Income earnings significantly associate with educational attainment (NCES 2015) and educational opportunities have become increasingly associated with family income levels, even net of standardized test scores (Putnam 2015). Particularly vulnerable are those who cannot invest in a college degree or the extended duration period often needed for successful adulthood launches (e.g., (Settersten and Ray 2010)).

Partially due to rising college enrollment, within-college differences are increasingly found to be important in predicting life course trajectories (Arum and Roksa 2014; Hamilton 2013; Hällsten 2010; Bozick 2007). At great risk are those ending with only some college, who can incur debt while pursuing college courses but without the degree to afford the interest, contributing to multiple financial strains and even bankruptcy (e.g., (Porter 2012, chp. 1, pp. 1–24, chp. 5, 85–100)). Moreover, emerging adults have varied cultural capital upon which to rely as they navigate their adult pathways. This leads to calling upon mixed, and sometimes overtly contradictory, advice as they attempt to make use of the large, bureaucratic, and impersonal settings of higher education and workplaces, and more generally rests futures too heavily on extant parent knowledge regarding complex issues (e.g., (Lareau 2011; 2015)).

Perceptions that adulthood transitions are merely a matter of individual choices and preferences, coupled with the hyper-self-focus of the life stage, can obscure the real social inequalities in adulthood pathways (e.g., (Osgood et al. 2005; Porter 2012; Radmacher and Azmitia 2013; Silva 2013)). Such misperception is enabled by rapid fluctuations in adulthood statuses during emerging adulthood complicating traditional social status measures. For example, month-to-month employment studies reveal that only 13 percent of university graduates had the same employer even one year later, and that 37 percent had a different employer at each of one, three, and five years after graduation (Krahn et al. 2014). Being among the rare minority with employment stability matters for future outcomes. One result of the extended transition to adulthood is the duration spent in low-wage labor positions (Carnevale et al. 2013). Even more troubling is the rising proportion of youth who are entirely disconnected from primary social institutions, namely school and work. This number rose by one-third in the previous ten years to nearly 15 percent in 2010 and is predictive of a range of problematic outcomes (Wight et al. 2010). Such vulnerabilities present challenges to sustaining participation in faith and giving.

Combined, these trends indicate the need for extra-familial organizations to contribute to the formation of emerging leaders in ways that span inequality and generational disconnects. However, Arum and Roksa (2010) find that 45 percent of college students in 24 higher education institutions demonstrate no significant improvement in their critical thinking, complex reasoning, or writing skills during first years of college. On average, it seems that the trends above, coupled with competing pressures of higher education, leave college graduates less prepared to launch successfully into leadership positions, or even to contribute successfully to organizations or be employed be them. In interviews with 30 different employers spanning 11 employment sectors, Konstam (2015) finds that managers experience a marked disconnect with their Millennial employees exemplified by this employer quote: "There is a tension between the values that many Millennials were taught when they were growing up and the harsh reality of what the 'real world' expects from them" (p. 163). Employers agree that Millennials lack needed skills and experience disillusionment with organizational realities.

Moreover, the extensive organizational participation of past generations supported previous transitions to adulthood roles by having non-familial adults to whom youth could turn for advice, support, and role modeling (Putnam 2000, 2015). As the pathway to adulthood has become less structured, regular civic and religious organizational participation has markedly declined. This decline in civic and religious participation has decreased the range of opportunities for youth to gain access to essential civic skills and moral values (Smith and Herzog 2009; Snell 2010).

For more information on these trends, see also Herzog and Price 2016; Glass et al. 2015; Lareau 2015; Sumner et al. 2015; Cherlin 2014; Cooper 2014; Dunkelman 2014; Pinker 2014; Sawhill 2014; Branje et al. 2014; Carbone and Cahn 2014; Barban and Billari 2012; Shulman and Connolly 2013; Buchmann 2012; Liefbroer and Elzinga 2012; Russell Sage Foundation 2012; Goldscheider 2012; Reynolds and Johnson 2011; Smith et al. 2011; Carlson and England 2011; Salmela-Aro et al. 2011; Massoglia and Uggen 2010; Mullen 2010; Peterson and Krivo 2010; Lareau and Conley 2010; Robette 2010; Macomber et al. 2009; Mayer 2009; Widmer and Ritschard 2009; Fuller 2008; Smith et al. 2008; Aassve et al. 2007; Billari et al. 2006; Hillmert 2005; Billari and Piccarreta 2005; Billari 2001; Arnett 2000; Gamoran 1992; Moen et al. 1992; Gove et al. 1989; Mare et al. 1984; Snell 2009.

3. Need for New Studies

Given these trends, more studies are needed that investigate social institutional leadership in guiding millennial youth in their transition to adulthood. For example, merging insights from the National Study of Youth & Religion (National Study of Youth & Religion 2013) and the Science of Generosity (e.g., (Herzog and Price 2016)) Figure 1 presents data on the religious and giving patterns of NSYR participants during their early emerging adulthood in Wave 4, collected in 2013. Figure 1 shows religious participation stability and change between Waves 3, when many participants were still living in their parents' homes, to Wave 4, when most were at least semi-independent from their parents' residences. There are three stable trends, of which stability in never attending (far left) is the highest, then stable sometimes attending (middle), and stable in regularly attending (far right). There is net decline in religious attendance during these waves, with the decline to never (left-middle) category being larger than the incline to regularly attending (right-middle). Thus, the trend is to further increases in religious "nones," or those who never attend religious services, which were already the largest group heading into emerging adulthood.

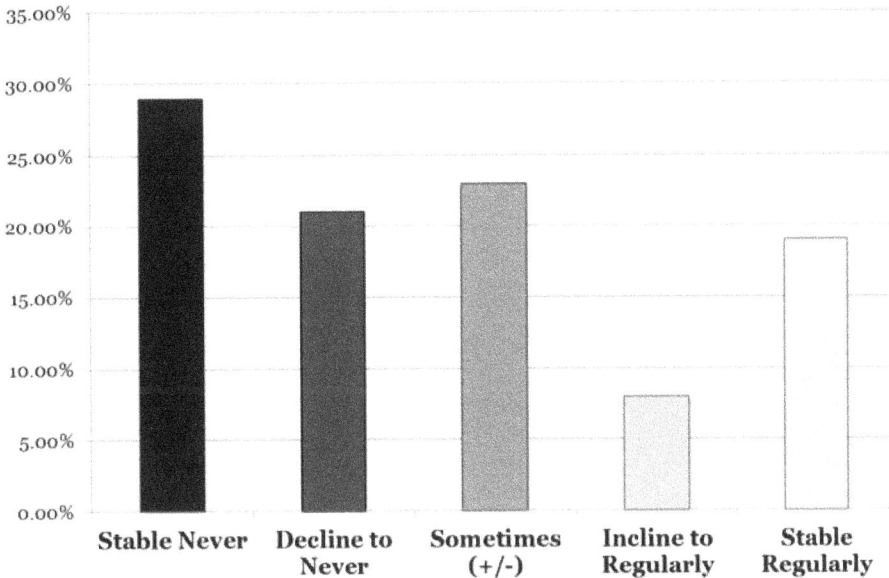

Source: National Study of Youth & Religion (NSYR) - Religious Participation Changes from Wave 3 (18 to 23 years old in 2008) to Wave 4 Changes (23 to 27 years old in 2013)

Figure 1. Religious Participation Over Time in Adulthood Transitions.

However, in assessing stability and change patterns in charitable giving during early emerging adulthood, the reverse trend is found. Figure 2 shows that 31 percent are a stable no for charitable giving between Waves 3 and 4, while 25 percent are a stable yes. However, only 10 percent decline from giving at Wave 3 to not giving at Wave 4. Conversely, 34 percent of emerging adults who were non-givers at Wave 3 became givers by Wave 4. Combining stability and change in religiosity and charitable giving, preliminary analyses show religious participation patterns related to giving stability. However, further investigation reveals a more complex, non-linear picture. Religious "nones" and sometimes attenders are about equal in those who decline from being a giver to not and in those who incline to becoming a giver across waves. Yet, inclines to becoming givers have a greater proportion of those who stably regularly attend or incline to becoming a regular attender across waves. Together, these results raise many questions, which we cannot yet well answer with existing data because previous studies reveal the need to inquire further about these issues.

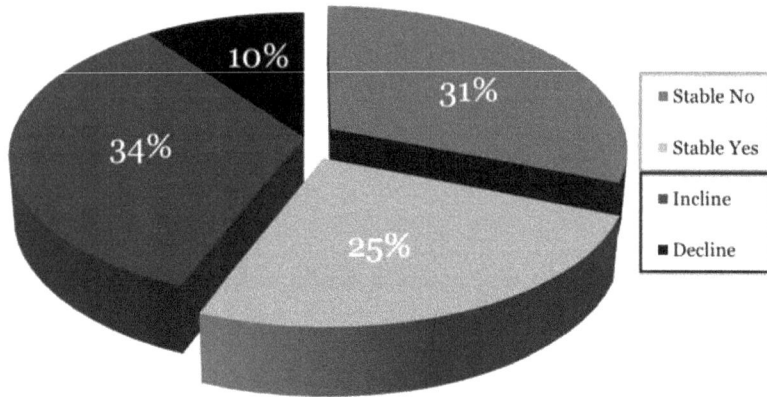

Source: National Study of Youth & Religion (NSYR) - Comparison of Status of Financial Giving to Charitable Causes from Wave 3 (18 to 23 years old in 2008) to Wave 4 Changes (23 to 27 years old in 2013)

Figure 2. Changes Over Time in Emerging Adult Financial Giving to Charitable Causes.

Examples of important questions raised by existing studies include: What propels emerging adults to start attending religious services or being charitably giving? What personal and social characteristics support emerging adults in maintaining their current religious and giving commitments through the fluctuations of early adulthood? What is lacking when emerging adults stop previous habits to attend religious services or charitably give once they begin adulthood and feasibly are more able to do both? How can people of faith and civic leaders help with successful adulthood launches? How are Millennials transforming faith and giving; are they involved in ways that are less formally organized and may be missed by typical measures?

My own research identifies work and school as two primary social settings that shape faith and giving, especially as emerging adults have multiple moves and become disconnected from other community organizations in the process. Thus, in asking and answering questions about faith and giving, it is necessary to also investigate emerging adult patterns with school and work. However, traditional academic investigation practices study each of these social institutions in disparate subfields and even different disciplines, causing a disconnect in knowledge gained from viewing emerging adults holistically, as full persons who experience life across an array of social settings simultaneously. Moreover, few studies have adapted data collection to accommodate the 21st century structure of these institutions. New studies are needed that build upon and connect prior knowledge on school, work, faith, and giving in investigating the changing reality of youth religiosity and spirituality.

4. Disjointed Contexts

Social and cultural trends have resulted in mostly de-institutionalized pathways to adulthood. Religious and civic organizations formerly provided locally based sites for cross class connections of youth to extra-familial supportive adults, but this is less the case today. Bifurcating inequalities coupled with declining organizational participation. Emerging adults transitioning to adulthood in more disorganized ways have divergent outcomes. Some have the cultural and social capital to navigate the complexities well. Others flounder and sometimes suffer in trying to establish stable adult lives. Formerly distinct organizations, such as churches, nonprofits, business, and universities increasingly share in common that the emerging leaders of the Millennial generation tend to distrust social institutions and operate more informally through networked communications. Religious and civic leaders, employers, and educators can feel disconnected from Millennials.

Yet Millennials are hyper-connected to each other, networked horizontally not laterally. Limited cross-generational contact causes disjoints in social institutional leadership preparation. Established leaders ask themselves: "Where are all the young people?" Emerging leaders *do not* ask themselves (enough): "Where is all the wisdom?" Established leaders of existing social institutions, such as pastors, often find themselves at a loss for how to impact the monumental social and cultural changes surrounding their organizations. Religious and civic organizations are sites for young people to have mentoring by extra-familial adults and to practice valuable organizational skills, such as generosity and commitment. But declining organizational participation by younger generations reduces access to these supports.

Formerly distinct organizations, such as churches, nonprofits, business, and universities now have in common changes ushered in by the Millennial generation, including changing values, different interaction styles, lower levels of organizational trust, and diverse desires from their participation. Religious leaders and Millennials can be disconnected from one another. Meanwhile, Millennials are hyper-connected with each other but often lack intergenerational mentoring and spiritual guidance. Limited cross-generational contact causes disconnects in religious leadership preparations. Established leaders often ask: "How can we engage more young people?" Often millennial emerging leaders ask: "What should I do next, and who can I turn to for guidance?" The disjuncture in these questions indicates that intergenerational connections and understanding can be mutually benefiting.

5. Book Aims and Commitments

A central aim of this book is to investigate with a deep commitment to and methodological support for *inclusivity*. This is a result of knowing that understandings of social life can be dramatically affected by paying attention only to our immediate contexts and reference groups, and of how skewed research results are if studying only those people who are most available for contact. Thus, the works included in this volume are intentionally varied in their geographical contexts, religious traditions, units of analysis, data collection techniques, and focus on religiosity, spirituality, charitable giving, or volunteerism.

A second aim of this book is to be receptive to *practice-based knowledge* and to conduct social science research in direct communication with young people, or those who have regular contact with young people. This is a result of a philosophy of science approach that is heavily influenced by community-based research, (Barnes et al. 2016) which is skeptical of knowledge constructed in academic "vacuums," and instead prioritizes a reverse of the traditional academic-practitioner hierarchy by recognizing community leaders as the experts and sees researchers as facilitators. Thus, many of the works in this volume give credence to the perspectives of laypeople, those who are not necessarily formally trained in religious theology, in order to learn from the perspectives of ordinary people and practitioners.

Third, this book aims to be *innovative* in its approach to studying the faith and giving of young people, in order to explore the possibility that social science is itself in need of reorganization. With humility and awareness that prior findings in social science may need updating, the call of this book is influenced by liberation theology approaches to pedagogy (Freire 2000). Thus, the contributors are receptive to *learning from research participants* their understanding of their activities. Rather than operating with approaches to studying social life that presume the most scientific knowledge is that which operates with a priori expectations that are tested to determine whether evidence positively supports hypotheses, the contributors to this volume were instead prepared to listen well to young people, interpret their data with theoretically informed approaches, and ready to learn from the empirical reality these studies present.

6. Chapter Summaries

The topics of the chapters include: religious nones, volunteerism, public religiosity, ecclesial worker marginalization, multi-faith workplaces, attitudes toward evangelization, charitable sporting events, religious giving, and youth socialization. The research locations, foci, and religious traditions are intentionally varied, resulting in data on Chinese and Japanese youth in the U.S.; black and white youth participation in the Chicago area; adolescent generosity in California; religious transmission of giving practices for youth in northern Indiana; religious youth leaders in the Detroit area; emerging adults in a college course preparing for religiously and culturally diverse workplaces in Northwestern Arkansas; emerging adults exploring religious identification in China; and the volunteerism of emerging adults in South Texas.

Interdisciplinary perspectives were welcomed. In addition to the core social science disciplines of sociology, psychology, political science, anthropology, and economics, insights were sought from human development, education, social work, history, human geography, management and business studies, law, international relations, philosophy, theology, and other relevant fields with applications to these social science questions. Empirical articles are the focus of the volume, and consideration was also given to important theoretical, historical, and philosophical submissions that contribute implications to social scientific inquiry on these topics.

In Chapter 1, sociologists Rhys H. Williams, Courtney Ann Irby, and R. Stephen Warner investigate the religious lives of young adults. They focus on youth organizational participation, and the ways this organizational involvement shapes religious identities and ideas about religious commitment. The black and white youth in the study are in the Chicago area, college-age, and Christians. Black youth tended to employ language of family, home, calling, and community, which highlighted the high degree of integration they had with the larger religious community. In distinction, the white youth in the study instead tended to chronicle their organizational biographies of involvement or disengagement, which highlighted their separation from the larger church community.

The study of Chapter 2 is based in China and also investigates attitudes about Christianity in college students. However, ethnologist Chao Wang finds that in the Chinese context, atheism is the mainstream belief system, and the youth describe their explorations with Christianity as a non-mainstream, non-family-engrained belief system. Though there has been a recent increase in the rate of exposure to Christian beliefs, the youth of this study do not evidence a complementary spike in religious affiliation. This highlights an inquisitive approach to religiosity that, as of yet, has not converted to deeper levels of belonging to a religious tradition.

In Chapter 3, scholars of education, Asian American studies, religious studies, and law, Russell Jeung, Brett Esaki, and Alice Liu investigate Chinese and Japanese American young adults by employing data from the Pew Research Center's 2012 Asian American Survey. Shifting away from a focus on belonging to religious denominations, this study investigates religious rituals and righteousness in ethical relations as "Asian-centric" forms of spiritual practices and orientations. This study complicates reports of rising religious nones by showing that these young adults, who are technically religious nones, engage in spiritual practices based on ancestor veneration and familial obligations, while also participating in religious festivals. Taken together, these first three chapters highlight (only some of) the complexities of religiosity and spirituality across diverse subcultures of youth and emerging adults.

The fourth chapter bridges to investigating institutional socialization of youth into religiosity and spirituality. the theologians and youth ministers, Michael McCallion, John Ligas, and George Seroka, study youth ministry practices within the Archdiocese of Detroit and find that this formal organization has a weak infrastructure for connecting with youth and young adults. Despite explicit claims to the opposite, the youth ministers report that they are not well-supported and feel marginalized in their ability to remain securely employed in the service of youth. Akin with broader organizational studies, this religious organization has a disconnect between its stated policy and actual practices, which serves to undermine concerted efforts to socialize youth and young adults into committed faith and frequent religious practices.

In Chapter 5, the focus on institutional socialization practices continues. Sociology and business lend insights to the research of Patricia Snell Herzog, DeAndre' T. Beadle, Daniel E. Harris, Tiffany E. Hood, and Sanjana Venugopal. They investigate college enrolled emerging adults who participated in a course aimed at preparing them to participate in multi-fait workplaces. Contrary to general cultural trends that find exposure to diverse religious orientations tends to undermine serious religious commitment, this study provides evidence that concerted effort, empathic connection with adherents of diverse faith traditions (including non-faith), mentoring that challenges cliché approaches to moral values, and personal reflection move emerging adults toward deeper levels of critical thinking that supports increases in cultural awareness without the byproduct of moral relativism.

Also employing a life course developmental approach, Chapter 6 investigates how less formalized social settings can contribute to religious and charitable outcomes. Psychologists Nathaniel A. Fernandez, Sarah A. Schnitker, and Benjamin J. Houltberg theorize a model for how participating in a charity marathon training may develop generosity among adolescents. Their model accounts for the complexity of motives by considering meaning-driven spiritual and moral motives, self-driven fitness motives, and relation-driven social motives. They theorize the mechanisms of change as: sanctification of activities, transcendent identity, positive emotions, cognitive dissonance, and group entitativity, which refers to the belongingness and cohesiveness of the group. An empirical model for investigating these effects on generosity is proposed.

In Chapter 7, consideration of the life course developmental effects of religious and spiritual socialization continues in a study of college-enrolled emerging adults in South Texas. Sociologists Reed T. DeAngelis, Gabriel A. Acevedo, and Xiaohe Xu investigate religious transmission across the life course as it relates to secular volunteerism while in college. While childhood religiosity relates to greater rates of volunteerism as an emerging adult, this relationship is mediated by whether emerging adults are religiously active. The implication is that childhood religious socialization, in the absence of continued religious participation, may be "necessary but not sufficient" in supporting giving time as an emerging adult.

The final empirical chapter, Chapter 8, continues an investigation of life course trends in religiosity and generosity. Sociologists Patricia Snell Herzog and Scott Mitchell investigate the intergenerational transmission of religious giving by studying how religiously involved parents, across different religious traditions, teach, model, or otherwise impart giving to their children. This study reveals that giving may have a "delayed onset," meaning it is patterned during childhood but may not be activated until later in the life course once adulthood is established.

The conclusion provides summaries of implications across these eight studies and interprets their relevance for practitioners who work with youth and emerging adults. The audiences for these implications are: college educators, religious and spiritual leaders, and parents. The conclusion also offers a section of remaining questions for studies investigating youth and emerging adults, within their changing religious, cultural, and social contexts.

Keywords: youth; emerging adults; faith; generosity; giving; volunteering; organizational participation

About the Journal: *Religions* is an international, open access, scholarly journal, publishing peer reviewed studies of religious thought and practice. It is available online to promote critical, hermeneutical, historical, and constructive conversations. *Religions* promotes interdisciplinary approaches to any of the world's religious and spiritual traditions. It publishes regular research papers, reviews, communications and reports on research projects. Religions aims to serve the interests of a wide range of thoughtful readers and academic scholars of religion, as well as theologians, philosophers, social scientists, anthropologists, psychologists, neuroscientists and others interested in multidisciplinary study of religions.

Acknowledgments: The author thanks Shauna Morimoto, Heather E. Price, Jared Peifer and Casey Harris for their input and discussions surrounding the ideas in this volume. Also instrumental was David King of the Lake Institute in the Lilly Family School of Philanthropy at Indiana University Purdue University Indianapolis, who generously funded a Lake Institute Emerging Scholar award that provided the time to craft the introduction to this volume. Special thanks as well to each of the contributors to the volume for their insights about youth and emerging adults.

Conflicts of Interest: The author declares no conflict of interest.

References

Aassve, Arnstein, Francesco C. Billari, and Raffaella Piccarreta. 2007. Strings of Adulthood: A Sequence Analysis of Young British Women's Work-Family Trajectories. *European Journal of Population / Revue Européenne de Démographie* 23: 369–88. [CrossRef]

Arnett, Jeffrey J. 2000. High Hopes in a Grim World: Emerging Adults' Views of their Futures. *Youth & Society* 31: 267–86.

Arnett, Jeffrey J. 2015. *Emerging Adulthood: The Winding Rose from the Late Teens through the Twenties*, 2nd ed. New York: Oxford University Press.

Arum, Richard, and Josipa Roksa. 2010. *Academically Adrift: Limited Learning on College Campuses*. Chicago: University of Chicago Press.

Arum, Richard, and Josipa Roksa. 2014. *Aspiring Adults Adrift: Tentative Transitions of College Graduates*. Chicago: University Of Chicago Press.

Barban, Nicola, and Francesco C. Billari. 2012. Classifying Life Course Trajectories: A Comparison of Latent Class and Sequence Analysis. *Journal of the Royal Statistical Society: Series C (Applied Statistics)* 61: 765–84. [CrossRef]

Barnes, Sandra L., Lauren Brinkley-Rubinstein, Bernadette Doykos, Nina C. Martin, and Allison McGuire, eds. 2016. *Academics in Action: A Model for Community-Engaged Research, Teaching, and Service*. New York: Fordham University Press.

Billari, Francesco C. 2001. The Analysis of Early Life Courses: Complex Descriptions of the Transition to Adulthood. *Journal of Population Research* 18: 119–42. [CrossRef]

Billari, Francesco C., and Raffaella Piccarreta. 2005. Analyzing Demographic Life Courses through Sequence Analysis. *Mathematical Population Studies* 12: 81–106. [CrossRef]

Billari, Francesco C., Johannes Fürnkranz, and Alexia Prskawetz. 2006. Timing, Sequencing, and Quantum of Life Course Events: A Machine Learning Approach. *European Journal of Population / Revue Européenne de Démographie* 22: 37–65. [CrossRef]

Bozick, Robert. 2007. Making It through the First Year of College: The Role of Students' Economic Resources, Employment, and Living Arrangements. *Sociology of Education* 80: 261–85. [CrossRef]

Branje, Susan, Lydia Laninga-Wijnen, Rongqin Yu, and Wim Meeus. 2014. Associations among School and Friendship Identity in Adolescence and Romantic Relationships and Work in Emerging Adulthood. *Emerging Adulthood* 2: 6–16. [CrossRef]

Buchmann, Marlis C. 2012. Review: Coming of Age in America: The Transition to Adulthood in the Twenty-First Century. Edited by Mary C. Waters, Patrick J. Carr, Maria J. Kefalas and Jennifer Holdaway. *American Journal of Sociology* 118: 517–19. [CrossRef]

Carbone, June, and Naomi Cahn. 2014. *Marriage Markets: How Inequality Is Remaking the American Family*. Oxford: Oxford University Press.

Carlson, Marcia, and Paula England, eds. 2011. *Social Class and Changing Families in an Unequal America*. Stanford: Stanford University Press.

Carnevale, Anthony P., Andrew R. Hanson, and Artem Gulish. 2013. *Failure to Launch: Structural Shift and the New Lost Generation*. Washington: Center on Education and the Workforce, Georgetown University, Available online: https://cew.georgetown.edu/cew-reports/failure-to-launch/ (accessed on 1 May 2017).

Cherlin, Andrew J. 2014. *Labor's Love Lost: The Rise and Fall of the Working-Class Family in America*. New York: Russell Sage Foundation Publications.

Cooper, Marianne. 2014. *Cut Adrift: Families in Insecure Times*. Berkeley: University of California Press.

Dunkelman, Marc J. 2014. *The Vanishing Neighbor: The Transformation of American Community*, 1st ed. New York: W. W. Norton & Company.

Freire, Paolo. 2000. *Pedagogy of the Oppressed*, 30th ed. London: Bloomsbury Academic.

Fuller, Sylvia. 2008. Job Mobility and Wage Trajectories for Men and Women in the United States. *American Sociological Review* 73: 158–83. [CrossRef]

Gamoran, Adam. 1992. Review: Getting Started: Transition to Adulthood in Great Britain. By Alan C. Kerckhoff. *American Journal of Sociology* 97: 1206–8. [CrossRef]

Glass, Jennifer L., April Sutton, and Scott T. Fitzgerald. 2015. Leaving the Faith How Religious Switching Changes Pathways to Adulthood among Conservative Protestant Youth. *Social Currents* 2: 126–43. [CrossRef] [PubMed]

Goldscheider, Frances K. 2012. The Accordion Family: Boomerang Kids, Anxious Parents, and the Private Toll of Global Competition by Katherine Newman. *American Journal of Sociology* 118: 821–22. [CrossRef]

Gove, Walter R., Suzanne T. Ortega, and Carolyn Briggs Style. 1989. The Maturational and Role Perspectives on Aging and Self through the Adult Years: An Empirical Evaluation. *American Journal of Sociology* 94: 1117–45. [CrossRef]

Hällsten, Martin. 2010. The Structure of Educational Decision Making and Consequences for Inequality: A Swedish Test Case. *American Journal of Sociology* 116: 806–54. [CrossRef]

Hamilton, Laura T. 2013. More Is More or More Is Less? Parental Financial Investments during College. *American Sociological Review* 78: 70–95. [CrossRef]

Herzog, Patricia Snell, and Heather E. Price. 2016. *American Generosity: Who Gives & Why*. New York: Oxford University Press.

Hillmert, Steffen. 2005. From Old to New Structures: A Long-Term Comparison of the Transition to Adulthood in West and East Germany. *Advances in Life Course Research* 9: 151–73. [CrossRef]

Konstam, Varda. 2015. Voices of Employers: Overlapping and Disparate Views. In *Emerging and Young Adulthood, Advancing Responsible Adolescent Development*. New York: Springer International Publishing, pp. 161–82.

Krahn, Harvey J., Andrea L. Howard, and Nancy L. Galambos. 2014. Exploring or Floundering? The Meaning of Employment and Educational Fluctuations in Emerging Adulthood. *Youth & Society* 47: 245–66.

Lareau, Annette. 2011. *Unequal Childhoods: Class, Race, and Family Life*, 2nd ed. Berkeley: University of California Press.

Lareau, Annette. 2015. Cultural Knowledge and Social Inequality. *American Sociological Review* 80: 1–27. [CrossRef]

Lareau, Annette, and Dalton Conley, eds. 2010. *Social Class: How Does It Work?* New York: Russell Sage Foundation Publications.

Liefbroer, Aart C., and Cees H. Elzinga. 2012. Intergenerational Transmission of Behavioural Patterns: How Similar Are Parents' and Children's Demographic Trajectories? *Advances in Life Course Research* 17: 1–10. [CrossRef]

Macomber, Jennifer Ehrle, Mike Pergamit, Tracy Vericker, Daniel Kuehn, Marla McDaniel, Erica H. Zielewski, Adam Kent, and Heidi Johnson. 2009. *Vulnerable Youth and the Transition to Adulthood*. Washington: The Urban Institute.

Mare, Robert D., Christopher Winship, and Warren N. Kubitschek. 1984. The Transition from Youth to Adult: Understanding the Age Pattern of Employment. *American Journal of Sociology* 90: 326–58. [CrossRef]

Massoglia, Michael, and Christopher Uggen. 2010. Settling down and Aging out: Toward an Interactionist Theory of Desistance and the Transition to Adulthood. *American Journal of Sociology* 116: 543–82. [CrossRef] [PubMed]

Mayer, Karl Ulrich. 2009. New Directions in Life Course Research. *Annual Review of Sociology* 35: 413–33. [CrossRef]

Moen, Phyllis, Donna Dempster-McClain, and Robin M. Williams Jr. 1992. Successful Aging: A Life-Course Perspective on Women's Multiple Roles and Health. *American Journal of Sociology* 97: 1612–38. [CrossRef]

Mullen, Ann L. 2010. *Degrees of Inequality*. Baltimore: Johns Hopkins University Press.

National Study of Youth & Religion. 2013. Available online: http://youthandreligion.nd.edu/ (accessed on 1 May 2017).

NCES. 2015. The Condition of Education 2015: Annual Earnings of Young Adults. U.S. Department of Education, National Center for Education Statistics. Available online: https://nces.ed.gov/fastfacts/ (accessed on 1 May 2017).

Osgood, D. Wayne, E. Michael Foster, Constance Flanagan, and Gretchen R. Ruth, eds. 2005. *On Your Own Without a Net: The Transition to Adulthood for Vulnerable Populations*. Chicago: University of Chicago Press.

Peterson, Ruth D., and Lauren J. Krivo. 2010. *Divergent Social Worlds: Neighborhood Crime and the Racial-Spatial Divide*. Baltimore: Russell Sage Foundation.

Pinker, Susan. 2014. *The Village Effect: How Face-to-Face Contact Can Make Us Healthier, Happier, and Smarter*. New York: Spiegel & Grau.

Porter, Katherine, ed. 2012. *Broke: How Debt Bankrupts the Middle Class*. Palo Alto: Stanford University Press.

Putnam, Robert D. 2000. *Bowling Alone: The Collapse and Revival of American Community*. New York: Simon & Schuster.

Putnam, Robert D. 2015. *Our Kids: The American Dream in Crisis*. New York: Simon & Schuster.

Radmacher, Kimberley, and Margarita Azmitia. 2013. Unmasking Class How Upwardly Mobile Poor and Working-Class Emerging Adults Negotiate an 'Invisible' Identity. *Emerging Adulthood* 1: 314–29. [CrossRef]

Reynolds, John R., and Monica Kirkpatrick Johnson. 2011. Change in the Stratification of Educational Expectations and Their Realization. *Social Forces* 90: 85–109. [CrossRef]

Robette, Nicolas. 2010. The Diversity of Pathways to Adulthood in France: Evidence from a Holistic Approach. *Advances in Life Course Research* 15: 89–96. [CrossRef]

Russell Sage Foundation. 2012. Chartbook of Social Inequality. Available online: http://www.russellsage.org (accessed on 1 May 2017).

Salmela-Aro, Katariina, Noona Kiuru, Jari-Erik Nurmi, and Mervi Eerola. 2011. Mapping Pathways to Adulthood among Finnish University Students: Sequences, Patterns, Variations in Family and Work-Related Roles. *Advances in Life Course Research* 16: 25–41. [CrossRef]

Sawhill, Isabel V. 2014. *Generation Unbound: Drifting into Sex and Parenthood without Marriage*. Washington: Brookings Institution Press.

Settersten, Richard, and Barbara E. Ray. 2010. *Not Quite Adults: Why 20-Somethings Are Choosing a Slower Path to Adulthood, and Why It's Good for Everyone*. New York: Bantam.

Shulman, Shmuel, and Jennifer Connolly. 2013. The Challenge of Romantic Relationships in Emerging Adulthood Reconceptualization of the Field. *Emerging Adulthood* 1: 27–39. [CrossRef]

Silva, Jennifer M. 2013. *Coming Up Short: Working-Class Adulthood in an Age of Uncertainty*. New York: Oxford University Press.

Smith, Christian, and Patricia Snell Herzog. 2009. *Souls in Transition: The Religious and Spiritual Lives of Emerging Adults*. New York: Oxford University Press.

Smith, Christian, Michael Emerson, and Patricia Snell. 2008. *Passing the Plate: Why American Christians Don't Give Away More Money*. New York: Oxford University Press.

Smith, Christian, Kari Christoffersen, Hilary Davidson, and Patricia Snell Herzog. 2011. *Lost in Transition: The Dark Side of Emerging Adulthood*. New York: Oxford University Press.

Snell, Patricia. 2009. What Difference Does Youth Group Make? A Longitudinal Analysis of Religious Youth Group Participation and Religious and Life Outcomes. *Journal for the Scientific Study of Religion* 48: 572–87. [CrossRef]

Snell, Patricia. 2010. Emerging Adult Civic Disengagement: A Longitudinal Analysis of Moral Values in Explaining Interest in Political Involvement. *Journal of Adolescent Research* 25: 258–87. [CrossRef] [PubMed]

Sumner, Rachel, Anthony L. Burrow, and Patrick L. Hill. 2015. Identity and Purpose as Predictors of Subjective Well-Being in Emerging Adulthood. *Emerging Adulthood* 3: 46–54. [CrossRef]

Tanner, Jennifer L. 2006. Recentering During Emerging Adulthood: A Critical Turning Point in Life Span Human Development. In *Emerging Adults in America: Coming of Age in the 21st Century*. Edited by Jeffrey J. Arnett and Jennifer L. Tanner. Washington: American Psychological Association.

Widmer, Eric D., and Gilbert Ritschard. 2009. The De-Standardization of the Life Course: Are Men and Women Equal? *Advances in Life Course Research* 14: 28–39. [CrossRef]

Wight, Vanessa R., Michelle Chau, Yumiko Aratani, Susan Wile Schwarz, and Kalyani Thampi. 2010. *A Profile of Disconnected Young Adults in 2010*. New York: National Center for Children in Poverty.

religions

MDPI

Article

"Church" in Black and White: The Organizational Lives of Young Adults

Rhys H. Williams [1,*], Courtney Ann Irby [1] and R. Stephen Warner [2]

[1] Department of Sociology, Loyola University Chicago, 1032 W. Sheridan Rd., Chicago, IL 60660, USA; cirby@luc.edu

[2] Department of Sociology, University of Illinois at Chicago, 1007 W. Harrison St., Chicago, IL 60607, USA; rswarner@uic.edu

* Correspondence: rwilliams7@luc.edu

Academic Editor: Patricia Snell Herzog
Received: 12 January 2016; Accepted: 30 June 2016; Published: 12 July 2016

Abstract: The religious lives of young adults have generally been investigated by examining what young people believe and their self-reported religious practices. Far less is known about young adults' organizational involvement and its impact on religious identities and ideas about religious commitment. Using data from site visit observations of religious congregations and organizations, and individual and focus group interviews with college-age black and white Christians, we find differences in how black and white students talk about their religious involvement; and with how they are incorporated into the lives of their congregations. White students tended to offer "organizational biographies" chronicling the contours of belonging as well as disengagement, and emphasizing the importance of fulfilling personal needs as a criterion for maintaining involvement. On the other hand, black students used "family" and "home" language and metaphors to describe how their religious involvement, a voluntary choice, was tied to a sense of "calling" and community. We show that this variation is aligned with organizational differences in black and white congregations that situate white youth as separate and black youth as integrated into the larger church community.

Keywords: young adults; race; religious commitment; identity; congregations

1. Introduction

Over the past few decades, studies of American religion have turned to youth to provide a new empirical context for some of the existing theoretical questions and debates within the subfield. While debates about whether American adults are becoming less religious have subsided as scholars have increasingly recognized more individualistic spiritual practices and shifts in patterns of institutional membership (e.g., [1–3]), research on religious youth and young adults has often continued to focus on just *how* religious young adults are by analyzing how often they attend religious services and comparing their beliefs to adults in their faith traditions [4–11]. This focus may stem from a paradox researchers have observed; that is, while attendance tends to decrease in adolescence and college, youth themselves often report that religious beliefs remain important and sometimes even increase during this period [12–14].

An underlying question within these studies is: How do we understand the differences in young adult religiosity? Do we conceptualize "young adults" from a life course perspective that emphasizes individual religious development and/or an intergenerational approach that explores unique differences in young adults' faith? In the present paper, rather than emphasizing points of difference between youth and their religious communities, we seek to place youth and young adults in their organizational contexts in order to understand dimensions of their religiosity. Towards this end, we build upon a smaller subset of studies that have explored how both the content of religious beliefs and the meaning of religious practices are shaped by youth's religious context. For example, Petts [15,16] and Regnerus [17] focus explicitly on family socialization patterns, and what those mean for religious participation. Bengtson et al. [18] explicitly studied the intergenerational transmission of faith identity and practice, noting conditions of both continuity and change.

More organizationally, Snell [19] examined the impact of participation in church youth groups on "life outcomes" such as moral values and continued church connection. Myers [20] focused specifically on differences in the "styles of youth ministry" between one black and one white Protestant Christian congregation in order to glean some lessons regarding how congregations can more effectively hold on to their youth. While Myers found some differences in youth ministry between the two congregations that resonate with our observations, he was less interested in the dynamics and developments of religious identity and commitment. Flory and Miller [21] offer a set of four congregational types that represent the new religious orientation of post-boomer young adults. Christerson, Edwards, and Flory [22] examine adolescents' attitudes towards and actual involvements in congregational life and the extent to which they vary by race to investigate how the primary socializing institutions reproduce racial inequality (and in that regard examine the family, schools, and peer groups as well). Recognizing that both the content of religious beliefs and the meaning of religious practices are shaped by youth's religious context, particularly the organizational context, we examine the ways in which youth and young adults are incorporated into the lives of their congregations and the attendant ways in which their discourses about religious identity and commitment also vary.

To analyze the relationship between private religiosity and communities, we examine black and white young Christians who are living in an "identity moment"—a period where the taken-for-granted dimensions of life and the social networks that reinforce them are addressed and, thus, at times challenged and reformulated (e.g., [11,23]). By exploring the racialized ways that young adults make sense of their often previously ascribed religious identities, we contextualize their personal discourses of religiosity within divergent modes of religious belonging and organizational practices of young adult ministries among black and white churches. Among the churches we studied, we found that black and white congregations implicitly conceptualized "youth" differently, which in turn affected how they imagined integrating them into their communities and thus produced dissimilar organizational practices. Many of the white churches we observed treated young people as a distinct "generation" with unique experiences and perspectives that church leadership believed required an autonomous structure of peer groups for successful ministry. Comparatively, many of the black churches we observed treated youth more as a "phase" or "stage" in the life-cycle, during which youth certainly have particular needs but that these needs require integration within the congregation and a multi-generational membership as opposed to segregation. Highlighting the importance of communities, and their organizational manifestations, in shaping personal forms of religiosity, we find that this divergent organizational context for youth aligns with racialized patterns in their talk about their personal religiosity.

In particular, we found that white college students adopt more individualized approaches to their religious involvement that emphasize what they personally receive from their involvement in congregations (see also [22], p. 138). While this "client" orientation in some ways reflects the "tinkering" [11] or "moralistic therapeutic deism" [8] that other scholars have identified as characteristic of young adult religiosity, we argue that it can be seen as much as a sign of continuity with their religious communities as a break from it. In comparison, we note that the tendency for black students to use family and community language and metaphors to personalize their religious involvement also can be seen as a sign of continutiy within the black church. To understand the organizational differences in how black and white congregations implicitly understand young people and their needs and roles in the congregation, as well as the individual-level discourses of white and black students, it is important to understand the historical contexts from which these collective religious identities emerge.

2. Religious Belonging in Black and White Christian Churches

As Shelton and Emerson ([24], pp. 4–5) note, "The legacy of race-based oppression and privilege has helped to fuel differences in black and white Christians' *religious sensibilities*...[and that] blacks and whites not only approach faith matters differently, but faith *matters* differently to blacks and whites" (emphasis original). In particular, they note that unlike white Protestants, who tend be more doctrinalinally oriented, black Protestants' faith is more experiential and seen as critical to survival and coping with suffering from everyday tribulations. More specifically among the faith lives of young adults, Christerson et al. [22] found this manifested in a "personalistic absolutism" among African-American teenagers, who often remain quite committed to the authority of their religious communities, and a "therapeutic individualism" among white teenagers who use a more individualized assessment of benefits and costs. Building upon Smith and Denton's [8] conception of "moralistic therapeutic deism", they note the significance of racial variation. Whereas white teens continued to fit this idea with their general orientation to God as someone that helps them in their problems and make them happy, African-American teenagers more often envisioned God as someone demanding something of them and an authority they must listen to in their lives. To contextualize the organizational and discourse differences that appear in our data, we briefly review the divergent ways religious belonging has been conceputalized within black and white Christian churches, as well as highlight the racialized ways that the sociology of religion has tended to conceptualize religious choice.

During the twentieth century, leading theoretical paradigms in the sociology of religion emphasized Americans' ability to freely choose how to identify and enact their religious faith within a deregulated religious marketplace (see, for example, [2,3,25–27]. As Edgell ([1], p. 249) notes, "Market theorists argue that modernity creates the conditions that foster religious privatization, pluralism, and voluntarism, causing religion to thrive—and, ironically, to retain much of its public significance." Despite the tendency within studies of youth and religion to highlight generational differences between young adults and the older adults of their religious communities, Christerson et al.'s [22] "therapeutic individualism"reflects a similar mode of religious belonging that emphasizes the authority of individuals to freely and creatively construct a faith of their own. Likewise, Manglos-Weber et al. [13] contend that young people are more likely to be "bricoleurs" in their religious lives.

While the literature on denominational growth and decline has not been explicitly limited to white Protestant denominations, much of the religious market theorizing that has been developed to account for such trends, including the experiences of youth, has presupposed a religious individualism characteristic of the white Protestant experience. Notwithstanding the observation that solidary groups may be agents in religious markets ([28], p. 1052, Table 1; [29]), studies of African American religion have largely proceeded outside of the main theoretical debates about persistence and change in American religion.

Studies of African-American Christianity note that because of its origins in conversions during the era of slavery, the "black church" has always dialectically operated as accommodative to the racialized system as well as resistant to it by offering its own form of self and community expression [24,30,31]. As opposed to a social agent characterized by free-will individualism, making decisions about how to worship and practice religion from an open marketplace, scholars of black religion have emphasized social actors that are embedded within interconnected elements of religious life (e.g., [32–34]). Mirroring language of the domestic private sphere, Frazier [35] argued that African-American religion has served as a refuge in a hostile white world. Rather than presupposing autonomous individuals confronting a religious market, this scholarship more often uses the metaphor of families. Conceptually focusing on how black churches operate as a "semi-involuntary" institution where social ties, including kin, constrain individuals' possible choices and action [36,37], studies of African-American religion have offered a different theoretical model of religious actors that challenges the perspective of free-will individuals entering public religious markets unencumbered. In fact, Christerson et al. [22] note that African-American teenagers were among the least likely to approve of picking-and-choosing from within own's faith or across different religious traditions. Barnes [38] also notes that youth programming has long been a standing feature within black churches and that they have often developed creative programming options, including in some cases dancing, drama, and gospel rap music.

By "shifting the center" [39] away from white Christians, towards theorizing from the experiences of black Christians, the more familial characteristics of religious identity, belonging, and commitment become apparent. Compared to religious marketplace conceptualizations of an individual that emphasizes their ability to autonomously and creatively choose from a religious market [2,3,40], Lincoln and Mamiya ([31], p. 5) observe a significant difference with how the black sacred cosmos conceptualizes "freedom".

> For whites, freedom has bolstered the value of American individualism: to be free to pursue one's destiny without political or bureaucratic interference of restraint. But for African Americans, freedom has always been communal in nature. In Africa, the destiny of the individual was linked to that of the tribe or the community in an intensely interconnected security system.

While the extent to which African-American religion maintains African elements is debated [30], Lincoln and Mamiya's observation highlights assumptions about autonomy that undergird theoretical accounts of religious choice. Whites' conceptualization of freedom emerges from what Feagin [41] calls the "liberty-and-justice frame" in which white Americans sought to gain their freedom during times that they oppressed and suppressed others. Furthermore, he argues the historical context of oppression, initially of slavery, formed a "home-culture" frame that resulted in the hybridization of African culture and North American experiences to create a distinct culture, including religion, which resisted oppression. Within this context, freedom is not about an individual but is about the collective (e.g., [32,33,42–44]). Furthermore, African Americans continue to occupy a precarious place in American society, in terms of economic and social security, and still face both explicit and implicit forces of marginalization. According to Shelton and Emerson ([24], p. 26), survival represents one of the five core building blocks in the Black theology. They write, "many African Americans Protestants believe that they as individuals and blacks as a group would not have made it in this country *but for the grace of God*" (emphasis original). Religion, thus, continues as a form of solidarity and a collective resource that can be both consoling and empowering.

Theorizing from the perspective of black religion also problematizes modernist assumptions of complete differentiation between religion and other public spheres [31]. On the one hand, studies of African-American religion demonstrate the interconnection between social institutions and how black churches and families exist in a "dynamic interactive relationship" in which "families constituted the building blocks for black churches and the churches through their preaching, teaching, symbols, belief system, morality, and rituals provided a unity—a glue that welded families and the community to each other" ([31], p. 311). Yet, on the other hand, black churches themselves offered an example of what Fraser ([45], p. 123) calls a "subaltern counterpublic" which consists of "parallel discursive arenas where members of subordinated social groups invent and circulate counterdiscourses to formulate oppositional interpretations of their identities, interests, and needs". The collective and familial dimensions of personal religiosity in the black church importantly come to bear on how congregations organize ministries for youth, as well as how black students discuss religion in their life. Lincoln and Mamiya [31] observed as "enduring institutions," black families and black churches have together both been charged with the care of African American youth. In the following analysis, we explore these themes further by examining how black and white churches situate and organize youth within their ministries. Next, we consider the points of continutity in how black and white students discuss their personal religiosity and their organizational experiences within their collective religious communities. Reflecting the marketplace and culturally individualist orientations of white Protestant congregations, white young adults approached their churches more as clients interested in what services, meanings, and experiences they could obtain. Comparatively, black young adults discussed their churches as a type of "home" or "family" that operated as an integral part of their self, even when they were not actively involved.

3. Data and Method

Our data come from interviews, organizational ethnographic observations within religious congregations, and ethnographic observations with families, all gathered within the general area of a large Midwestern metropolitan area. The data in this paper are drawn from a larger study that includes Muslims, Hindus, and Latino/a Christians, but we focus here on black Protestants and white Christians (both Protestant and Catholic). We studied young people in two general categories—"youth", who were basically in the 13–17 years old range, and "young adults" who were generally 18 years old up to about 24. More significantly, the "youth" we engaged were living at home and we interacted with them as parts of their families, whereas the "young adults" were college students and generally living away from home. Both sets of young people were involved with religious organizations or interested in being interviewed about their religious involvements and their engagement with religious organizations that were run by, or seemed particularly attractive to, young people. There is a range of levels of involvement among the individuals in our study. We recruited interviewees through public advertisements, announcements in sociology classes, and announcements at religious groups on two college campus that largely draw their students from the metro area. We recognize that we were more likely to get student participants who were involved with religious groups than not, but are not troubled by that "bias" in the samples; we wanted to explore the various meanings and practices of organizational involvement. Thus, we do not have the ability to assess what makes some youth religiously involved and others not, and we do not have a collection of young adults who are completely uninterested in or disengaged from religion. However, we can examine some of the organizational and familial dynamics in which young people are involved, how they articulate religious commitment, and how that aligns with the religious identities they come to claim and how they conceptualize religious commitment. Our ethnographic and interview data reveal the important role that religious institutions can play in how young adults formulate senses of who they are, what they believe, and the languages they use to articulate those connections.

Using a variety of methods, we gathered four types of data on a number of different populations of youth and young adults, religious organizations that serve them, and families who are involved with congregations. First, we have data from 14 focus groups of college students—students from two public universities that draw most of their student bodies from the metropolitan area. The groups were recruited through public advertising on the college campuses, and through campus-based religious organizations. The groups were organized by gender and by race/ethnicity/religion. Three groups were composed of black Christians (one with six black men, one with seven black women, one with six black women) and three groups were composed of white Christians (one with seven white men, one with three white men, and one with six white women). The participants in the black focus groups were all Protestant, except for one person; the white groups had Catholics and Protestants, with a slender majority being Catholic. Second, we conducted formal, one-on-one, in-depth interviews with 52 young adults (mostly college students), of which 13 were white men, 19 were white women, six were black men, and 11 were black women (there were also two Hispanic women and one Asian-American man). A small number of the interviewees had been in the focus groups, but most had not; most interview recruitment occurred through campus, non-religious, channels.

Third, we did institutional ethnographic work through multiple site visits with religious organizations. Specifically, we attended worship services, classes, and youth activities at religious organizations that catered to, or were run by, or seemed to attract, youth. This meant, in practice, primarily congregations and their youth programs, but it also included campus ministries and some young adult-organized voluntary organizations. We located these sites in two phases; first, we canvassed the metropolitan area with the help of graduate assistants and undergraduate interns for a wide variety of organizations that we or our student assistants had heard about. We visited a total of 40 Christian congregations or organizations and did at least one field observation at each of them. After finding some institutions that particularly seemed to fit our needs in terms of their vibrant youth activities and membership (and that were happy to have us study them in more depth), we chose a sample for extended study. Thus, we focused on seven particularly vibrant organizations, of which one was white Protestant, one was black Protestant, and two were multi-ethnic Protestant (the remaining three were Hindu or Muslim). We did multiple visits to these organizations and often individual interviews with their youth ministry leadership.

Finally, we have what we call "family" data, gathered by spending entire days with families, participating with them in their religious involvements, but also sharing meals and informal relaxing time. Understanding how the main "religious" day is organized, at both the congregation and the home, importantly helped us obtain a clearer sense of how religious faith is transmitted to children. Further, the time spent in church also complemented our ethnographic observations about the ways in which youth and young adults were incorporated into, and in turn used, the church. We contacted the families through references from their churches' pastors. Relevant to this paper, we spent time with two black Protestant and two white Protestant families. We watched how religion was practiced in the home and by the family in their respective religious institutions, usually spending a full day with the family on the day of their major religious practice. The families all had youth under-18 years old living at home, and allowed us to see the direct connection between family practices and religious organizations.

Our ethnographic and interview data reveal the important role that religious institutions play in helping to formulate young adults' senses of who they are, what they believe, and the languages they use to articulate those connections. Of course, we want to be careful about making generalizations about racial differences that are too sweeping; but we have also seen differences in the way black and white college-age young adults' talk about their religion and their church involvement. Additionally, we have seen distinct differences in the way black and white churches respond to the youth in their midst.

4. The Dynamics of Congregational Organization

In our observations, black youth were integrated into the congregational community across generations—they are and remain part of a larger community just as they stay more connected to extended family. Comparatively, white youth were often treated as if they were distinct from other generations, with development of their personal autonomy as the highest good. The structure and functioning of the organization is an important mediating dynamic between the demographic realities of class and risk, and the outcomes and narratives that young adults embody and employ when they reflect on their religious lives.

4.1. Ministering to a Different Generation: White Churches' Organizational Practices

We began to notice in our site visits that the mostly white, mostly middle-class parents and religious educators who set the tone for the Mainline Protestant churches in the last quarter of the 20th century had clearly incorporated lessons and assumptions about generational succession into their programming. Intensely aware of rapid technological and cultural change and sensitive to the embarrassment many of their teenage children express upon being seen in their company in public, many parents despaired of the possibility of sharing the meaning of their faith with their children. Their churches' post-college-age youth workers, in turn, felt pressured to do what the parents felt they could not, a task that was regarded by their employers as well within their grasp due to their younger age and presumed fluency in youth culture, especially the music, of their young charges. However, many of these youth workers themselves employed the language of a "generational gap" to explain their own perceived difficulties in reaching youth ten or even five years younger than themselves.

One result of these impulses was the organizational creation of alternative institutional programs like one we came to call "Connexions" and another we call "Soul Station"—generation-specific groups that would meet on their own, plan and run their own events (often in isolation from the church's adult membership), and in the extreme end up running almost a de facto parallel congregation. Connexions met in the church building of a white Evangelical Protestant (but not fundamentalist) suburban church, but not in the sanctuary. It had its own dedicated rooms that were decorated and appointed by youth and their leadership. They ran their own worship and educational programming. They focused relentlessly on finding the new, on treating religious community as peer-based, and giving a distinctly youthful and "non-traditional" version of what "church" is. The pastor leading Connexions, indeed, worried about keeping the constituency young (it did include some young adults as well as teenage youth), and was constantly changing the music lest it get dated. He was also well-read in the "generations" popular literature and spoke easily about Gen X versus Gen Y versus Millennials. The Connexions pastor, in an interview, did not know for certain what happened to Connexions participants once they "aged out" of the program—did they "graduate" to the parent church, or find another? It was a concern voiced by the parent church's senior pastor but not a central issue for Connexions itself.

With the considerable resources of the parent church, Connexions put on high quality services with professional sound, musicians, stage craft for their skits and plays, and the like. They were not just entertainment, there was serious theological content, but they were well thought out, very smoothly done, and usually used plenty of humor. The programs, often on Saturday evenings and sometimes on Tuesdays, were unusual in that congregants did not just enter the meeting room upon arrival. Doors were closed "pre-show" and there was usually a small line when they opened about 30 min prior to start. Two ushers would hand out programs (often just 5×7 cards) in welcome; many had coffee or lattes from the nearby church coffee bar.

Soul Station was connected to another large Evangelical Protestant congregation, that also identifies with the Reformed tradition, in a different suburb. Similarly, it used the church, but not the sanctuary, for its meetings, usually on Saturday evenings. Participants in Soul Station gathered after dark by the fountain in a garden court lit by scores of candles. Slides were projected on screens on two sides of the room, illuminating scenes of traditional religious iconography. The fountain would burble softly in the background throughout the meeting, whether anyone was speaking or a group was making music or, most strikingly for a Protestant church, there was a long period of silent contemplation. The candles suffused the air with the smell of their burning wax. Most people sat on the cool, wrought-iron chairs that had been set out, but people would move around to sit on fabric cushions, benches, and even the hard polished slate floor. The people were young, the atmosphere heavily sensory.

Soul Station began with a handful of upper-middle class young adults, some of whom grew up in the church, others who did not but who were looking for a place to worship with people their own age. Part of the philosophy behind Soul Station is that internal change by the participants will lead to external consequences for the larger community. It describes itself as a "worship-driven" community in that its primary focus is to provide a space for young adults to freely worship and experience the presence of God.

Connexions and Soul Station are two types of programs, one more verbal and discursive, one more sensual and affective, that have been lifted up by many as an answer to the generational crevasse between youth, and young adults, and their parents. They offer intense religious experiences, but are distinct and separate. These types of organizational arrangements also mark the campus ministries of many white religious groups, whether Baptist, Presbyterian, or Catholic. The Baptist Student Union at one of the universities at which we did interviews ran events, held services, and sponsored social gatherings at which the lead author and his graduate assistant were regularly the oldest persons there; it was a constituency that was almost entirely white. Another Baptist church near the campus, also overwhelmingly white, had programs catering to members of the university community and many younger members, but the campus' Baptist Student Union itself ran independently of those efforts. While we heard frustrations from youth leaders about reaching young people, and even from senior congregational leaders who feared losing their young people, we also continued to see and hear evidence of organizationally disengaged young adults—with assumptions about keeping youth somewhat segregated that seemed unexamined.

We note that age-stratified involvement is multi-faceted in many white churches. For example, a significant number of our white interviewees reported going to church camps, one- or two-week summer getaways for young people, with young adult camp counselors and programming oriented toward youth. This is partly a class-oriented activity, not explained totally by race, but it is yet another feature of many white churches that reinforces the idea that youth development needs significant amount of time separate from adults and surrounded by peers.

4.2. Keeping Them with Us: Black Churches' Organizational Practices

By contrast, we found a fundamentally different way of doing "youth ministry" at an African American church we call "Southside". At the "youth night" event one evening, there were plenty of young people at the church, both youth and young adults, both young women and young men. There was loud music–singing to the beat of guitars, drums, and keyboards, performed by a band composed of young church members, with many of the non-performing young men still crowding around the instrumentalists and the women predominating among the singers. Young people gave many of the Scriptural readings, led many of the prayers, and constituted the signature presence on the stage. It was "their" night, as they proclaimed.

However, the evening's central talk, or sermon, was not given by one of the church's young members, but rather by a youthful-looking/young middle-aged woman who was an invited guest. Her talk was based on a teaching relevant to the young people's lives and the challenges they faced. It was filled with references to pop culture and "church-appropriate" slang. But even beyond the featured speaker, the young people were not on their own. There were scores of grown-ups in the hall, many of them parents of the youth on stage but many of them not. The senior church leadership was also there—not actively leading things, but sitting on the side, attentive and watchful.

This wasn't an "autonomous" youth event. Young people clearly planned much of it, and were active and featured participants. However, this was a night for the young people to demonstrate to the rest of the congregation their growing religious competency. This was a night where they demonstrated their mastery in this phase of the life-cycle of growing into adult church membership. This wasn't a distinct generation constituting its own version of "church". It was young people, with the active assistance of an adult audience, demonstrating that they were preparing to carry on the work of the congregation—and its traditions—into the future.

One of the elders of the church who happened to be there that night also happened to be an acquaintance of one of the authors, and she gladly accepted our offer of a ride home. During the lengthy drive back to her home we talked about the events of the evening, and she spent some time talking about her presence at the church's "youth night". She was single at the time, and not a parent of any of the young people. But she is a long-time member of the congregation, personally devoted to the church and its pastor (it takes her two train rides, a bus ride, and a half-hour walk to get from her home to church on Sunday mornings). As she explained it, as one of the active adults in the congregation, she feels called to be a witness to the youths' public religious commitment, which, in turn, meant being part of an appreciative audience and keeping tabs on what they were up to. As social analysts, we recognized that her role was one of both support and surveillance, or perhaps we might say, monitoring.

This particular church was not idiosyncratic among African American congregations, as we found consistently an "intergenerational ethic" in black churches in our study. Church leaders and youth departments stressed that children belong in worship, an expectation that is alternately a burden on families (when the kids just don't want to be there) and an opportunity for them (a safe place to bring them). One congregation we attended fairly frequently, that we dubbed "One Accord Missionary Baptist Church" (OAMBC) made that practice possible by informally setting aside the balcony at the back of the church for families as a place with a more relaxed standard of decorum, where grown-ups were freer to come and go, to take little kids to the bathroom, wipe their noses and tie their shoes, where older children could quietly read a book, and still older youth could sneak pre-flirtatious looks at one another. Significantly, those in the balcony joined with everyone else in the march to the offering plate, and the children of almost every age were expected to have something to put in it.

From time to time, youth workers at OAMBC led an hour of "children's church" at the rear of the balcony, where primary grade children were given other things to do during the sermon. In addition, there was also a nursery for the youngest kids, which some parents took advantage of on and off during the 2 h or so of the Sunday service. But no other activity of religious significance goes on in the congregation during worship. Just as children are supposed to be in worship, so adults are expected to be in Sunday School during the preceding hour, even if, from week to week, only about a third of them are. Age-graded classes study the same syllabus of Biblical texts according to what the pastor called a scheme of "graduation, not generation". All the classes come together before worship for a collective review session, where a delegation from one of the classes, who may be middle-aged or pre-teen, summarizes the lesson as they understand it.

Every fourth Sunday at OAMBC was Youth Day, where the young people would take on just about every role in worship other than the pastor's—they act as ushers, readers, soloists, devotional leaders—both in the morning service and in the evening. With the proud help of their coaches, they often performed contemporary dance. Because fewer people regularly returned in the evening for the second service, the pastor and other elders would often make a special appeal to the congregation at the morning service, "please come out to support our youth." Like any congregational worship service, youth night is for people of all ages.

The intergenerational ethic went both ways. Kids were expected to make at least an effort to participate in worship, and grown-ups were expected to appreciate the kids' dancing. The pastor insisted that elders must be willing to experiment with new worship styles even as he equally insisted that youth mind their manners. Whether an inspirational speech given by a teenager or a dowager, the speaker was supposed to be given respectful attention. Deference is owed to the wisdom that is supposed to come with age, even when, again as is often the case in immigrant churches, some of the teenagers have a better command of and comfort with English than some of their Sunday School teachers.

We do note that one church where we did extended observations, OAMBC is a mid-sized congregation, with about 300 weekly service attenders. They have a professional full-time clergy person, and some part-time staff (such as the music director), but it is not a large or mega-church. Southside Church, the congregation that was the site of the earlier vignette above, however, was indeed a large congregation with several professional clergy. While congregational size and the attendant resources that brings, surely affecteds the programming choices that are made, we are convinced this intergeneration ethos can be found in African-American churches along the size spectrum. The intergenerational ethic is dramatically different from the generationally specific offerings of the many white middle class churches where youth have their own celebration service. When we asked the pastor's wife at one African-American congregation whether youth have activities of their own, she very emphatically said that they do not. "They need supervision and guidance," she said.

Combined with insights from the "family" data we generated by spending time with two African-American families, it is clear that "family" was understood expansively and "fictively", not narrowly and specifically; the idea is not limited to the nuclear family or even necessarily blood relations. Married couples are neither privileged as the norm nor overly burdened with sole responsibility for their children. Women's Month and Men's Month mean that responsibility for worship cuts across families, being shared by members of the same gender of all ages. Many of the parents are single mothers, many of the children come on their own or with friends and cousins, and grandparents pitch in. Unlike many white Protestant churches, where mothers bear the burden of shushing their toddlers or whisking them out of church before their fussiness upsets others, children at our Black Church sites were both given greater latitude and admonished by other, non-parental grown-ups as they saw fit. On one of our visits, right after the offering, the pastor at OAMBC announced that he had "a little policing" to do, and he scolded the youth in the balcony for talking and eating during the service. He said that it sometimes helps if you tell people what's expected of them so that they can correct themselves. For today, he concluded, "I'm the Daddy here."

We must reiterate that the extended family community we observed at the black churches we studied is constructed, not given, intentional and not merely "traditional". One congregation we saw has a church bus that traverses over a hundred square miles to pick up parishioners every Sunday. Ammerman [46] also observed that African American churches regularly draw their congregants from wide geographical regions. People go to considerable effort to "choose" their church, and get there once or twice a week, but they do not consider their involvement as the purely voluntary act of isolated and autonomous individuals. They are "called" to belong. It is a set of institutional arrangements, an integration of generation and participation that leads to a distinctive discourse about religion, about church as organization and community, and about the nature of social relationships.

5. Black and White Young Adult Discourse

College is a period of exploration, doubt, sometimes experimentation. The received patterns of religion, whether belief or practice, have to be—at the very least—consciously decided upon. Particularly for those who go away to college, parents are no longer around to "force" one to go to church (see [23]). At this age, personal autonomy is often both an issue and a value—reinforced by peers and often by parents themselves. In religious belief and religious practices, this autonomy produces a particular "talk" about searching, choices, and attempting to discern what is best for oneself (see, e.g., [47]). There is often a great deal of what might be called "church shopping" by those young adults who want to be connected to a congregation, even if the person wants to stay within their denomination of origin. And yet, in individual interviews and in focus group sessions with black and white college students, we found some distinct differences in how young adults talk about their religious involvements and beliefs, and how these in turn reflected distinct religious identities. Here, we focus on examples of the "talk", or what we would call the "discourse"—the sets of assumptions, phrases, and metaphors—that black and white students used to explain and understand their own church involvement or lack thereof.

5.1. White Students' Organizational Biographies—Client Orientation

The major difference we found is that white students discussed their religious involvements in terms of what they "needed" from a religious organization at that point in their lives. They often presented us with what we call "organizational biographies" that chronicled and described the contours of their belonging. They tended to see religion's positive influence in their lives in terms of personal life and happiness, and expressed their doubts in terms of personal questioning. They often recognized that church involvement gave them skills and experiences that could be useful to them in life. Not surprisingly, we also often heard the suspicion of organized religion and its institutions that is so common in contemporary American society. In that sense, they have what might be called a "client" orientation to the church, and treat their involvement in it as largely voluntary, personalistic, and for their own benefit. We should note that we are not necessarily alleging cynicism or selfishness to these young adults; indeed, there was a consistent theme in our interviews in which respondents assessed congregations and other religious choices based on how well they embodied or expressed religious truth. However, we note that white students consistently assumed that they themselves were competent and authentic judges of that.

We began our individual interviews by asking respondents to draw a "time line" of their religious lives and their involvement with religious organizations. It is important to recognize that we were seeking information on organizational involvement, and thus it is not surprising that we solicited talk about churches and organized religion from both white and black students. Of course, most of the organizational biographies we elicited also involved talk about parents, families, and family life, as well as the transition from their childhood pasts to their current religious participation and involvements. That was our purpose. What caught our interest were the differences in the discourse, which we highlight in these sections.

First, while white students often described childhood experiences in the church, as well as times of crisis in which they turned to religion, for many of them church involvement could be distinct from religion. For example, some students separated "organized religion" from "true" religious beliefs, and often made the well-known and much commented upon (e.g., [8,22]) distinction between "religion" and "spirituality". The emphasis from white students repeatedly returned to individual autonomy and personal decision making, with a basic attitude that considered religious organizations as potentially useful but largely optional. For example, consider these quotes from several different interviews or focus groups:

> "going to church no more would make you a good Christian than going into a garage would make you a car." (white female focus group member)

> "I actually asked my mom why I have to go to church if I believe...She said she thought that going to church made everybody come together...You know, like, I was like, whatever." (white female focus group member)

> "I don't ever remember questioning the existence of God, but I started to question the institution." (white male focus group member)

> "Well, I don't really believe in organized religion at all" (white male interview)

Clearly, these students remain concerned with religion—after all, they attended our focus groups or agreed to do (uncompensated) interviews about religion—but there is a certain amount of "anti-institutionalism", or at least a suspicion of organizational authority, in their words. There is a clear subtext of assuming individual autonomy about spiritual and religious issues, a reserving for themselves the options of making their own decisions about truth, just as they are beginning to make decisions about their own lives separately from their parents.

> "I still call myself Baptist but I don't agree with everything in the established religion. I kind of just got my own little thing, you know." (white woman focus group member)

This woman offers a construction that resonates with Bellah et al.'s [48] famous "Sheilaism", wherein an individually tailored spiritual system is her focus. Others voice a concern with the translation from beliefs into ethical conduct and a keen eye for the potential for alleged hypocrisy between beliefs and behavior. That "religion" is often social, but "spirituality" can be individualized leads them to portray the church as an institution as irrelevant to them or sometimes as an actual hindrance to spiritual development. One can see that here:

> "You don't have to go to church to be religious...I tend to like the word spiritual better than religion because to me the word religious has a lot of dogma attached to it." (individual interview, white woman)

> "I asked [my friend] where she was going and she said the training...I said what...are you training for? And she said to go to church...I was like, to do that is so stupid! If you talk about religion as being accepting of all kinds of different people then they shouldn't make them train to be good enough to come and worship God." (individual interview, white woman)

When these white college-age young adults did look for a church, they focused on one that fit what they perceived as their spiritual needs and evaluated their involvement based on the extent to which the institution seems to be serving them well. Church is not necessarily a place that functions to give them a needed community. One young woman described her search for a church in terms of how it suited her personally:

> "it's not about going to church, it's about personal relationship...it's not forced. ... [my friend] asked me, 'do you want to go to a church that teaches you what I'm teaching you?'...I went with him to the church...it was really cool...it was really good for me at first. ... [but] there were problems with the people there. They were too judgmental. If you did things a little different, they wouldn't like it. ... So, it became too judgmental for me and I stopped going to that church after about five years. ... let me tell you what I did after I left...I worked on my own personal relationship with God. I did it with my friends. We had our own church. ... we all would get together and have our own church." (individual interview, white woman)

Five years of involvement is not insignificant in the life of a college student. However, her organizational commitment was determined by her perception of her own spiritual requirements. Namely, as she saw her spiritual needs change, she changed her organizational involvement.

Distinct from, even if sometimes connected to, the general questioning of institutionalized religion was a narrative that portrayed the varying forms and periods of involvement in terms of individual needs and outcomes. For example, an interview with one white man elicited:

> "I think it was good that I went when I did because I think if I hadn't of gone then I may have picked a different path in life. I think it was a good choice. Even though I didn't stick with it, and I don't necessarily believe it, it still taught me some good things. I got better friends. But not now, not in the present, it doesn't really help. Actually I think that every major theme of being Baptist, I think I'm the opposite now."

Or a young white woman explained: "I saw that when I needed it I went there, then I found out that I didn't need it anymore...I felt that I could have a place in the universe without it." Yet, another white young man said:

> "I'm only concerned with my own spiritual growth, not with my religious...interaction. Well, I mean,...I have my friends who are Christian and I try to keep up with them, and, go to Bible study, and make sure we're all growing, but, see what I mean? I'm...only in it right now to make sure I'm spiritually sort of on track, you know what I mean." (individual interview white man)

One can see that this young man values spirituality, and even maintains an involvement with others. But the emphasis is on his personalized growth, not a community, and he places himself as the clear judge of what is best for accomplishing that growth.

We note that not all the commentary was negative, by any stretch. In the following quote from an interview with a white man, he places great value on his religious involvement. Importantly, however, these very positive comments are framed in terms of individual needs and outcomes:

> "Looking back on it, I haven't been [religious]. I am now. I have found myself in the church. There was a time when I started dropping out. I stopped going to church as much. I still went because my mom was the secretary. I lost that connection with my church. I don't know how spiritual I had ever been. Now I just see things in a different light. Coming down here [college], I've found a different church. And as much as I've found God, I've found myself. I've realized I wasn't really close to God. I went to church because I was expected to."

In summary, the discourse of the white students, as well as their abilities to narrate developed organizational biographies, are framed around assumptions about individual value, autonomy, and choice. There was often genuine spiritual seeking, and a great concern with religious truth and ethical behavior. However, there was little concern if that seeking produced a distancing from a religious community, and a clear willingness to assess any organization's value as distinct from what the religious and spiritual message might be.

5.2. Black Students' Organizational Biographies—Called to Belong

Black students, on the other hand, voiced far less suspicion of religion or its institutions. They often credited religion and church involvement with helping them in college, either by keeping them out of trouble or by providing a support system for them. Black students often discussed church involvement using "family" language and metaphors—that is, with the same kinds of terms that one uses for familial blood relationships. Family relationships are not entirely voluntary—we may not like family but we are pretty much stuck with them. Black students regularly used the language of personal "choice", and they repeatedly noted that when at college and not being "forced" to attend church by their parents, they often did not. Yet, black students often did a remarkable amount of "church shopping"—after all, these are kids who are away at college. In addition, when they explained the "church homes" they did find, they used the language of the "home church"—the place where they felt as enmeshed in familial-type relationships as they did when they lived with their families of origin.

Several of the black students had not found a church home at the time of the interview, and some reported not attending as much as they did while living at home (as did white students). They noted the importance of making their own choices as a way of authenticating the genuineness of their religious lives. Yet, their criteria and qualifications for what counted as an appropriate church differed from their white peers because personal happiness and satisfaction alone were not enough to justify religious involvement. Rather, being part of a community, making a public witness (not just personal morality), and finding the types of relationships that family can offer permeated their discussions. Here are some examples that are explicit about the connection to "home":

> "I wish I was involved a little bit more, like in a community. Like back at home." (individual interview black woman)

> "I am still in the process of looking for a church home...I really do not desire to forsake the fellowship of believers...it's really very hard for me not to be in fellowship." (black woman focus group member)

Others used the language of "home" less, but were explicit about aspects of what we might call "community":

> "My spiritual growth...needs...some feeding. It's not just about me getting fed, obviously. It's also about what I give back by coming to worship the Lord as well." (black women focus group)

> "I got down here and started enjoying the Voices of Inspiration Choir [in which she participates]. So really for me, it was like church was basically just on Sunday. That was it. As far as Bible study, we would go every now and then. But now that I've come down here [to college] I go more often. It's more close knit."

In addition, there was clear recognition that it was not easy to balance the searching, and the choice, with the rewards of the sense of connection:

> "I'm glad I go to church now, like she [another focus group participant] said she doesn't go to church now. That can be good because you can drag yourself crazy looking for the right church, but I like going to church." (black women focus group)

It was not uncommon to hear black students provide a more instrumental rationale for their involvement. For example:

> "Getting involved in church down here has kept me out of trouble. I have gotten involved in church activities. It keeps me focused on God and on my studies and on my grades...I am just thankful that I stayed in church when I came to college." (individual interview black woman)

However, the goals in this quote are not articulated as personal spiritual development, or personal happiness alone. Church involvement is a discipline that keeps the respondents pointed toward their goals. Thus, we regularly found black young people who were engaged in practices of "church shopping" and who used individual religious authority (for example, to decide whether any particular church is preaching the "Word of God") to discern the usefulness and appropriateness of any given religious congregation. But organization and religious authority matter, distinct from the sentiments common among the white students that regularly separated the two. Furthermore, collective identity and connections to a community matter, with a clear sense that the community can enforce parameters of belief and behavior that benefit the person.

5.3. Religious Involvement and the Language of Family

We do not want to overdo the talk of racial differences, as many themes crossed races in the young people's discourses. Issues with the transition from living at home to attending college were common, as was the use of personal authority to assess the appropriateness or worthiness of a organized religion or a specific congregation (however, Christerson et al. [22] use survey data to show that this is more common among white than among black teenagers). One shared theme was the considerable discussion of religion and family life. But even in that discourse, there was an important distinction—white students often spoke of their church history and involvement in terms of their family—but they meant their blood kin, such as parents, siblings, and their own prospective children. For white students, the connection between family and religion centered more on whether and how they wanted their own families to be involved with religion. While black students certainly mentioned this view, their discussions of family did not end there and often had much more to do with extended family, especially female relatives such as grandmothers and aunts. Moreover, for black students, discourses about family were often used to describe what church is and should be—church was so often described with metaphors of it being "family" or relationships that are "called" rather than chosen.

Thus, for example, many white students saw enough value in their religious upbringing to want to pass at least some of it on to their own prospective children:

> "I will regulate my [future] kids...I learned a lot of my morals at church, a lot of what's right. I learned what the Church thinks is right anyway...It was good for me, and was...a positive thing in my life. So I would want my kids to experience that as well. And if they didn't want to I wouldn't make them." (individual interview white man)

> "I'll make my kids go, but not every Sunday." (individual interview white man)

Note that these quotes show white students affirming aspects of their personal history, and the determination to recreate much of their own family life in future families, but they still separate institutional authority from personal choice and emphasize autonomy in decision-making. The church in these scenarios is seen as a useful guide to life, but not a necessity and not a source of binding rules and moral precepts—for example:

> "I am happy that they made me go when I was little, but I am not so sure that I am happy that they made me do it once I entered high school...I think once your reach a certain age, you are to the point when you can decide for yourself." (white man focus group)

Church involvement is a matter of family connection, for both black and white students. However, compare the following discussion about raising children in the church among black students with the white students' quotes about children that were listed above:

"[W]hen I have children, I want us to go to church together. I won't tell them they have to go to a Pentecostal church or a Baptist church or Catholic. They can choose where they want to worship the Lord." (individual interview black woman)

"I'm going to feed them [giving children religious instruction] until they're fat and they can't take no more. I'm going to guide them until they feel they can make the right decisions. I'm not going to try to be a new-age parent—'oh, I'm not going to do this to my kids because it's a different age.' I will guide my kids to the light." (black woman focus group)

"The people in my church I have known them ever since I was a little girl. We all grew up together...it's not just like just religion, it's my friends and my family are there. We are like a community within a community. We are all there. We are all there to support each other." (black woman focus group)

The black students see religious involvement as integral to their identity. They believe it supports them, provides them with personal discipline, and reminds them that they are public representatives of the faith. Where white students sometimes worried about a potential "stigma" of church membership that would restrict or inhibit their relationships with others, black students discussed church membership as a type of "insulation" that helped them resist temptation (especially, we heard in one focus group, the temptation of "cute guys"). Church involvement, in summary, is a social factor for black students, not just a personal one. And while family connection is important to both groups, black students conceptualized church relations in family terms, as what used to be called by sociologists "fictive kin". We would hear respondents say things such "the organist at church is my auntie"—but the woman was not a blood relation (the sister of her parent). Instead, the older woman, was a respected authority figure who also had the emotional connection and the sense of responsibility toward the younger woman that an older woman would have. Just as fellow church-goers are "sister" or "brother"—or just as South Asian students we observed called elders from their community "uncle" or "aunt" whatever their familial status—the relationships formed within church had the binding power of blood ties. Church involvement is "like a family" as well as being "with family". One doesn't "choose" family—it is not a social contract from which a dissatisfied party can withdraw and move on to find a different and better deal [48]). Family is locative, but transcends the particulars of place and time—it is grounding, constraining, and empowering.

Obviously, developing personal autonomy, trust in one's individual judgment, and the like are important processes and life skills. In addition, they are key skills needed by those in the contemporary middle-class. Both black and white students were developing and using those skills, but in ways that had important differences. Many of the white youth we talked to do not face as risky a world as many of the black students who are trying to make it in college. The community has been a great source of resources and resilience for African Americans, and the church in particular is often a bulwark for protecting children and young people from "the street" (see [33]). Religion greatly matters for urban black communities, but as in the case of immigrant groups, it has become less something that can be taken for granted and more something that has to be worked at (see [34,43]). Urban black neighborhoods have more than their share of people at the socio-economic margins, and those people who have achieved or are trying to achieve middle-class status are more precariously perched there than are white families. This is where religion matters most for promoting positive outcomes for young people [38,42,44]. Precisely where young people are disadvantaged, religious involvement can make the biggest difference in their capacity to take advantage of opportunities and skirt dangers.

6. Conclusions

Studies of the religious lives of young adults have tended to implicitly emphasize the differences between them and their parents and their religious communities by either stressing the life cycle dimension of being a "young" adult or the generational factors that shape a unique experience. The relative emphasis on continuity between young people and adults varies. For example, Smith and Denton [8] conclude that most of the youth they talked to were actually pretty close to their parents' religiosity. Not surprisingly, as youth age, they often change their religious beliefs and practices, as Smith and Snell [9] and Pearce and Denton [14] demonstrate, but often that change is not radical. Similarly, Bengtson et al. [18] tell a story that emphasizes intergenerational continuity. Nonetheless, some of the religious change experienced by young adults is thorough and dramatic—and often those who begin as most highly religious become least involved later (a finding in both Smith and Snell and Pearce and Denton).

More encompassingly, Flory and Miller [21] and Wuthnow [11] posit a fundamental generational difference in the ways that young adults now engage religious belief and practice, though they differ in the content of the new patterns. That is, Flory and Miller see an "expressive communalism" as the typical religious orientation of the post-boomer generation, while Wuthnow sees young adults who are in the "after baby boomer" generation as fundamentally "tinkerers" who put together religious lives from whatever they have at hand—a *bricolage* of beliefs and practices that are suited to individualized needs (see also [13,22]) find both personalistic and communal orientations in the youth they study—white youth much more likely to be individualist in belief and questioning of institutional authority, while black and Latino/a youth are more oriented toward community and family, and more trusting in the religious authority of those communities.

We have offered an argument that stresses the differences between black and white youth/young adults, but that simultaneously shows a basic continuity with their communities of origin—rooted in the ways in which they participate in religious organizations. Thus, while we show racial variation among young adults, we argue that it is built upon a continuity with their congregations and communities of origin.

It would be tempting to over-interpret our findings. We did not set out to discover the different ways in which African American and white Americans either do or talk about religion. We recognize that class differences, and differences in religious traditions, complicate any generalization that is too sweeping. We cannot address why some young people get or stay involved with religious organizations and others do not. While we grounded our analysis of the discourses of white and black students in the ways in which various congregations practice "youth ministry", we also recognize that cultural and social locations, as well as economic class, are powerful contexts that shape the ways in which we talk and act. Furthermore, we also saw many similarities in the interviews between black and white students—they wrestled with their own faith commitments, and they were testing a certain amount of autonomy now that they were not living at home and thus had less direct familial pressure to get up and out on Sunday mornings. Many were less observant than they had been earlier in their lives.

That said, we found two distinct sets of differences: first, the uses of individualized, "client" language by white college students to describe their organizational biographies versus the use of "family"and "home" language by black college students to describe their immersion in religious communities; and second, the generational segregation of youth into age-graded ministries in many white churches versus the age-integrated activities in black churches that focused on youth demonstrating their religious "chops" for their elders in settings that combined moral support with adult supervision. We do not think these differences are coincidental.

Pushing our empirical observations more conceptually, we witnessed differences in what we term the "dynamics of commitment". A long thread of analysis of American cultural and religious history has contrasted individualized versus communal approaches to connecting to groups (e.g., [48–50]). On one hand, there is the "social contract" language of classical liberalism, in which society is conceptualized as an aggregation of individual connections. These connections are basically "contracts" in which people exchange varieties of personal and social "goods". The implication of a contract is that once it becomes perceived as not a good deal for one of the parties involved, they renegotiate or perhaps leave. On the other hand, "covenant" language portrays social groups as bound together by a collective identity and a collective commitment to the survival of the group. In the Judeo-Christian religious tradition, this was a pact initiated by God; but it is more than a simple contract—it binds individuals into a "people" who have collective and individual responsibilities and who are bonded through both good and ill fortune.

At the level of understanding young adults' discourse about their own religious involvements, we have revealed distinct hints of both contractual and covenantal thinking. When white students found a congregation not to their liking, or upholding values or practices they could not abide, or felt that their personal journeys were not being well served, they disengaged. When black students—even those not very active at the time—discussed their own involvements they were conscious of the ways in which church connections were family-like, and communal. They served to keep individuals on the right path, a path that was understood as benefiting the collective as well as the individual.

Acknowledgments: These data come from the Youth and Religion Project, R. Stephen Warner, P.I. and Rhys H. Williams, co-P.I. The data gathering was supported through generous funding from the Lilly Endowment, Indianapolis, Indiana, USA. The authors thank Craig Dystra and Christopher Coble of the Religion Division of the Endowment for their support. Previous drafts of this paper were presented to the Center for the Study of Religion and Society at the University of Notre Dame and the 2013 Annual Meeting of the Society for the Scientific Study of Religion in Boston. The authors appreciate the useful feedback in both settings, as well as from guest editor Patricia Snell Herzog and the anonymous reviewers.

Author Contributions: Warner and Williams, with the assistance of graduate student research assistants and undergraduate interns, gathered the ethnographic and interview data. Irby worked as research assistant to Williams and cleaned, coded, and analyzed much of the interview data. Williams wrote the first draft of the paper, Warner added substantial ethnographic and interview material, and Irby added interview material and wrote the first draft of the literature review.

Conflicts of Interest: The authors declare no conflict of interest. The funding sponsors had no role in the design of the study; in the collection, analyses, or interpretation of data; in the writing of the manuscript, and in the decision to publish the results.

References

1. Edgell, Penny. "A Cultural Sociology of Religion: New Directions." *Annual Review of Sociology* 38 (2012): 247–65. [CrossRef]

2. McGuire, Meredith B. *Lived Religion: Faith and Practice in Everyday Life*. New York: Oxford University Press, 2008.

3. Roof, Wade Clark. *Spiritual Marketplace: Baby Boomers and the Remaking of American Religion*. Princeton: Princeton University Press, 1999.

4. Dean, Kenda Creasy. *Almost Christian: What the Faith of Our Teenagers Is Telling the American Church*. New York: Oxford University Press, 2010.

5. Hoge, Dean R., William D. Dinges, Mary Johnson, and Juan L. Gonzales, Jr. *Young Adult Catholics: Religion in the Culture of Choice*. Notre Dame: University of Notre Dame Press, 2001.

6. O'Connor, Thomas P., Dean R. Hoge, and Estrelda Alexander. "The Relative Influence of Youth and Adult Experiences on Personal Spirituality and Church Involvement." *Journal for the Scientific Study of Religion* 41 (2002): 723–32. [CrossRef]

7. Regnerus, Mark D., Christian Smith, and Brad Smith. "Social Context in the Development of Adolescent Religiosity." *Applied Developmental Science* 8 (2004): 27–38. [CrossRef]

8. Smith, Christian, and Melinda Lundquist Denton. *Soul Searching: The Religious and Spiritual Lives of American teenagers*. New York: Oxford University Press, 2005.

9. Smith, Christian, and Patricia Snell. *Souls in Transition: The Religious and Spiritual Lives of Emerging Adults*. New York: Oxford University Press, 2009.

10. Uecker, Jeremy E., Mark D. Regnerus, and Margaret L. Vaaler. "Losing my religion: The social sources of religious decline in early adulthood." *Social Forces* 85 (2007): 1667–92.

11. Wuthnow, Robert. *After the Baby Boomers: How Twenty- and Thirty-Somethings Are Changing the Nature of American Religion.* Princeton: Princeton University Press, 2007.

12. Barry, Carolyn McNamara and Larry Nelson. "The Role of Religion in the Transition to Adulthood for Young Emerging Adults." *Journal of Youth and Adolescence* 34 (2005): 245–55. [CrossRef]

13. Manglos-Weber, Nicolette, Margarita Mooney, Kenneth Bollen, and J. Micah Roos. "Relationships with God among Young Adults: Validating a Measurement Model with Four Dimensions." *Sociology of Religion*, 2016. [CrossRef]

14. Pearce, Lisa and Melinda Lundquist Denton. *A Faith of Their Own: Stability and Change in the Religiosity of America's Adolescents.* New York: Oxford University Press, 2011.

15. Petts, Richard J. "Trajectories of Religious Participation from Adolesence to Young Adulthood." *Journal for the Scientific Study of Religion* 48 (2009): 552–71. [CrossRef]

16. Petts, Richard J. "Parental Religiosity and Youth Religiosity: Variations by Family Structure." *Sociology of Religion* 76 (2015): 95–120. [CrossRef]

17. Regnerus, Mark D. *Forbidden Fruit: Sex and Religion in the Lives of American Teenagers.* New York: Oxford University Press, 2007.

18. Bengtson, Vern L., Norella M. Putney, and Susan Harris. *Families and Faith: How Religion Is Passed Down Across Generations.* New York: Oxford University Press, 2013.

19. Snell, Patricia. "What Difference Does Youth Group Make?: A Longitudinal Analysis of Religious Youth Group Participation and Religious and Life Outcomes." *Journal for the Scientific Study of Religion* 48 (2009): 572–87. [CrossRef]

20. Myers, William R. *Black and White Styles of Youth Ministry: Two Congregations in America.* New York: Pilgrim Press, 1991.

21. Flory, Richard, and Donald E. Miller. *Finding Faith: The Spiritual Quest of the Post-Boomer Generation.* New Brunswick: Rutgers University Press, 2008.

22. Christerson, Brad, Korie L. Edwards, and Richard Flory. *Growing Up in America: The Power of Race in the Lives of Teens.* Stanford: Stanford University Press, 2010.

23. Clydesdale, Tim. *First Year Out: Understanding American Teens After High School.* Chicago: University Chicago Press, 2007.

24. Shelton, Jason E., and Michael O. Emerson. *Blacks and Whites in Christian America: How Racial Discrimination Shapes Religious Convictions.* New York: New York University Press, 2012.

25. Finke, Roger, and Rodney Stark. *The Churching of America, 1776–1990.* New Brunswick: Rutgers University Press, 1992.

26. Finke, Roger, and Laurence R. Iannaccone. "Supply-Side Explanations for Religious Change." *The Annals of the American Academy of Political and Social Sciences* 527 (1993): 27–39. [CrossRef]

27. Stark, Rodney, and Roger Finke. *Acts of Faith: Explaining the Human Side of Religion.* Berkeley: University of California Press, 2000.

28. Warner, R. Stephen. "Work in Progress toward a New Paradigm for the Sociological Study of Religion in the United States." *American Journal of Sociology* 98 (1993): 1044–93. [CrossRef]

29. Warner, R. Stephen. *A Church of Our Own: Disestablishment and Diversity in American Religion.* New Brunswick: Rutgers University Press, 2005.

30. Baer, Hans A., and Merrill Singer. *African American Religion: Varieties of Protest and Accommodation.* Knoxville: University of Tennessee Press, 2002.

31. Lincoln, C. Eric, and Lawrence H. Mamiya. *The Black Church in the African American Experience.* Durham: Duke University Press, 1990.

32. Barnes, Sandra L. "The Black Church Revisited: Toward a New Millennium DuBoisian Mode of Inquiry." *Sociology of Religion* 75 (2014): 607–21. [CrossRef]

33. McRoberts, Omar M. *Streets of Glory: Church and Community in a Black Urban Neighborhood.* Chicago: University of Chicago Press, 2003.

34. Speakes-Lewis, Amandia, LeRoi L. Gill, and Crystal George Moses. "The Move Toward American Modernity: Empowerment and Individualism in the Black Mega Church." *Journal of African American Studies* 15 (2011): 236–47. [CrossRef]

35. Frazier, E. Franklin. *The Negro Church in America.* New York: Schocken Books, 1974.

36. Ellison, Christopher G., and Darren E. Sherkat. "The Semi-Involuntary Institution Revisited: Regional Variations in Church Participation Among Black Americans." *Social Forces* 73 (1995): 1415–37. [CrossRef]

37. Ellison, Christopher G., and Darren E. Sherkat. "Identifying the Semi-Involuntary Institution: A Clarification." *Social Forces* 78 (1999): 793–802. [CrossRef]

38. Barnes, Sandra L. "The Least of These: Black Church Children's and Youth Outreach Efforts." *Journal of African American Studies* 12 (2008): 97–119. [CrossRef]

39. Collins, Patricia Hill. "Shifting the Center: Race, Class, and Feminist Theorizing about Motherhood." In *Shifting the Center: Understand Contemporary Families*, 3rd ed. Edited by Susan J. Ferguson. New York: McGraw-Hill, 1994/2007, pp. 371–89.

40. Hammond, Phillip E. *Religion and Personal Autonomy: The Third Disestablishment in America.* Columbia: University of South Carolina Press, 1992.

41. Feagin, Joe R. *The White Racial Frame: Centuries of Racial Framing and Counter-Framing.* New York: Routledge, 2010.

42. Barnes, Sandra L. "Black Church Culture and Community Action." *Social Forces* 84 (2005): 967–94. [CrossRef]

43. Gilkes, Cheryl Townsend. "Plenty Good Room: Adaptation in a Changing Black Church." *The Annals of the American Academy of Political and Social Science* 558 (1998): 101–21. [CrossRef]

44. Patillo-McCoy, Mary. "Church Culture as a Strategy of Action in the Black Community." *American Sociological Review* 63 (1998): 767–84. [CrossRef]

45. Fraser, Nancy. "Rethinking the Public Sphere: A Contribution to the Critique of Actually Existing Democracy." In *Habermas and the Public Sphere*. Edited by Craig Calhoun. Cambridge: MIT Press, 1992, pp. 109–42.

46. Ammerman, Nancy Tatom. *Congregation and Community.* New Brunswick: Rutgers University Press, 1997.

47. Cherry, Conrad, Betty A. DeBerg, and Amanda Porterfield. *Religion on Campus: What Religion Really Means to Today's Undergraduates.* Chapel Hill: University of North Carolina Press, 2001.

48. Bellah, Robert N., Richard Madsen, William M. Sullivan, Ann Swidler, and Steven M. Tipton. *Habits of the Heart: Individualism and Commitment in American Life.* Berkeley: University of California Press, 1985.

49. Bromley, David G., and Bruce Busching. "Understanding the Structure of Contractual and Covenantal Social Relations: Implications for the Sociology of Religion." *Sociological Analysis* 49 (1988): 15–32. [CrossRef]

50. Williams, Rhys H. "Covenant, Contract, and Communities: Religious and Political Culture in America." *International Issues* 37 (1994): 31–50.

religions

MDPI

Article

Research Note: College Students' Attitudes toward Christianity in Xi'an, China

Chao Wang

Institute For Western Frontier Region of China, Shaanxi Normal University, No.199, South Chang'an Road, Yanta District, Xi'an 710062, China; wangchao@snnu.edu.cn; Tel.: +86-1399-1213-104

Academic Editor: Patricia Snell Herzog
Received: 26 January 2016; Accepted: 10 May 2016; Published: 20 May 2016

Abstract: Atheism is the mainstream belief system in contemporary China. In recent years, a growing number of Chinese have converted to different religions, particularly Christianity. In this study, we conducted a survey in the region of Xi'an to investigate the following three questions: How common is Christianity among college students in Xi'an? How many of them have converted to the Christian faith? How do they gain their knowledge of Christianity? It is a popular notion in China that many college students have, in recent times, converted to Christianity. However, our survey results do not provide support for this. While many students encounter Christian faith on university campuses, especially through organizations such as The Fellowship, students in this survey report low religious affiliation.

Keywords: college students; Christianity; survey; China

---

1. Introduction

Between 1982 and 2001, the number of Catholic, Protestant, and Islamic affiliates increased from 10 million to 60 million in China. The nonstatistical affiliates of Buddhism and Daoism are about 10 million in number. The white paper on religious belief in China (Baipishu) shows that there are 100 million people in China who believe in religion. Related statistics are debatable as some suggest that 300 million followers of religion is a more approximate number. According to surveys, 70–80 percent of the affiliates began to convert from the 1980s onwards, and of them 30 percent are young people [1]. As Professor Fenggang Yang observed: "In the reform era since 1979, all kinds of religions have revived and are thriving. Christianity has been the fastest-growing religion for decades" [2]. Published estimates of the proportion of Christians in the Chinese population range from approximately 1 percent in some relatively small-sample public opinion surveys to about 8 percent in reviews of membership reports from churches and church leaders (including unregistered churches) within China. The Pew Forum's demographers estimate that the 2010 Christian proportion of China's population is likely to be approximately 5 percent (or 67 million people of all ages). This figure includes non-adult children of Chinese affiliates and unbaptized people who attend Christian worship services [3]. What about young people's religious faith, or college students' faith? In the early 2000s, one-third of the population with religious beliefs were young people, which is around 30–40 million [4]. As part of the religious revival since the Reform era, Christianity has gained popularity in China. An increasing number of people have become Christians, especially in coastal towns and developed cities.

How common is Christianity among the young people in universities, especially in Xi'an, a city in Northwestern China? To answer this question, we conducted a survey aiming to learn the basic trends in the percentage of Christians among college students and their attitudes toward Christianity. We asked all participants about how they came to know about Christianity. Was it the church or other Christians that led them to develop an awareness and understanding of Christianity? Among the affiliates, we asked them when they started believing in the Christian message and why. Additionally, we questioned them on how their religious practices take place on campus. How do they get exposed to the Christian faith on campus? How do they spread their knowledge of Christianity to other students?

To gain answers to these questions, we randomly selected 1000 students from 12 universities in Xi'an. The universities were selected for their different specialties including liberal arts, science, and language studies. The selected universities are distributed in different parts of the city. Since the sample is randomly selected, we hoped to balance the ratio between male and female participants; the grade ranges were from freshman to graduate students; and the ethnic groups comprised both Han and minorities. This general survey aimed to understand the religious beliefs of college students and to find out if Christianity was popular on campus.

The questionnaires were distributed twice to students on campus, and they had to fill them in during classes. First, when 250 students were pre-tested, we found that some questions that were based on previous questionnaires did not get clear answers, and we made additions and changed some of them. Then, later we distributed 750 changed questionnaires. Therefore, the total number of statistics had little variation for the different questions. We received 950 questionnaires in return, for a 95 percent response rate. The following are the results of the statistical analysis of 950 questionnaires. SPSS was used for data analysis.

2. Religious Affiliation in China

A number of studies have already investigated religious affiliation in China generally. For example, Stark and Wang find that Christianity is widespread in China, with the rate of Chinese claiming affiliation rising in recent decades [5]. However, these scholars also find that there is a general reluctance of many Chinese to admit affiliation with Christianity. In this sense, claiming affiliation is still a relatively undesirable status socially. They find that many Chinese have a personal faith in Christianity but tend to underreport more public forms of religiosity, such as affiliation with a specific religious tradition.

Less studied is the extent to which this broader pattern in China is true among young Chinese. In particular, religiosity among college students is important for predicting future patterns in China. However, no studies that we are aware of have given particular attention to religious affiliation among college students, especially not in Xi'an. Xi'an is located in the interior of the country and as a "university city" has a large concentration of universities. Thus, this study has particular relevance.

3. Survey in Xi'an, China

3.1. Student Characteristics

We selected different universities in Xi'an to distribute the questionnaires to get a varied sample with regard to gender, grade, major, and nationality. However, students were not chosen on the basis of any specific characteristic.

Gender: The total number of valid questionnaires was 950, of which 364 were male respondents, 562 female, and 24 non-indicated, accounting for 38.3 percent, 59.2 percent, and 2.5 percent, respectively. The proportion of girls was relatively high, which corresponded with the overall proportion of girls in the universities.

Grade: Of the students who answered the questionnaire, 155 were postgraduates, 782 undergraduates, 2 college students, and 11 undesignated, accounting for 16.3 percent, 82.3 percent, 0.2 percent, and 1.2 percent, respectively. Most of the respondents were undergraduates, showing that they formed the main group among college students.

Majors: The numbers of students majoring in different disciplines were as follows: In the arts, there were 317 students majoring in humanities and social sciences, 139 in foreign languages, and 8 in art and sports. This comes to a total of 464 students, which accounts for 48.8 percent of the sample. In addition, there were 428 students majoring in science and engineering, and 46 majoring in medicine, with a combined total of 474 students comprising 49.9 percent of the sample. Finally, there were 12 students without a designated major who comprised 1.3 percent of the sample of college students in this study.

Minorities and Han: The number of students from among the Han nationality, minorities, and the undesignated were 823, 121, and 6, accounting for 86.6 percent, 12.7 percent, and 0.6 percent, respectively. This reflects the overall situation in the country. The number of students among minorities was slightly higher because some surveys were concentrated in minorities' classes.

These randomly selected students reflect the overall trends among college students in Xi'an, and the different variables in the sample were conducive to a representative survey.

3.2. Students' Faith Profiles

Other researchers who surveyed the number of college students who affiliate with religions showed results with the proportion of affiliates varying from 3.5 percent to 44 percent. A higher proportion of college students was found in the coastal region, underdeveloped areas, and minority areas who affiliated with a religion. [1] Xi'an is not a coastal region, nor is it underdeveloped, nor is it in the minority area; thus, we know little about the proportion of students who affiliate with religion there.

From Figure 1, it is evident that "No Faith" is the option of the highest number of students, the second is Buddhism, and the third is Islam. Very few responded saying "Christianity". The proportion of all students who affiliate with a religion is 14 percent, while 86 percent are non-affiliates who responded with "no faith" or no answer. This 14 percent lies in the median range from 3.5 percent to 44 percent.

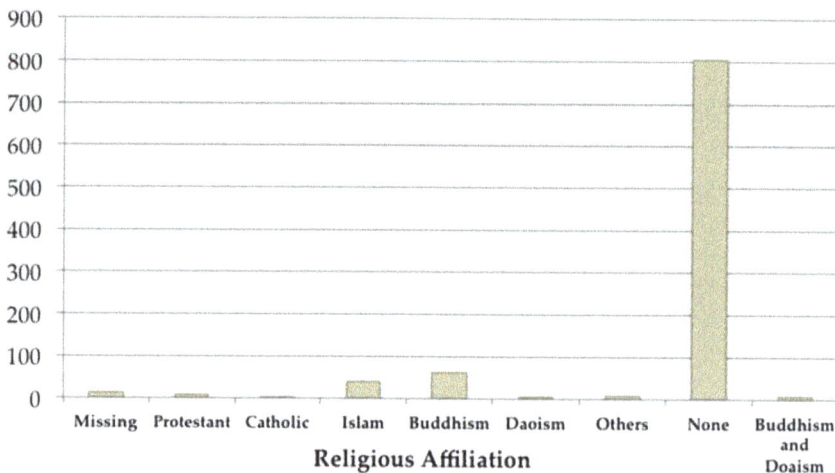

Figure 1. Religious affiliation among college students.

The difference between the number of affiliates and non-affiliates is quite significant. Among those surveyed, the number of affiliates was 133 out of 950, making up 14 percent, of which 11 were Protestant and Catholics among the 950, accounting for 1.2 percent. The number of non-affiliates was 804, accounting for 84.6 percent; the incomplete questionnaires were 13, accounting for 1.4 percent. The general scenario is that a very small proportion of them are Protestant or Catholic, with most of them subscribing to no religion. The number of students believing in traditional Chinese Buddhism and Daoism together or other religions (including Tibetan Buddhism, Confucianism, and Folk Religion) is 83. There were 39 students who believe in Islam.

The survey produced the following results. Of the college students surveyed in this study, 84.6 percent reported they have no religion; 8.7 percent reported Buddhism, Daoism, Buddhism and Daoism, or Folk religion; 4.1 percent reported Islam; 1.2 percent reported Protestant or Catholic; and 1.4 percent did not respond to this question. These results are the same as the data of the CFPS (Chinese Family Panel Studies) 2012 generated by the Institute of Religion and Culture of Beijing University. Their data showed that only 10 percent of Chinese regard themselves as affiliated with religion. Most respondents (89.6 percent) think they have no religious faith. Buddhism, with numbers almost double those of other religions, is still the most influential religion in China, with 6.75 percent of the interviewees regarding themselves as Buddhist. Furthermore, the CFPS data indicated that 1.9 percent of Chinese are Christians, which equates to approximately 26 million Christians living in China now. This makes Christianity the second largest religion of the Han ethnic group [6]. The outcomes of two surveys are similar. The reason that Islamic affiliates outnumbered Christians here is that more minority students were interviewed.

However, the Pew Forum's data indicates that 5 percent of the Chinese population numbers approximately 67 million people. Meanwhile, the CFPS's survey indicated a 1.9 percent Christian population proportion in China, while our survey indicated a 1.2 percent proportion of Christians among college students. We consider that the Pew results differ based on the use of estimated data. Moreover, both the definition of particular religions and the method of survey used are different in each of the studies. It is possible that, under Communist rule in China, some religious people do not admit their faith, so that the true data is higher than the survey results suggest.

In that survey, the results do not appear to be significantly influenced by the factors of gender, grade, and subject major. However, the ethnic factor is more significantly related to the expression of religious faith, especially for the followers of Islam or Tibet Buddhism. "Most Chinese Muslims belong to one of several ethnic groups that are overwhelmingly Muslim. The 2000 Chinese census included a measure on ethnicity. While not all members of these ethnic groups would necessarily identify as Muslim, the Census figures provide a reasonable and generally accepted approximation of the size of China's Muslim population" [7].

Table 1 presents the results of the survey in this study and shows that most of the students do not follow any faith. The Han students' main faith is Buddhism, Daoism, or both of them together. The minorities' faith is mainly Islam and Buddhism (including Tibetan Buddhism). The Protestant designation is more popular among the Han than among the minorities. Among the minorities, 59 out of 121 have religious faith, accounting for 48.76 percent, almost half, but among the Han, 85 out of 822 have religious faith, accounting for 10.34 percent. This comes close to the national figures—100 million of the 1.3 billion Chinese. Of course, this includes Han and minority figures; only the Han total 10.34 percent in this survey.

Table 1. Ethnic groups and religious affiliation.

Faith	Han	Minorities	Missing	Total
Missing	11	1	1	13
Protestant	7	1	0	8
Catholic	2	1	0	3
Islam	1	38	0	39
Buddhism	47	14	0	61
Daoism	4	1	0	5
Others	6	1	1	8
None	737	62	5	804
Buddhism/Daoism	7	2	0	9
Total	822	121	7	950

In Figure 2, a higher ratio of religious identity among ethnic minorities is demonstrated (59 of 121; 48.76 percent). Most in this group believe in Islam, Buddhism, and Tibetan Buddhism. Han and other minorities believe in other religions. Non-affiliation is high. Hardly any of the students identified themselves as Christians. Knowing this, the next question is whether the small number of Christians have made an impact on others in terms of their views about Christianity and about the missionary work associated with some Christians in China.

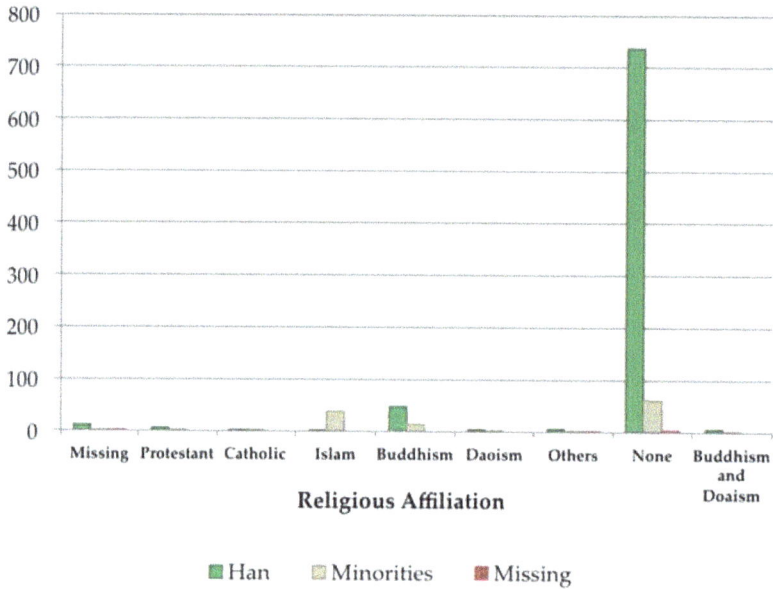

Figure 2. Religious affiliation by ethnic group.

3.3. College Student Views about Christianity

From among all the students who took the survey, 306 of 901 (34 percent) have respect for the Christian faith, 466 of 901 (51.7 percent) oppose Christian missionaries; only 17 of 901 (1.9 percent) consider it to be a religion of superstitions; and 111 of 901 (12.3 percent) have no idea. From this we realize that most students respect the Christian faith, but do not like missionary activities. Moreover, the superstition response, which was the common view of religion in the past, is equated with religion by few students today. These results are displayed in Table 2.

Table 2. Students' attitude toward Christianity.

Missionary Attitude	Frequency	Percentage	Valid Percentage	Cumulative Percentage
Missing	1	0.1	0.1	0.1
Respect	306	32.2	34.0	34.1
Oppose missionary work	466	49.1	51.7	85.8
Think are superstitious	17	1.8	1.9	87.7
No idea	111	11.7	12.3	100.0
Total	901	94.8	100.0	100.0

Table 3 preliminarily investigates whether there appears to be a difference in attitudes toward Christianity between religious affiliates and non-affiliates. Among the 762 respondents who followed "no religion", 247 reported "respect", accounting for 32.41 percent, and 402 respondents, accounting for 52.76 percent, opposed missionary activities. Only 14 people, accounting for 1.84 percent, reported their opinion that Christianity is superstitious. Among those who identified themselves as Protestant or Catholic, almost all of them stated that they respected the Christian identity. Among followers of Islam, Buddhism, Daoism, and other religions, only three people thought Christianity was superstitious. This meant that most students respected the Christian faith, few considered the religion to be superstitious, but most, among both religious affiliates and non-affiliates, opposed missionary activities. This is a general trend in contrast to other variables that include gender, grade, major, and ethnic group. People who believe in a religion and those who do not have different attitudes toward the Christian faith; among the religious affiliates, Christians and non-Christians have different attitudes.

Table 3. Attitudes toward Christianity among religious affiliates.

Faith	Respect	Opposed to Missionary Work	Think Are Superstitious	No Idea	Missing	Total
Missing	6	5	0	1	0	12
Protestant	6	0	0	0	0	6
Catholic	1	1	0	1	0	3
Islam	16	18	1	3	0	38
Buddhism	23	28	2	7	0	60
Daoism	0	5	0	0	0	5
Others	2	3	0	1	0	6
None	247	402	14	98	1	762
Buddhism/Daoism	5	4	0	0	0	9
Total	306	121	17	111	1	901

The proportion of students who are respectful and neutral toward those having Christian beliefs was 85.6 percent while those thinking of them as superstitious accounted for only 1.8 percent, and 11.7 percent were indifferent. Overall, this indicated that, although they are not Christians, the vast majority of them adopt an accepting or neutral attitude toward Christianity. This is because the majority of students believe that it is acceptable for college students to have religious beliefs. That is to say, most the college students generally accept the religious affiliates.

Students' attitudes toward Christianity are more respectful than antagonistic. While most of the students reported not liking missionary activities, they also indicated that young people are generally accepting of religious culture and have great regard for the social role of religion in the contemporary era. That is the reason for their interest in Christianity. However, the acceptance does not necessarily lead to affiliation with the Christian faith and following its beliefs—not publicly at least. Some young people who often attend the activities in a church or a fellowship group do not particularly believe in the Christian message [8]. Thus, most of these college students do not affiliate with Christianity. But are they interested in learning about it?

3.4. Students' Interest in Learning about Christianity

As discussed above, most students respect Christianity, but are not personally interested in converting. If they had not been exposed to Christianity, would they have been interested in learning about it? Table 4 shows that most of these students have no interest in learning about Christianity: 399 out of 950, accounting for 44.3 percent. Only 196 of the 950 answered "yes," accounting for 21.8 percent. The other 304 out of 950 marked "no idea," accounting for 33.8 percent.

Table 4. Students' interest in learning about Christianity.

Christianity Interest	Frequency	Percentage	Valid Percentage	Cumulative Percentage
Missing	1	0.1	0.1	0.1
Yes	196	20.6	21.8	21.9
No	399	42	44.3	66.2
No idea	304	32	33.8	100
Total	900	94.7	100	100

Does knowledge about Christianity relate to interests in learning about it? From Table 5, we see that, among those with the most understanding, 2 out of 5 are interested, 1 out of 5 are not interested, and among those who had little understanding, 37 out of 84 are interested, and 19 out of 84 are not interested. With an average understanding of Christianity, 86 out of 277 showed interest, 101 out of 277 had no interest. Among those with little understanding, 62 out of 373 showed interest, 169 out of 373 had no interest. Therefore, students who know more about Christianity are more interested in learning about it than students who knew very little about it.

Table 5. Understanding about and interest in Christianity.

Knowledge of Christianity	Interested in Learning about Christianity				Total
	Yes	No	Don't Care	Missing	
4	2	1	2	0	5
3	37	19	28	0	84
2	86	101	89	1	277
1	62	169	142	0	373
0	9	109	43	0	161
Total	196	399	304	1	900

(0–4, the level from knowing nothing to knowing the most).

The chart in Figure 3 reads from left to right, the green bar indicating "interest" and the yellow indicating "no interest". The students who have more knowledge of Christianity are interested in learning more about Christianity. Note that the green bar is higher than the yellow bar in column "4" (learn most) and "3" (learn more).

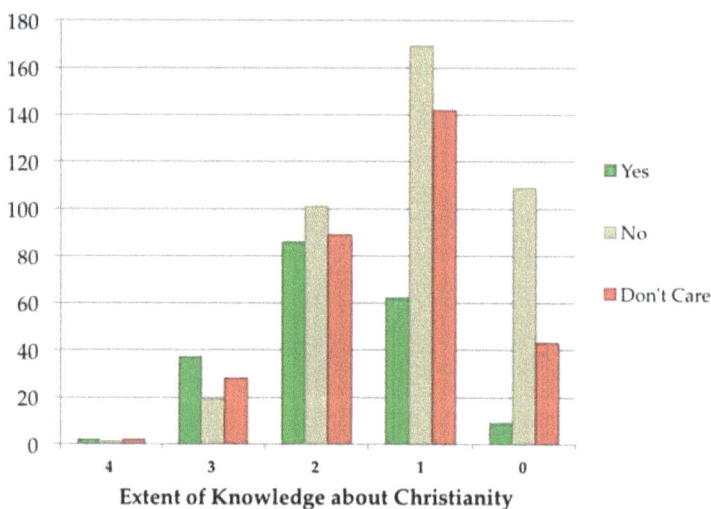

Figure 3. Students' understanding about and interest in Christianity.

Comparing the results from different disciplines in Table 6, we see that students majoring in the Arts (Liberal Arts, Foreign Languages, and Sports) are more numerous in our respondent group than students in the Sciences (Science and Technology and Medicine). Of students in the Arts, 112 of 196 (57.14 percent) are interested in learning about Christianity, whereas, among students in the Sciences, 79 of 196 (40.31 percent) are interested in learning about Christianity. Meanwhile, among the students with "no interest", this trend is reversed. The Sciences group (220 of 399 respondents, accounting for 55.14 percent) has more students with no interest than the Arts group (165 of 399, accounting for 43.86 percent). Therefore, the discipline in which students are majoring appears to be an important factor that is related to interest in learning about Christianity.

Table 6. Academic major and interest in learning about Christianity.

Major	Interested in Learning about Christianity				Total
	Missing	Yes	No	Don't Care	
Missing	0	5	4	0	9
Liberal Arts	0	87	112	99	298
Science and Technology	1	68	200	151	420
Foreign Language	0	22	61	36	119
Sports	0	3	2	3	8
Medicine	0	11	20	15	46
Total	1	196	399	304	900

Are different attitudes connected to the interest in learning about Christianity? We see from Table 7 that the students who respect Christianity are also those interested in learning about it and *vice versa*. Overall, college students' interest in learning about Christianity is related to the extent to which they have an understanding of the faith, their attitude toward Christians, and the discipline in which the students are majoring. The number of students who have an interest, have no interest, or are indifferent is 196 (20.6 percent), 399 (42 percent), and 305 (32.1 percent), respectively. Those who have clearly expressed no interest account for 42 percent (nearly half), and those who are interested are possibly those who only have a superficial interest, showing a low level of participation in Christian activities; their interest is mainly satisfied indirectly from books.

Table 7. Attitude toward Christians and interest in learning about Christianity.

Major	Interested in Learning about Christianity				Total
	Yes	No	No Idea	Missing	
Missing	0	0	1	0	1
Respect	122	85	97	1	305
Oppose missionaries	68	239	159	0	466
Superstitious	2	14	1	0	17
No idea	4	61	46	0	1111
Total	196	399	304	1	900

3.5. Students' Knowledge of Christianity is Related to Communicating with Christian Friends

To investigate correlates of student knowledge of Christianity, Figure 4 first presents the results of the student knowledge rating. From Figure 4, it is clear that most students report that they know very little about Christianity; more than half of them (the yellow and purple) know little to nothing. "Just so-so" knowledge of Christianity is represented by the brown khaki section. "Know quite a bit" and "very familiar" are green and blue, respectively.

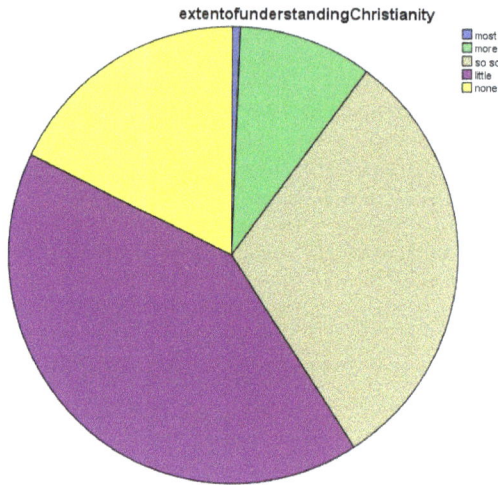

Figure 4. Students' understanding of Christianity.

When students had a connection with religion, their knowledge about Christianity was higher. Table 8 presents the results of crosstabulations analyzing knowledge of Christianity and whether students have Christian friends and shows greater knowledge among those with Christian friends. Thus, interest and understanding of Christianity are linked, perhaps because interest promotes learning about faith, or perhaps because learning about faith promotes interest. Both possibilities may be true. The causal order is unknown from this cross-sectional analysis, but this preliminary analysis has established that there appears to be a relationship between the two. Next, we investigate possible sources of religious exposure.

Table 8. Knowledge of Christianity and Christian friends.

Christian	Extent to Which Students Know about Christianity					
Friends	Most	A little	So-so	Very little	Not at all	Total
Missing	0	0	2	3	0	5
Yes	5	56	193	219	57	530
No	0	28	82	151	104	365
Total	5	84	277	373	161	900

Table 9 shows that students who have Christian friends understand Christianity more than those who have no Christian friends. We understand this to mean that having Christian friends is related to students' knowledge of and interest in learning about Christianity.

Table 9. Understanding of Christianity and participating in Christian activities.

Christian	Extent of Understanding about Christianity					
Activities	Most	A little	So-so	Very little	Not at all	Total
Missing	0	1	1	1	0	3
One	0	11	38	35	3	87
Two	0	9	12	19	0	40
Three or more	2	21	24	6	0	53
Nil	3	43	202	312	158	718
Total	5	85	277	373	161	901

Understanding of Christianity may also be related to the degree of participation in religious activities. Among the five students who understand Christianity quite well, three have not participated in Christian activities; 43 out of 85 students who understand Christianity well have not participated in Christian activities; and 202 out of 277 students who have little understanding have not participated in Christian activities. This indicates that their level of understanding is not necessarily linked to their level of participation. Perhaps instead college students' understanding of Christianity results from textbooks, the Internet, film, and television or from having Christian friends and classmates, without any formal contact with Christianity or Christians. This seems likely since the survey regarding their intent shows that even those students who have participated in Christian activities do not necessarily show a high degree of interest in Christianity. Thus, further investigation is needed into the sources of religious exposure.

3.6. Sources from Which Students Learn about Christianity

College students reporting religious affiliation appear to have learned about Christianity from different sources than non-affiliates. Most affiliates attribute their knowledge about Christianity to their family (47.9 percent), friends (18.8 percent), or from attending religious meetings (10.4 percent). Non-affiliates attribute their knowledge of Christianity to reading religious books (18.8 percent), browsing the Internet (18.8 percent), or being introduced through friends (17.6 percent). This indicates that affiliates obtained their religious knowledge from their surroundings, and nearly half from family members. The non-affiliates attribute their religious knowledge to reading books and browsing the Internet. Both affiliates and non-affiliates rarely attribute it to religious broadcasts, leaflets, or religious organizations [9].

According to this survey, most students learned about Christianity through social networks and the Internet, books, relatives, friends, and religious classes, among others. In addition, a large proportion of college students have not participated in any Christian activities. Their understanding of Christianity continues to come from the Internet, books, and other external sources, which makes it clear that college students' contact with Christianity is very limited. This is because the total number of university students believing in Christianity in Xi'an is smaller, and the non-affiliates show no willingness to learn more about Christianity from their Christian classmates and friends, thus preventing the further spread of the Christian faith among students.

Leaflets distributed on campus and through fellowships continue to play an important role in introducing Christianity to college students. A fellowship on the campus may be accepted by young students because it is a relaxing place for socializing without a religious discipline or rules. This could help facilitate being around religious affiliates. The members of a fellowship actively build friendly relationships with students and invite them to take part in activities to learn about Christianity. This is a way for students to learn by communicating directly with Christians.

The activities of Christians are not only in the church but also outside the church. The Christian way of life for college students involves being in the fellowship first, not the church. The house church and the fellowship have become more popular than traditional churches for young people. When we surveyed people in fellowships, house churches, and traditional churches, we found that more youth Christians (including college students) gathered in a fellowship or house church rather than in a traditional church. House churches in Xi'an attended by young people (including college students) can number from fewer than 10 communicants to more than 200. However, few young people attended traditional churches. In addition, when interviewed, the young people indicated that the fellowships and house churches were more attractive for them than were traditional churches.

Table 10 shows that the main ways in which students participate in religious activities is by visiting temples, churches, and mosques, where a majority of the Buddhists and Muslims hold their religious activities. Christians organize and participate in more meetings or classes. Most Christians attend the parties of affiliates or take online learning classes, while Buddhists are more likely to participate in other forms of religious activities demonstrating that spiritual advancement is greater than other organizational expressions.

Table 10. Ways of participating in religious activities.

	Missing	1. Temple, Church, or Mosque	2. Party of Affiliates	3. Online Learning Class	4. Others	1&2	2&3	3&4	1,3&4	Total
Missing	0	0	0	0	1	0	0	0	0	1
Protestant	0	2	3	1	2	0	0	0	0	8
Catholicism	0	0	1	0	0	0	1	0	1	3
Islam	1	10	2	1	1	2	0	0	0	17
Buddhism	0	12	3	0	7	1	0	1	0	24
Daoism	0	1	0	1	2	0	0	0	0	4
Other Religions	0	1	0	0	2	0	0	0	0	3
Buddhism and Daoism	0	0	0	1	1	0	0	0	0	2
Total	1	26	9	4	16	3	1	1	1	62

We see from Table 11 that almost 25 percent of the students encountered the missionaries between one and three times or more. This shows that fellowships have been communicating with college students frequently. As outlined above, most students do not approve of missionary activities, but some of them are interested in learning about the culture of Christianity. Students are invited to attend fellowships around the campus to experience Christian culture, without having to participate in religious activities. This seems to provide a more comfortable atmosphere for participating in social events with Christians.

Table 11. Number of encounters with missionaries on campus.

Missionary Encounters	Frequency	Percentage	Valid Percentage	Cumulative Percentage
Missing	2	0.2	0.2	0.2
Once	101	10.6	10.7	10.9
Twice	82	8.6	8.6	19.5
Thrice or more	58	6.1	6.1	25.6
None	705	74.2	74.4	100
Total	948	99.8	100	100

Table 12 shows that, while the absolute number of females invited to participate in fellowship activities was greater than the absolute number of men, the gender ratio was nearly equal: women numbered 141 out of 561, accounting for 25.13 percent, and males numbered 92 out of 363, accounting for 25.34 percent.

Table 12. Number of encounters with missionaries by gender.

Gender	Number of Encounters					
	Once	Twice	Thrice	None	Missing	Total
Missing	0	5	0	3	15	23
Male	2	39	34	19	269	363
Female	0	57	48	36	420	561
Total	2	101	82	58	704	947

Thus, it seems from these initial descriptive statistics that there are potentially interesting patterns in knowledge about, understanding of, and exposure to Christianity.

4. Summary of the Survey Results

Most of these college students do not believe in religion. Christianity is not popular among them in Xi'an. As the Pew report showed, "three-quarters of the religiously unaffiliated (76 percent) also live in the massive and populous Asia-Pacific region. Indeed, the number of religiously unaffiliated people in China alone (about 700 million) is more than twice the total population of the United States" [7]. Christians comprise 5 percent of the population in China, according to the Pew Forum estimates. At present, most young Christians attend fellowships or house churches, and an increasing number of college students are also interested in experiencing cultural Christianity. However, the proportion of Christians remains low among all students.

In a survey taken in the Guizhou province in recent years, most college students believed in a religion before they went to university or college, nearly 76.92 percent. Moreover, 23.08 percent developed their faith during college; meanwhile, 61.54 percent followed the faith as practiced in their family. In addition, they were influenced by their surroundings more than those who had a strong religious inclination [10].

The situation was found to be similar in Guizhou, Xi'an, and other cities in China. The proportion of affiliates in religion among Chinese in general is not high, but the actual number has been increasing. Buddhism and Christianity are more acceptable to college students. Some students feel that religion plays a positive role in society. They have a tolerant attitude toward religion [11].

Most students are interested in religion. Most of them get their religious knowledge, especially Christianity, from books or websites, but they have no contact with any Christians. One of the professors said that, on the one hand, young students had passionate feelings about religion that manifest themselves in such aspects as religious festivals, traveling to religious locations, experiences in temples, and religious cultural searching, religious food, and superstitions; on the other hand, the same students do not understand the scriptures or doctrine. They also had less religious fervor.

Most of the students are not familiar with the religion they believe in. Only 3 percent understand their religious rules and texts well, and 16 percent of them do not even know about their religion [12]. Therefore, religious beliefs of college students can be of three types: they believe in God but do not belong to an religious organization; they are interested but not strongly committed; they have the culture but are not engaged in the spiritual realms of religion [1].

Finally, we understand the ways in which they get exposure to religion, specifically Christianity: Some of them receive fliers and frequently receive invitations to join a study circle on campus. The missionary effort is greater than it was in the past; a stronger effort is being made to introduce Christianity to more students.

5. Discussion

Why are there fewer Christians in Xi'an when compared to other religious groups? Why do most college students have no knowledge of religion? Why do they have no interest in learning about Christianity? It is partly the atheistic environment in China that is responsible for most people being disinclined to religious thinking. They also do not make contact with religious people. Especially in Xi'an, an inland city in Northwestern China, people are more traditional than those in coastal cities and thus less receptive to Christianity and thoughts from other religious cultures. This is a common phenomenon in China.

Conversely, religion is nowadays experiencing a revival in China; all religions have spread quickly. As we know, in the past thirty years, after several decades of severe repression, new manifestations of religion have been appearing throughout China. Tens of thousands of temples have been reopened or rebuilt. Millions of people have returned to Buddhism, and, once again, huge numbers of Chinese are pursuing their traditional folk religions and worshipping at their ancestral shrines. Meanwhile, tens of millions of Chinese have embraced Christianity, with thousands more converting every day and more than forty new churches opening every week. [5] Therefore, some people think that Christianity has spread rapidly in all cities in China.

How can we reconcile these two different phenomena? Some scholars contend that the surveys indicate lower numbers of Christians in China, such as in Xi'an, because individuals do not admit their faith to others under communist rule. Indeed, how many college students are believers? There is no consensus.

Meanwhile, Christianity has spread unevenly in different cities in China. In 1919, at the beginning of the Christian missionary effort, Chinese Christians in seven coastal provinces outnumbered those in other provinces, accounting for 71 percent of the total Christian population. The downstream areas of the Changjiang River are home to approximately 80 percent of all Chinese Christians [13]. Professor Xing Fuzeng's view is that, in the 20th century, the spread of Christianity in China was unbalanced, with several provinces witnessing quicker growth and Chinese Christians congregating in 4–5 provinces, not including the Shaanxi Province. The Christians in Shaanxi comprised 0.98 percent of the province's population in 1997 [14]. At present, according to data obtained from the local government, the ratio of Christians in the Shaanxi Province or Xi'an City is always lower than in some coastal cities.

In 2015, there were approximately 360,000 Christians in the Shaanxi Province, accounting for 1 percent of the province's total population of 37,000,000 [15]. Moreover, there are 83,000 Christians in Xi'an, accounting for 0.95 percent of the city's total population of 8,700,000 [16]. The proportion of Christians in Xi'an is lower than in other cities. It is, therefore, reasonable to conclude that the ratio of Christians among college students in Xi'an is also lower than in some other cities.

In addition, young people seldom express their religious fervor as compared to the older people. College students are more interested in the attractions around them and often consider religion to be strange. At the same time, religious faiths have rules while students prefer to live easily and without limitations. In one report (Data of CFPS2012), the author indicates that: In general, few people with college degrees believe in religion; Compared with Christian believers, Buddhists tend to be younger and better educated; In Christian, people over the age of 40 believing in Christianity are more numerous than younger believers, people with a higher level or lower level of education believing in Christianity are more numerous than middle level education believers [6].

Based on the various surveys or estimates, some people think the proportion of Christians in Xi'an should be higher, other people do not think so, whose opinion correctly represents the current trend? This depends on the quality of the survey. In this survey, the finding that Christianity is followed by a low rate of college students reinforces the results of the CFPS2012 Report. We consider that these results reflect the detailed monitoring of religious activities in China. According to related laws and regulations, religious activities can only be held in special places. In essence, displaying religious beliefs and religious practices is prohibited in public, a law which is applicable to university campuses. To be exposed to a religion, a person must first have a chance encounter with believers. Therefore, the first step to make a cognitive connection to Christianity is important. As Ying Xiong said in his article:

> The more mature faith is based on cognition (thoughts). When you think God is believable, you begin to believe ... you rely on what you believe in your feeling and spirit, you are convinced and then you are the real follower, moving from your thinking to your activities ... therefore, faith is the process from initial belief (often feeling) to being convinced. The people who go through the entire process are the real affiliates [17].

Members of Christian fellowships on campus have become more active in missionary work; thus, students have become exposed to more fliers and have received more invitations from missionaries. In this way, fellowship members provide more opportunities to college students to learn about Christianity. In contrast to traditional missionaries, the fellowship uses certain initiatives and adapts itself to a young person's way of thinking. The initiative involves making friends with students, adapting to them by decreasing the emphasis on religious rules, and creating an inviting space for young people to learn about Christianity. For most people who convert to Christianity, it is not the faith or the search for the meaning of life that leads them to convert, but their feeling/thinking that a Christian is a good person and that it is good to be in contact with Christians. Therefore, deeply communicating with a Christian does not begin with the so-called "quest of the spirit" but with real experience [18], and that is why young people more easily accept this faith model.

6. Limitations

It could alternatively be that people who do believe personally in Christianity are still unlikely to report affiliation due to this being a relatively un-socially desirable status to report [5]. If this is the case, then their low levels of affiliation reported in this survey may not attempt to examine accurately religious affiliation and participation among Xi'an college students.

It is also worth noting that, as a cross-sectional survey, the causal direction of the relationships reported is unknown. For example, interest in Christianity could promote greater understanding, or *vice versa*. What is indicated by this survey is that the two are related. This provides initial evidence that investigations of this type can be fruitful.

7. Conclusions

In summary, we have found that, despite reports of high and growing rates of Christianity in China, college students in Xi'an still report relatively low rates. What appears to be changing is the degree of participation in, interest about, and understanding of Christianity through multiple forms of exposure to small groups of Christians on college campuses.

Conflicts of Interest: The author declares no conflict of interest.

References

1. Baolian Jin, and Junxue An. "A ponder on college students' religious belief in the new period." (对新时期大学生宗教信仰问题的思考). *Journal of Shenyang Agriculture University (Social Sciences Edition)* 13 (2011): 37–40.
2. Fenggang Yang. *Religion in China-Survival and Revival under Communist Rule*. Oxford: Oxford University Press, 2012, p. 83.
3. Pew Forum on Religion & Public Life. "Global Christianity—A Report on the Size and Distribution of the World's Christian Population." December 2011. Available online: http://www.pewforum.org/2011/12/19/global-christianity-exec/ (accessed on 19 December 2011).
4. Suju Li, and Qifei Liu. *The Young People and Religion Hot*. (青年与"宗教热"). Beijing: China Youth Publishing Group, 2000, p. 19.
5. Rodney Stark, and Xiuhua Wang. *A Star in the East: The Rise of Christianity in China*. West Conshohocken: Templeton Press, 2015.
6. Yunfeng Lu. "Report on contemporary Chinese Religions based on Data of CFPS2012." *The World Religious Cultures* 1 (2014): 11–25.
7. Pew Forum on Religion & Public Life. "The Global Religious Landscape—A Report on the Size and Distribution of the World's Major Religious Groups as of 2010." December 2012. Available online: http://www.pewforum.org/2012/12/18/global-religious-landscape-exec/ (accessed on 18 December 2012).
8. Xiuli Han. "Analysis of the religious mentality of youth." (当代青年宗教心理解读). *China Religion* 7 (2003): 34–35.
9. Tu Min-xia. "The religious needs of youth in the social transformation—An investigation on the religious beliefs of Guangzhou youth." (社会转型期青年的宗教需求研究—广州青年的宗教信仰调查分析). *Journal of Beijing Youth Politics College* 4 (2012): 5–14.
10. Yongshen Lu. "Research on the religious faith of college students and young teachers in universities—A case of Guizhou province." (高校青年教师和大学生宗教信仰问题研究—以贵州省高校为例). Paper presented at The Conference Proceedings of Social Science Academic Annual Meeting of Guizhou, Guiyang, China, 11 November 2011 to 22 December 2011.
11. Qiongru Sun. "Review and Prospect of the research on College Students' religious belief." (大学生宗教信仰问题研究回顾与展望). *China Youth Study* 11 (2008): 63–67.

12. Lianming Xu. "Youth religious fashion: Fashion interpretation of the youth religion in China." (青年宗教时尚: 我国青年宗教热的时尚化解读). *China Youth Study* 5 (2013): 73–78.

13. Milton T. Stauffer, ed. *The Christian Occupation of China: A General Survey of the Numerical Strength and Geographial Distribution of the Christian Forces in China*. (1901–1920年中国基督教调查资料，原《中华归主》修订版). Revised in Chinese. Made by the Special Committee on Survey and Occupation, China Continuation Committee 1918–1921. Translated by Yongchun Cai, Yong Wen, Qi Duan, and Zhouhuai Yang. Beijing: China Social Science Press, 2007, p. 728.

14. Fuzeng Xing. "The distribution of christianity in mainland China in 20th century." (20世纪中国内地基督教的区域分布). In *The Regional History of Chinese Christianity*. (中国基督教区域史研究). Edited by Jianming Chen and Jiahui Liu. Chengdu: BASHU Press, 2008, p. 15.

15. "Christianity in Shaanxi Province." (陕西省基督教基本情况). Available online: http://www.sxmzzj.gov.cn/newstyle/pub_newsshow.asp?id=29003565&chid=100228 (accessed on 14 December 2009).

16. "Christianity in Xi'an." Available online: http://w.xa.gov.cn/ptl/def/def/index_1276_4152_ci_trid_1804755.html (accessed on 25 August 2015).

17. Ying Xiong. "Psychological guidance of youth religious belief." (青年宗教信仰心理及其引导). *Youth Exploration* 5 (2015): 87–92.

18. Cao Lijuan, and Huang Jian. "The Faith and Life Practice of a Young Christian—Based on the Case Study of a Young Christian from a Family Church." (青年基督徒的信仰与生活实践). *Contemporary Youth Research* 7 (2012): 42–47.

religions

MDPI

Article

Redefining Religious Nones: Lessons from Chinese and Japanese American Young Adults

Russell Jeung [1,*], Brett Esaki [2] and Alice Liu [3]

[1] Asian American Studies Department, San Francisco State University, 1600 Holloway Avenue EP103, San Francisco, CA 94132, USA

[2] Department of Religious Studies, Georgia State University, P.O. Box 3994, Atlanta, GA 30302-3994, USA; besaki@gsu.edu

[3] Educational Studies, Ohio State University, 127 Arps Hall, 1945 North High Street, Columbus, OH 43210, USA; alice.x.liu@gmail.com

* Author to whom correspondence should be addressed; rjeung@sfsu.edu; Tel.: +1-415-338-7586; Fax: +1-415-338-0500.

Academic Editor: Peter I. Kaufman
Received: 13 June 2015; Accepted: 27 July 2015; Published: 30 July 2015

Abstract: This analysis of Chinese and Japanese American young adults, based on the Pew Research Center 2012 Asian American Survey, examines the religious nones of these ethnic groups. Rather than focusing on their beliefs and belonging to religious denominations, it highlights their spiritual practices and ethical relations using an Asian-centric *liyi* (ritual and righteousness) discourse. Despite being religious nones, these groups have high rates of ancestor veneration and participation in ethnic religious festivals, as well as strong familial and reciprocal obligations. These findings indicate that, similar to other American Millennials, these groups may be better understood by how they do religion than in what they believe.

Keywords: religious nones; spiritual but not religious; Chinese Americans; Japanese Americans; Asian Americans; millennials

1. Introduction

According to the 2014 American Religious Landscape Study, the number of Americans unaffiliated with any religion has risen stunningly by over 40% in the past seven years, from 16.1% to 22.8%. The report accounted for this change by noting the generational replacement of Catholic and Mainline individuals by Millennials who are religious "nones". Regarding this major shift in Americans' religious identities, it states:

As the Millennial generation enters adulthood, its members display much lower levels of religious affiliation, including less connection with Christian churches, than older generations. Fully 36% of young Millennials (those between the ages of 18 and 24) are religiously unaffiliated, as are 34% of older Millennials (ages 25–33). [1]

An emerging field of scholarship now seeks to explain why so many Americans, especially Millennials, are rejecting religious affiliation [2].

Two groups of ethnic Americans, however, have historically been religiously unaffiliated instead of shifting to this category. Both Chinese Americans and Japanese Americans—at 52.1% and 32.5%—have the highest rates of religious nones in the United States [3]. Their young adults under 30 have even greater proportions of being unaffiliated, at 65.6% and 44.4%.

We suggest that the Western conceptualization of religion along the dimensions of belief and belonging are less than adequate in understanding these religious nones. Instead, we argue that an East

Asian *liyi* spiritual discourse, which emphasizes moral rituals (li) and right relationships (yi), is a more appropriate framework to discuss and analyze the spirituality of Chinese and Japanese Americans. Even for the second, third, and fourth generations of these groups who are acculturated, an emphasis on rituals and relationships better accounts for their spiritual realities. Chinese Americans may be characterized with a hybridized "familism" and Japanese Americans with a "natural religion" of reciprocal obligations that shape their ultimate aims and ethics. Further, we posit that this discourse can be a helpful way to describe the emerging outlooks of American Millennials who are religious nones.

2. American Religious Nones

The emerging research on American religious nones, those who do not affiliate with any religious tradition or identity, offers typologies and social characteristics of this group. The Pew Research Center has divided this umbrella group into three subgroups: atheists, agnostics, and nothing in particular. The nothing in particular category has been further conceptualized and categorized, including the use of a range of terms: unchurched believers [2], humanists [3], spiritual but not religious [4], and liminals [5]. American religious nones are more likely to be male, unmarried, college educated, and residing in the West [6]. Four other characteristics mark the religiously unaffiliated, which provide explanations for their growth in the last two decades. They are (1) demographic shifts; (2) religious socialization; (3) political trends; and (4) cultural turns towards individualism.

First, as this Special Issue on religion and young adults observes, the rise of the nones is attributed to generational replacement as Millennials enter adulthood and older Americans, who were more religious, pass away. The Pew Research Center suggests that "These generational differences are consistent with other signs of a gradual softening of religious commitment among some (though by no means all) Americans in recent decades" [4].

Second, Baker and Smith assert that the religious socialization of those who are unaffiliated significantly correlates with their subsequent religious identification as adults [2]. Religious nones are more than three times likely than others to have an unaffiliated mother or father, who long serve as their primary reference group. Their parents' non-affiliation, in turn, shapes the extent to which they bring their children to religious institutions [7]. Religious nones were much less likely to attend organized religious services as twelve year olds than those religiously affiliated.

Third, Hout and Fischer observe that American religious nones tend to retain traditional religious beliefs, but are disenfranchised by organized religion [8]. They correlate highly with political liberals who have disaffiliated from religion and have been alienated by the incursion of conservative Christian politics within the last few decades. Similarly, Baker and Smith find that both atheists and unchurched believers share strong opposition to religion in the public sphere [2]. Thus, their growth of religious nones is a political act of disaffiliation, an expression of antipathy both to organized religion in general and to some churches' stances on divisive issues such as same-sex marriage [9].

Finally, the overall privatization of religion within the United States has promoted the development of personal spirituality, which may be independent of traditional religions. Peter Berger has maintained that increased pluralism destabilizes religious belief and organizations. The availability of alternatives to a single, unified religious worldview opens new options, including secularism and individually crafted spirituality [10]. As religious institutions decline, Americans continue to retain spiritual beliefs and individual religious practices in a bricolage fashion, which Bellah *et al.* have described as "Sheilaism" [11]. Among Millennials, the increase of religious individualism in the United States is an overall cultural trend, which follows secularization trends in Europe [12].

These explanations address the shift towards religious nones, but do not explain why Chinese and Japanese Americans have been historically religiously unaffiliated. To better theorize their religious patterns, a reconceptualization of religious nones is necessary.

3. Conceptual Issues in the Categorization of Religious Nones

Western sociological conceptualizations of religion focus on belief and belonging. Since American Judeo-Christian faith traditions emphasize belief in religious teachings and in membership to denominations, these paradigmatic assumptions about religious participation have been valid and reliable. The rise of religious nones, then, is thus assumed to relate to nonbelief and nonbelonging. For instance, the title of Baker and Smith's article, "None Too Simple: Examining Issues of Religious Nonbelief and Nonbelonging in the United States" reflects this paradigm [2].

Current research on religious nones debates the appropriate classification, terminology, and measurement of this category. The General Social Survey (GSS) automatically assigned persons according to their belief on a fundamentalist-moderate-liberal continuum. Refining this classification system may better identify distinctions among the "other" category [13]. For example, by measuring religious affiliation at the congregational level, rather than at the broader denominational level, Dougherty, Johnson and Poulson find that the percentage of religious unaffiliated is significantly lower while the numbers of Americans who are Evangelical is higher [14]. In contrast, Smith and Kim argue that these numbers do not indicate better measurement of nones and evangelicals, but simply a measurement of different responses [15].

Even while being contested, the belief and belonging religious paradigm is dominant and it assumes binaries between belief and non-belief, belonging and non-belonging. Hence, the spiritual but not religious category assumes a bifurcation of two concepts: religion is tied to organized, traditional faith traditions and spirituality is connected to hybridized, individualistic orientations toward the transcendent [16].

Asian American sociologists of religion also employ the belief and belonging paradigm, especially when studying Christianity. Fenggang Yang includes four elements in his definition of a religion which highlights belief: (1) a belief in the supernatural; (2) a set of beliefs regarding life and the world; (3) a set of rituals manifesting the beliefs; and (4) a distinct social organization of moral community of believers and practitioners [17]. Carolyn Chen prioritizes belonging, as she defines religion as "living traditions of meaning grounded in institutionalized communities [18].

One issue regarding this belief and belonging religious paradigm is that East Asians, such as Chinese and Japanese, have historically conceptualized and employed very different terms for their spiritual practices. For example, Chinese rarely use the term, "religion" for their popular religious practices and they also do not use the vocabulary that they believe "in" gods or truths [19]. Their linguistic schemas are based on the facts that Chinese popular religion has no sacred text or doctrines, hierarchical priesthood, or rites that express particular beliefs [18,20]. Instead, Chinese popular religion is better conceptualized around spiritual practices and forms of sociality, that is, around ritual and relations (*liyi*). Adam Chau's title, *Miraculous Response: Doing Popular Religion in Contemporary China*, names this religious orientation away from belief and belonging and toward enacting ritual and relations [21].

Likewise, Japanese culture has been greatly influenced by Chinese religions and Confucian philosophy, including the importance of reciprocal obligations. Categorizing these practices as religious or not religious has been the struggle of sociologists of religion, given that Japanese have responded in surveys that they are not religious, yet they regularly perform ritual obligations [22].

In examining Japanese rituals and relations, Toshimaro Ama defines Japanese "natural religion" as the practices which includes these reciprocal obligations, folkloric beliefs, and the value of being "ordinary"—practices, which Japanese do not categorize as religious [23]. They relate to a broad cultural ideal of maintaining community harmony, such as hosting, anticipating others' concerns, prioritizing care for others, respecting family and ancestors, and humility.

By examining the moral rituals of Chinese and Japanese American young adults, as well as their understanding of virtuous relationships, we better distinguish and capture their religious sensibilities and values. Categorization as religious nones does them a disservice; they do lead devout lives of devotion and commitment—even the atheists. Data from the Pew Research Study, "Asian Americans: A

Mosaic of Faiths" demonstrates how a redefinition of religion may be helpful in not only understanding this grouping, but American Millennials overall [24].

4. Methodology

This study analyzes survey data made available by the Pew Research Center. Phone interviews were conducted of 728 Chinese Americans and 523 Japanese Americans in early 2012. In analyses, we will provide unweighted figures in percentages. The use of percentages conforms to PEW's own analyses of its data for ease of cross-study comparison and simplifies the range of possible responses. We were not able to weight the figures by age because the age groups do not match either PEW or Census reports, and not able to weight religious affiliations because there are also no available figures on Asian American religious affiliations broken down by age outside of the data we are examining.

In our sample, 157 of the Chinese Americans (21.5%) were under 30 years of age. Atheists made up 13.3% of this group and nothing in particulars comprised 36.3%. Among the Japanese American respondents, 36 were under 30 years old. In this group, two were atheists, one was agnostic, and thirteen were nothing in particular. Due to the small sample size of Japanese Americans, we can only make preliminary observations about Japanese American young adults and primarily, nothing in particulars. The percentages of religious nones who are under 30 are greater than the overall group: 5.6% of young Japanese Americans are atheists and 36.1% were nothing in particular, as compared to 2.7% and 25.8% of all Japanese Americans, respectively.

Since atheists and nothing in particulars are the categories that make up the largest proportions of Chinese Americans, this study compares them to identify both similarities and differences in rituals and relationships. It also details how Chinese and Japanese American religious nones, who are young adults (under 30 years of age), stand in relationship to their overall subpopulations.

5. Findings

5.1. Belonging

Using the survey categories provided by the Pew Research Center, young adult Chinese and Japanese Americans are more likely to be unaffiliated than the average young American (Pew Research Center 2010). Over 1/3 of Chinese Americans (36.3%) and Japanese Americans (36.1%) self-identify themselves at "nothing in particular," as compared to 18% of all American young adults. Young Chinese Americans (13.3%) were four times more likely and Japanese Americans (5.6%) were two times more likely to be atheist than the average American (3%) (Figures 1 and 2).

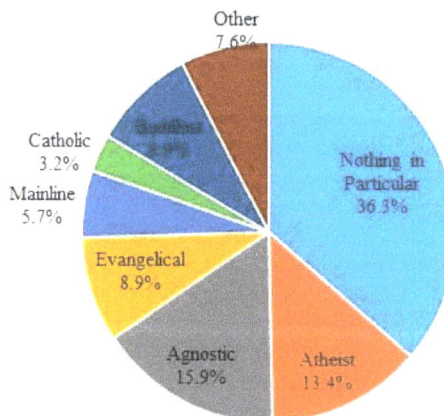

Figure 1. Religious Affiliation of Young Chinese Americans.

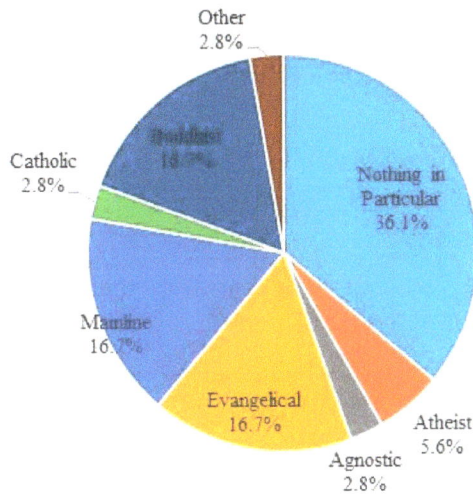

Figure 2. Religious Affiliation of Young Japanese Americans.

Compared to their ethnic subpopulation, these Chinese American Millennials are also more likely to be atheists. Overall, Chinese Americans included 8.7% who were atheist. On the other hand, the percentage of all Chinese American nothing in particulars (37.4%) was roughly the same as the Millennials. Among all Japanese Americans, only 2.7% were atheist and 25.8% were nothing in particular.

5.2. Beliefs

As religious nones, Chinese and Japanese American young adults have much more variegated beliefs than other Asian Americans or other Americans their age. Overall, they rate religion as less important to them than those who do affiliate with religion. Among Chinese Americans, only 19.0% of atheists and 15.8% of the nothing in particulars view religion as "somewhat important" to them and none said it was "very" important to them. Among all Chinese Americans, 20.6% said religions was "very" important and 25.1% said it was "somewhat" important. Of the young Japanese Americans, 15.4% of the nothing in particulars considered religion somewhat important (7.1% of all Japanese American atheists). In contrast 12% of American young adults who were religious nones stated that religion was "very" important to them (Figure 3).

In terms of belief in God or universal spirit, religious nones clearly varied again. Among Chinese American young adults, 43.9% of the nothing in particulars believed in God, but only 23.8% of atheists did, in contrast to the 63.5% of Chinese Americans overall who believed in God. Even more Japanese American nothing in particulars, at 53.8%, believed in God (21.4% of all Japanese American atheists). On the other hand, 36% of American Millennials who were unaffiliated were certain in their belief of God [25] (Figure 4).

Although large percentages believed in God, Asian Americans had much lower rates of belief in heaven. When asked about a heaven where people are eternally rewarded, 19.0% of Chinese American atheists and 29.8% of nothing particulars expressed their belief as compared to 46.0% of all Chinese Americans. Young adult Japanese American nothing in particulars were slightly higher at 38.5%. In contrast, almost half (46%) of American religious nones who are young adults believed in heaven (Figure 5).

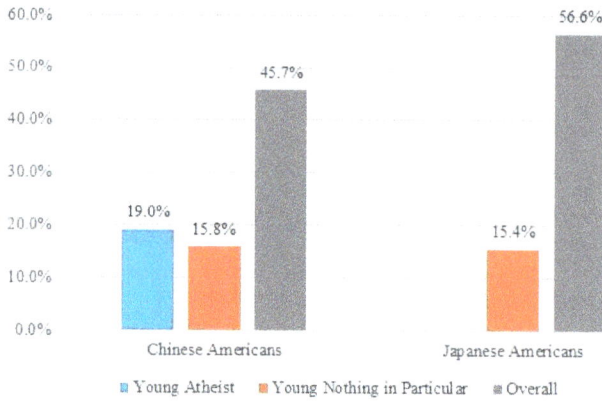

Figure 3. Importance of religion.

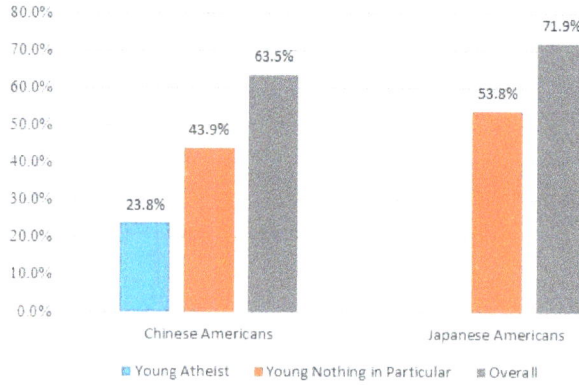

Figure 4. Belief in God or universal spirit.

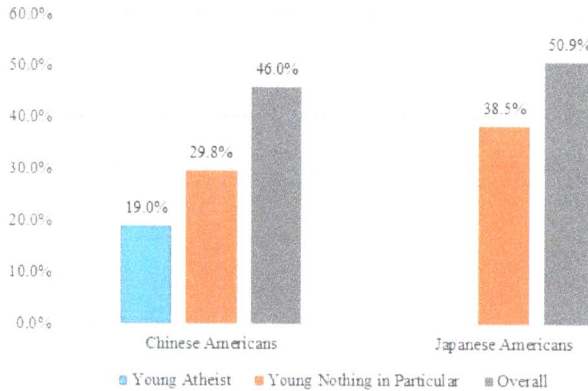

Figure 5. Belief in heaven.

While these Asian Americans may not espouse belief in God and Western religious concepts as European and African Americans might, they do believe in East Asian supernatural forces. Regarding *qi*, or spiritual energy located in physical things, 19.0% of Chinese American atheists and 38.6% of nothing particulars did, in comparison to the 39.3% of all Chinese. Japanese American nothing in particulars had an even higher percentage at 46.2% (Figure 6).

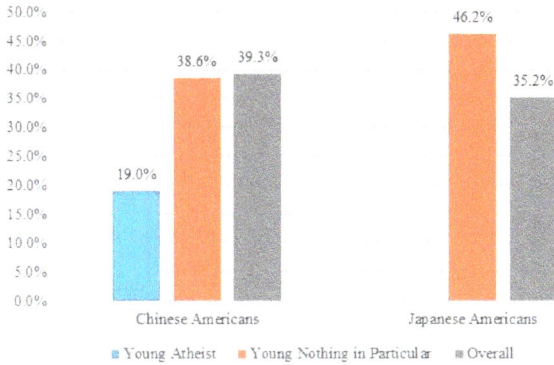

Figure 6. Belief in spiritual energy.

Likewise, large percentages of Asian American religious nones believed in ancestral spirits, even the atheists. In fact, Chinese and Japanese Americans were more apt to believe in ancestral spirits than in God. One third of Chinese American atheists (33.3%) and 43.9% of nothing in particulars acknowledged that their deceased relatives continued to exist. Indeed, a higher rate of Chinese American nothing in particulars believed in ancestral spirits than the average Chinese American (40.0% believing). Of the young adult Japanese Americans, 38.5% of the nothing in particulars believed in ancestral spirits (21.4% of all Japanese American atheists) (Figure 7).

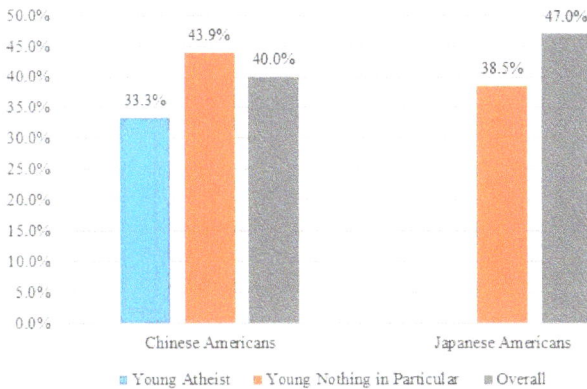

Figure 7. Belief in ancestral spirits.

5.3. Practices

Since Chinese and Japanese Americans have high rates of nonbelief and nonbelonging, they rarely attended religious services, prayed, meditated, or fasted. Only 7.1% of Chinese American nothing in particulars pray more than a few times a week and none of the Chinese American atheists pray this much. Japanese Americans pray slightly more often, but still at low rates, with 15.4% of nothing in particulars praying weekly and 23.1% praying a few times a month. However, both groups do continue to maintain spiritual practices with Asian roots. These practices include both family home rituals and ethnic festivals.

For example, Chinese continue to maintain home shrines despite their religious non-affiliation. In terms of keeping a shrine for prayer at home, 23.8% of Chinese American atheists and 12.3% of nothing particulars had one. Japanese American young adults, on the other hand, were less likely to have a shrine. In general, 10.9% of all Chinese Americans and 17.6% of all Japanese Americans kept a home shrine (Figure 8).

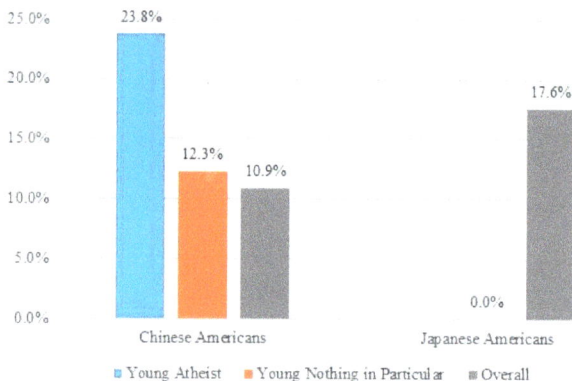

Figure 8. Has home shrine.

Although they do not necessarily espouse Christian beliefs, high rates of Chinese Americans celebrate Christmas. Of the Chinese religious nones who are Millennials, 57.1% of atheists and 70.2% of nothing in particulars practice this religious holiday, lower than all Chinese Americans (81.9%). The young Japanese Americans of all affiliations were unanimous in their celebration of Christmas at 100% (Figure 9).

Even higher rates of Chinese Americans celebrate Lunar New Year. Nine of ten Chinese American atheists (90.5%) and 90.9% of nothing in particulars practice this ethnic festival, higher than the overall Chinese American rate of 83.5%. Unlike Chinese Americans, Lunar New Year is not a traditional festival for Japanese Americans, yet 46.2% of young nothing in particulars celebrate it. These figures are higher than the overall Japanese American population, of which 27.1% celebrates this holiday (Figure 10).

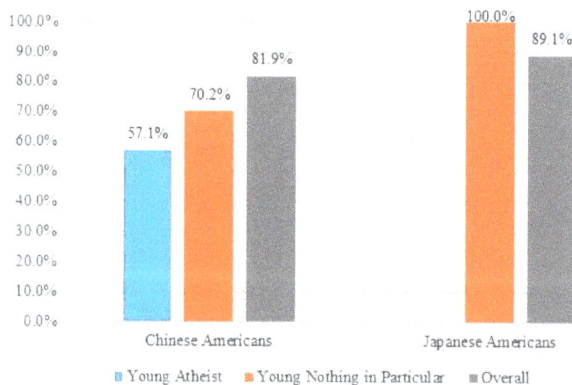

Figure 9. Celebrates Christmas.

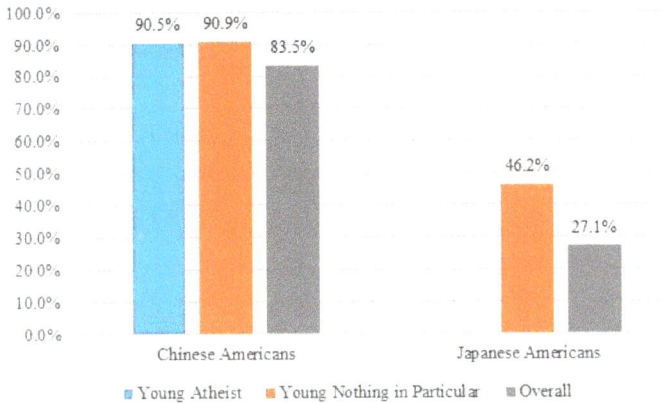

Figure 10. Celebrates Lunar New Year.

5.4. Relationships and Ethics

Even though Chinese and Japanese Americans do not have rates of religious belonging, belief, or practices, they hold very high values for close family bonds and reciprocal relationships.

When asked about their most important goals, Chinese and Japanese American young adults valued being good parents slightly higher than other Americans. Among Chinese Americans, 57.1% of atheists and 49.1% nothing in particulars rated this as their top life goals, as compared to 56.7% of Chinese American overall. A similar percentage, 55.6% of young Japanese Americans, valued being a good parent as a top goal, including 23.1% of nothing in particulars, and 100% of the atheists (85.7% of atheists overall). Though the figure for nothing in particular seems low, 69% responded the next tier response of "very important" goal, leading to 92.3% responding very important and most important. About half (52%) of Millennials overall rated being a good parent as a top goal [26] (Figure 11).

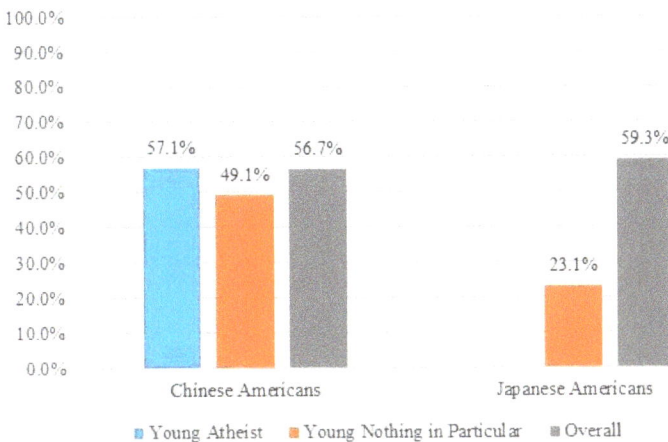

Figure 11. Top goal: being a good parent.

Having a successful marriage is the next highest rate goal, with 23.8% of Chinese American atheists and 43.9% of nothing in particulars citing this value. About half of Chinese Americans in general (45.7%) agreed about the importance of marriage. For young Japanese Americans, 38.5% of nothing in particulars held marriage as a top goal (57.1% atheists overall). Only 30% of American Millennials rated marriage this highly (Figure 12).

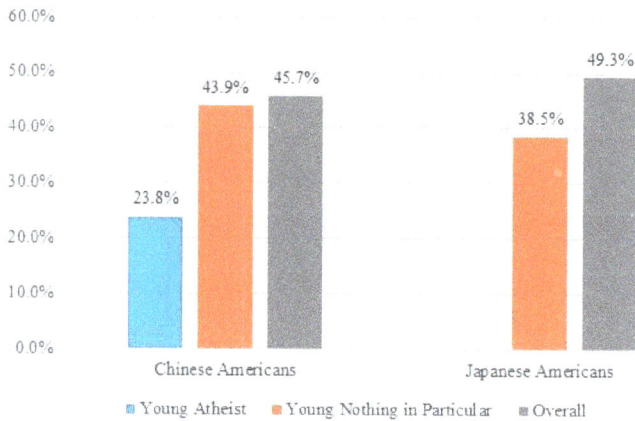

Figure 12. Top goal: having a good marriage.

While young adults are at a stage in life to focus on their careers, career is not as an important goal for Asian Americans as their family lives. Only 9.5% of Chinese American atheists and 19.3% of nothing in particulars identified career as one of their top goals, as compared to 16.8% for all Chinese Americans. Similarly for young Japanese Americans, 15.4% of nothing in particulars held their career as a top goal (no Japanese American atheists cited as a top goal). These percentage rates are comparable to other American young adults, of whom 15% wanted a successful, high paying career (Figure 13).

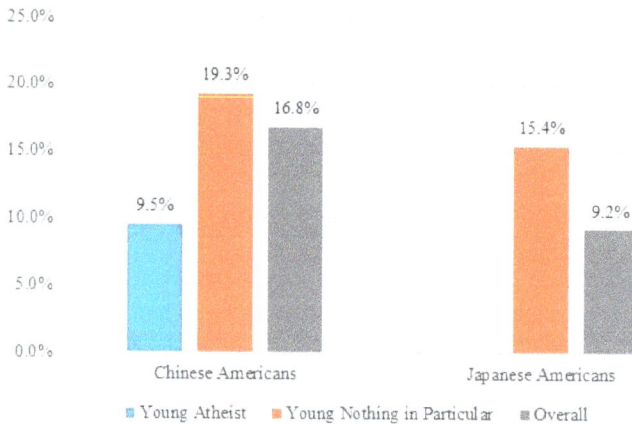

Figure 13. Top goal: having a successful career.

One out of ten Chinese American atheists (9.5%) and 19.3% of nothing in particulars listed helping others in need as one of their most important goals. More Japanese American youth held this as a top goal, with 30.8% of nothing in particulars and both young atheists. Overall, 21.0% of all Chinese Americans and 21% of American Millennials rated this value highly (Figure 14).

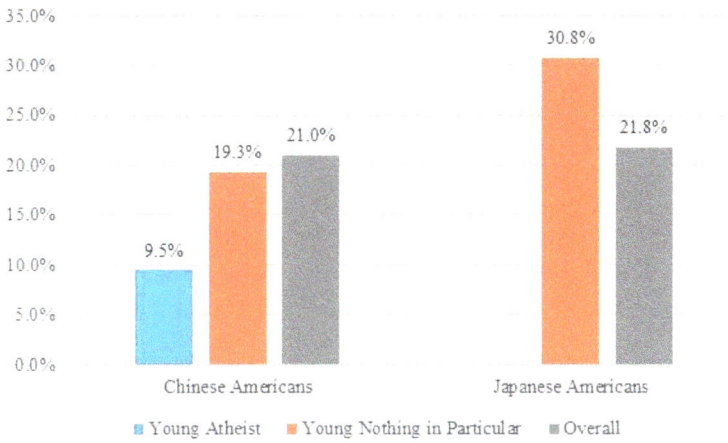

Figure 14. Top goal: helping others in need.

Another way to rate family bonds is valuing parental influence over major decisions. Chinese American young adults state that their parents should have some or a lot of influence in their careers and even marriage choice. In fact, 38.1% of atheists and 64.9% of nothing in particulars believe their parents should have some or a lot of say in their choice of careers. Six out of ten Chinese Americans overall (62.9%) feel parents should have such career influence (Figure 15).

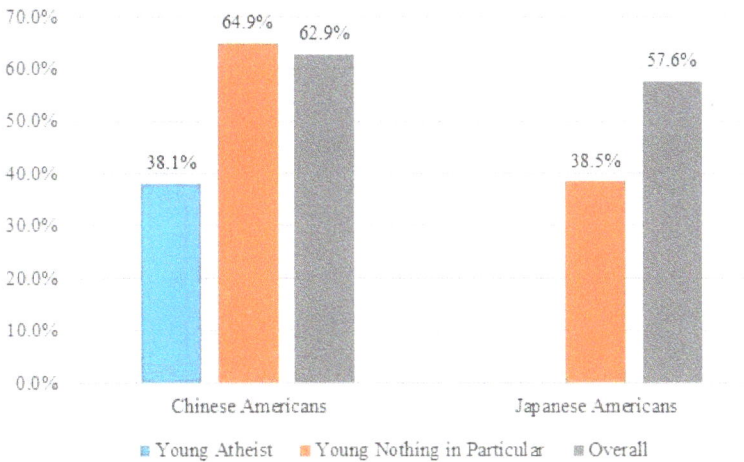

Figure 15. Values parental influence in career.

Similarly, 42.9% of atheists and 65.0% of nothing in particulars believe their parents deserve some influence in their choice of spouse, as compared to 56.8% of Chinese Americans who do. By contrast, young Japanese Americans felt that their parents should have less influence over their choice of career, with 38.5% of nothing in particulars. In regards to choice of spouse, 30.8% of Japanese American nothing in particulars felt their parents should have a say (Figure 16).

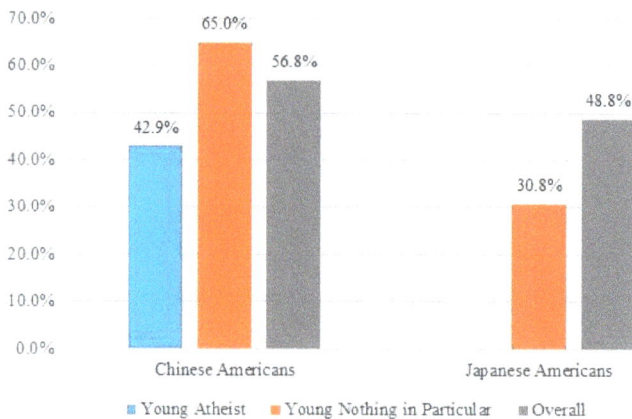

Figure 16. Values parental influence in spousal choice.

Along with having strong family bonds, Chinese Americans and Japanese Americans feel that their respective groups get along well with other racial groups in the United States. Young Chinese Americans feel that they get along well with whites, with 85.7% of atheists and 80.7% of nothing in particulars expressing that the groups get along pretty well or better. In general, 85.0% of Chinese Americans also state the same. Young Japanese Americans responded at higher rates, with both atheists (92.9% of all Japanese American atheists) and 84.6% of nothing in particulars feeling this way. And, for all Japanese Americans, the figure is 91.8% (Figure 17).

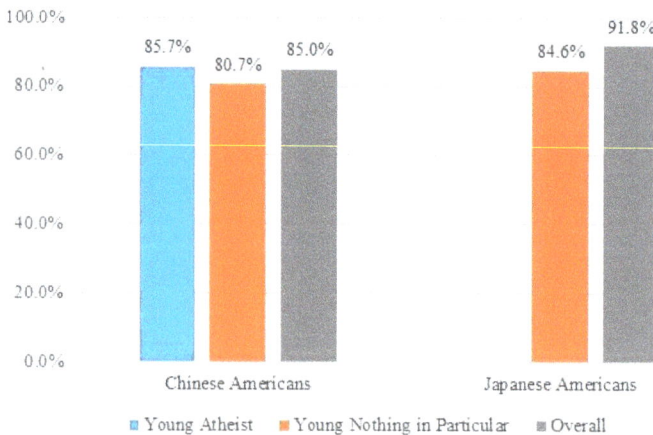

Figure 17. Getting along with whites.

In reference to blacks and the Chinese American community, 52.4% of atheists and 52.7% of young nothing in particulars felt that Chinese Americans get along pretty well or higher, as compared to 52.7% overall. Young Japanese Americans again responded higher with 71.4% of all atheists, 69.2% of nothing in particulars, and 67.7% of the total feeling that Japanese Americans get along with black Americans (Figure 18).

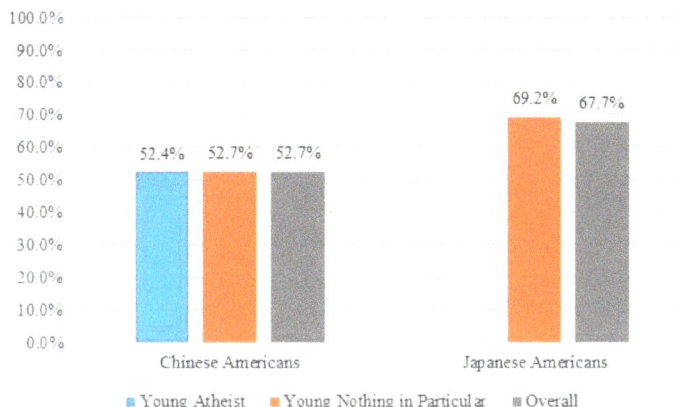

Figure 18. Getting along with blacks.

In regards to politics, both young adult Chinese and Japanese Americans tend to identify as moderate, would consider abortion legal in all or most cases, and feel that homosexuality should be accepted by society. Both the Chinese American atheists and nothing in particulars identify as moderate (as opposed to liberal and conservative) at 38.1% and 40.4%. Young Japanese Americans similarly identify as moderate with 23.1% of nothing in particulars doing so. Note that for all Chinese Americans 38.3% are moderate and 35.8% of all Japanese Americans identify as moderate, the highest response for any political ideology (Figure 19).

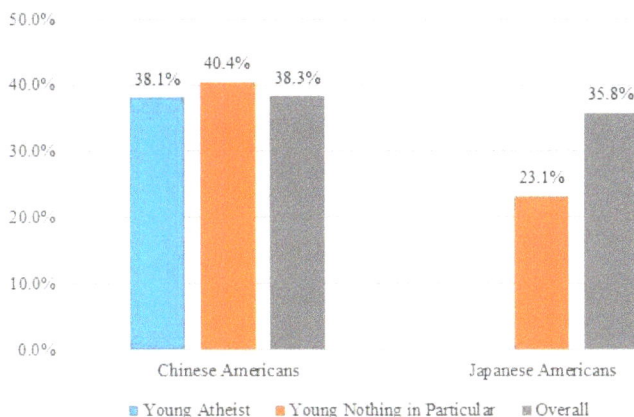

Figure 19. Moderate political ideology.

Young Chinese American religious nones tend to consider that abortion should be legal in all or most cases, with 100% of atheists and 61.4% of nothing in particulars agreeing to these statements. Two thirds of Chinese Americans (66.1%) also believe the same. Young Japanese Americans respond similarly with 92.3% of nothing in particulars assenting (Figure 20).

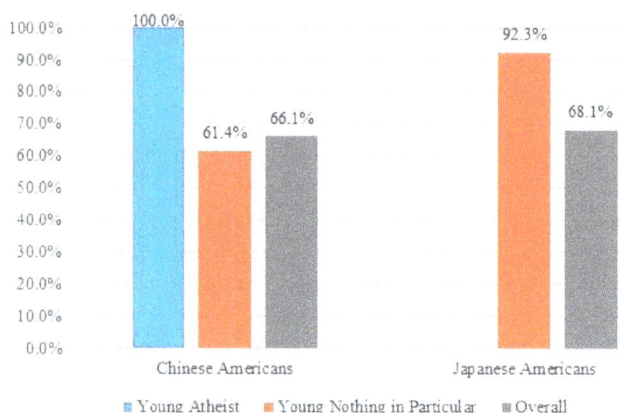

Figure 20. Supports legal abortion.

The issue of homosexuality diverges slightly for Chinese and Japanese Americans. Of young Chinese Americans, 95.2% of atheists and 75.4% of nothing in particulars feel that society should accept homosexuality. In contrast, only 54.8% of Chinese American total sample think the same. Young Japanese Americans feel strongly that society should accept homosexuality with 92.3% of nothing in particulars responding in this way, and 68.1% of all (Figure 21).

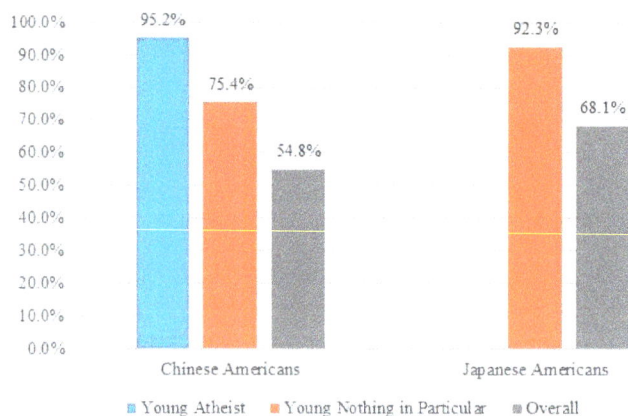

Figure 21. Supports homosexuality.

6. Discussion

Chinese and Japanese American young adults have higher rates of religious nones than their ethnic groups overall, as well as their American counterparts of the same age. We suggest that three key factors explain why Asian Americans are the racial group with the highest percentage of religious nones in the United States.

First, 46.4% of the Chinese Americans surveyed came from the People's Republic of China, where atheism is the official doctrine of the Chinese Communist Party. The government regulates religion so that only five major religions are recognized. On the other hand, it labels Chinese popular religion as *mixin*, or superstition. The Cultural Revolution (1966–1979) sought to eradicate bourgeois elements, including all religion. Consequently, all religious venues were shut down, religious leaders were persecuted, and believers had to make public renunciations [17]. As a result of these policies, a large portion of Chinese Americans from China identify as religious nones.

Second, religion has been historically intertwined with the western colonization of Asia. In fact, the term "religion" itself was imposed on Japan in the mid-nineteenth century, when the United States and European nations used a military envoy to force the nation to accept trade treaties. Included in these treaties was the "freedom of religion", which meant that Christians were free to missionize Japan. Religion was narrowly translated as "doctrines", leaving many Japanese rituals, obligations, and emotions outside of "religion" [27]. It also left the term with negative connotations of divisiveness and consumptive aggression. As a result, Asians—and those who became Asian American—often disassociate themselves from the concept of religion and from Christianity, which was considered an imposed, Western religion.

Third, despite their religious nonbelonging, significant portions of both atheists and nothing in particulars maintain beliefs, practices, and ethics that are consistent with Asian popular religious practices. However, these religious rituals and relations have no sociological category that fit them.

Among young atheists, almost one fourth (23.8%) of Chinese Americans believed in God. On the other hand, 1/3 of them believed in ancestral spirits, which is not a belief that atheists are known to hold. A higher rate of Chinese American nothing in particulars, at 43.9% believed in God and the same percentage believed in ancestral spirits. In fact, young Chinese American nothing in particulars were more likely to believe in ancestral spirits than the overall Chinese American population.

Beliefs are similarly strong among Japanese American young religious nones, with 53.8% of nothing in particulars expressing a belief in God or universal spirit. The numbers of young atheists is too small, but 21.4% of all Japanese American atheists expressed this belief, which is similar to the Chinese American figure. Young Japanese American atheists asserted belief in ancestral spirits and the spiritual power of yoga (not noted above), though the small sample cannot convey the extent of belief, except to say that atheists do hold beliefs.

Even though unaffiliated young Chinese Americans do not pray or attend religious services much at all, a small percentage do maintain home shrines where they may venerate their deceased ancestors. Japanese Americans have two traditions of home shrines that can be traced to an organized religion—the *butsudan* (Buddhist) and the *kamidana* (Shinto). However, in practice both shrines can be utilized for memorial and fortune rituals not specific to a religious organization; consequently, those who continue these rituals need not identify with the organization, and those who reject religious affiliation can continue these rituals [28]. Whether Chinese and Japanese Americans do pray or make offerings at these shrines was not asked. Further, altars are not an element of any religion named in sociological surveys. Subsequently, these ethnicities cannot affiliate with any religious grouping, and instead usually identify religiously as "nothing in particular".

Following ethnic family traditions, Chinese American religious nones are more likely than the average Chinese American to celebrate Lunar New Year, a time when families come together to honor deities and ancestors. It also includes several rituals to bring good fortune and taboos to keep away bad luck. As another key festival of Chinese popular religion, these rituals are often employed to instill moral values and ethical behavior among its adherents. However, like ancestor veneration they are not part of a named religion, so participants do not classify themselves as belonging to any one faith tradition.

This familism is also reflected in how the Millennial Chinese and Japanese American religious nones seek to be good parents and in how they relate to their own parents. Like other Millennials, being a good parent is the top life goal for Chinese and Japanese Americans. Indeed, Chinese American Millennials do not necessarily seek to become autonomous adults but include their parents in their major decisions. They may believe that since their parents sacrificed so much for them in the immigration process that they have an obligation to consider their parents' wishes in their career choices.

Japanese American Millennials hold the value of family relationships but differ in their interpretation of what results from a functioning family. In Japanese popular religion, correct family and community relationships are supposed to emanate the feeling of warm togetherness and gracious hospitality. In this sense, parental influence over career and spouse feels a bit heavy-handed, and correspondingly no young atheists responded that parents should influence them and young nothing in particulars responded in the thirty percent range.

Responses to questions about holidays, relations with other racial groups, and political stances reveal aspects of this warm hospitality for Japanese Americans. All young Japanese Americans celebrate Christmas, including the unaffiliated. This unanimity illustrates how they may see Christmas as the holiday with the most opportunity to practice hospitality, to have a heartfelt experience with extended family, and to honor parents, elders, and children alike. Young Japanese Americans responded that they get along well with whites and blacks. In this way, young, unaffiliated Japanese Americans cultivate warm hospitality among their friends and colleagues in addition to their family.

The value for hospitality is further illustrated by young Japanese Americans' moderate political identity and support of homosexuality. Being "moderate" concurs with the image of Japanese Americans being open to others and not excluding others, be they conservative or liberal. They are also open to different sexual orientations, with young Japanese American nothing in particulars feeling that society should accept homosexuality. By welcoming sexual orientations and races, mitigating authoritarian pressure, and taking advantage of the common, jolly holiday of Christmas, young Japanese Americans can be unaffiliated yet practice elements of Japanese popular religion.

7. Conclusions

Chinese and Japanese American Millennials who are religious nones maintain spiritual practices and ethical behaviors that are unique hybridizations of their ethnic backgrounds and American upbringings. We suggest that to better capture the nature and character of their religious behavior, a *liyi* religious discourse of ritual and relationships is more appropriate than one of belief and belonging.

A distinguishing feature of *li*, which can be translated as Chinese rites or religious rituals, is that they instill normative, proper morals [29]. Rituals of Chinese popular religion, such as ancestor veneration, New Year meals, or cleaning gravesites, are what people should do with pious and serious effort to preserve social order. Not only do these rituals act as concrete guides to follow, but also they may have the power to bring about the moral transformation of the individuals performing them. As stated earlier, Chinese traditionally do not "believe in" religion, but instead they "do" religion.

Japanese popular religion includes similar rituals, some inherited from the Chinese, in order to create a family and community filled with warmth and hospitality. In addition, the term "religion", translated as "doctrines", was forced onto Japan by colonialism in the mid-nineteenth century. As a result, religion does not include rituals and feelings of togetherness, and it connotes divisiveness and consumptive aggression. Japanese do not "believe in" religion, but "do" it.

Yi, translated roughly as righteousness or justice, is a moral disposition to do good and the ability to feel what is right and wrong [30]. Indeed, some acts ought to be performed simply because they are the correct and right thing to do. This concept particularly relates to how one relates to others with loyalty and righteousness, as epitomized by General Guan Yu, a Chinese historical figure who was deified. Overseas Chinese especially revere Guan Yu as he reflected the brotherhood and mutual support that they valued in foreign lands [31]. Likewise, Japanese Americans learned to support each other as a family and community through the racist eras of the Exclusion Act of 1924 and World War II. They spread slogans such as "patience and perseverance" and "for the sake of the children" which mean self-sacrifice for the emotional well-being of the family [32].

A focus on rituals and righteousness in relations illuminates how Chinese and Japanese Americans do religion. While the religious nones of these groups may not belong to any religious traditions or espouse Judeo-Christian beliefs, they do maintain certain rituals for their "rightness" and they relate to family and others in highly moral ways. In other words, the rituals and righteousness of Asian

Americans provide their ultimate morals and manners. These spiritual practices make up what we term "Chinese American familism" [33]. For Japanese Americans, the rituals and righteous relations are reflected in their hospitality and warmth in relationships.

Likewise, those identifying as religious nones vary so much in their religious orientations that a redefinition of religion is required, including a renewed focus on religious practice [34,35]. Nancy Ammerman observes that the discourses of spiritual but not religious individuals tend to converge around an ethical spirituality, one where "real spirituality is about living a virtuous life, one characterized by helping others, transcending one's own selfish interests to seek what is right" ([16], p. 272). Her study demonstrates that Americans overall also believe that true religion concerns more with what they do and how they relate than what they believe or with whom they belong.

Despite self-identifying as religious nones, Chinese and Japanese American young adults do maintain hybridized spiritual rituals and value righteous relations. A focus on their *liyi* religious repertoire can similarly illuminate how American Millennials do spirituality in our changing religious landscape.

Acknowledgments: The authors wish to acknowledge Seanan Fong and Helen Jin Kim for their insights on Asian American religious nones and *liyi* religious discourse.

Author Contributions: Russell Jeung co-wrote the paper. Brett Esaki co-wrote the paper. Alice Liu analyzed the data and prepared the figures.

Conflicts of Interest: The authors declare no conflict of interest.

References

1. Pew Research Center. "America's Changing Religious Landscape: Christians Decline Sharply as Share of Population; Unaffiliated and Other Faiths Continue to Grow." Available online: http://www.pewforum. org/2015/05/12/americas-changing-religious-landscape/ (accessed on 13 May 2015).

2. Joseph Baker, and Buster Smith. "None Too Simple: Examining Issues of Religious Nonbelief and Nonbelonging in the United States." *Journal for the Scientific Study of Religion* 48 (2009): 719–33. [CrossRef]

3. Barry Kosmin, and Ariela Keysar. "American Nones: The Profile of the No Religion Population, A Report Based on the American Religious Identification Survey 2008." In *American Nones: The Profile of the No Religion Population.* Trinity College Faculty Report; Hartford: Institute for the Study of Secularism in Society & Culture, 2009.

4. Pew Research Center. "Nones on the Rise." 9 October 2012. Available online: http://www.pewforum.org/ 2012/10/09/nones-on-the-rise/#_ftn4 (accessed on 6 January 2015).

5. Chaeyoun Lim, Carol McGregor, and Roger Putnam. "Secular and Liminal: Discovering Heterogeneity among Religious Nones." *Journal for the Scientific Study of Religion* 49 (2010): 596–618. [CrossRef]

6. Joseph Baker, and Buster Smith. "The Nones: Social Characteristics of the Religiously Unaffiliated." *Social Forces* 87 (2008): 1251–63. [CrossRef]

7. Christel Manning. "Unaffiliated Parents and the Religious Training of Their Children." *Sociology of Religion* 74 (2013): 149–75. [CrossRef]

8. Michael Hout, and Claude S. Fischer. "Why More Americans Have No Religious Preference: Politics and Generations." *American Sociological Review* 67 (2002): 65–90. [CrossRef]

9. Nicholas Vargas. "Retrospective Accounts of Religious Disaffiliation in the United States: Stressors, Skepticism, and Political Factors." *Sociology of Religion* 73 (2012): 200–23. [CrossRef]

10. Peter Berger. *The Homeless Mind: Modernization and Consciousness.* New York: Random House, 1973.

11. Robert Bellah, Richard Madsen, William M. Sullivan, Ann Swidler, and Steven M. Tipton. *Habits of the Heart: Individualism and Commitment in American Life.* Berkeley: University of California Press, 2007.

12. Robert Wuthnow. *After the Baby Boomers: How Twenty- and Thirty-Somethings Are Shaping the Future of American Religion.* Princeton: Princeton University Press, 2007.

13. Brian Steensland, Jerry Z. Park, Mark D. Regnerus, Lynn D. Robinson, W. Bradford Wilcox, and Robert D. Woodberry. "The measure of American religion: Toward improving the state of the art." *Social Forces* 79 (2000): 291–318. [CrossRef]

14. Kevin Dougherty, Byron Johnson, and Edward Polson. "Recovering the Lost: Remeasuring U.S. Religious Affiliation." *Journal for the Scientific Study of Religion* 46 (2007): 483–99. [CrossRef]
15. Tom Smith, and Seokho Kim. "Counting Religious Nones and Other Religious Measurement Issues: A Comparison of the Baylor Religion Survey and General Social Survey." GSS Methodological Report No. 110; Chicago: University of Chicago, 2007, p. 110.
16. Nancy Ammerman. "Spiritual but Not Religious? Beyond Binary Choices in the Study of Religion." *Journal for the Scientific Study of Religion* 52 (2013): 258–78. [CrossRef]
17. Fenggang Yang. *Religion in China: Survival and Revival under Communist Rule.* New York: Oxford University Press, 2012.
18. Carolyn Chen. *Getting Saved in America: Taiwanese Immigration and Religious Experience.* Princeton: Princeton University Press, 2014, p. 42.
19. Vincent Goosaert. "1898: The Beginning of the End for Chinese Religion? " *Journal of Asian Studies* 65 (2006): 307–36. [CrossRef]
20. Fan Lizhu. "Popular Religion in Contemporary China." *Social Compass* 50 (2003): 449–57. [CrossRef]
21. Adam Chau. *Miraculous Response: Doing Popular China in Contemporary China.* Stanford: Stanford University Press, 2008.
22. Winston Davis. *Japanese Religion and Society: Paradigms of Structure and Change.* New York: State University of New York, 1992.
23. Toshimaro Ama. *Why Are the Japanese Non-religious? Japanese Spirituality: Being in a Religious Culture.* Lanham: University Press of America, 2005.
24. Pew Research Center. "Asian Americans: Mosaic of Faiths." 19 July 2012. Available online: http://www.pewforum.org/2012/07/19/asian-americans-a-mosaic-of-faiths-overview/ (accessed on 6 August 2015).
25. Pew Research Center. "Religion among the Millennials." 17 February 2010. Available online: http://www.pewforum.org/2010/02/17/religion-among-the-millennials/ (accessed on 6 January 2015).
26. Pew Research Center. "Millennials: A Portrait of Generation Next." 10 February 2010. Available online: http://www.pewsocialtrends.org/files/2010/10/millennials-confident-connected-open-to-change.pdf (accessed on 6 January 2015).
27. Michihiro Ama. "Immigrants to the Pure Land: The Acculturation of Shin Buddhism in Hawaii and North America, 1898–1941." Ph.D. Dissertation, University of California, Irvine, CA, USA, 2007.
28. Jane Iwamura. "Altared States: Exploring the Legacy of Japanese American Butsudan Practice." *Pacific World: Journal of the Institute of Buddhist Studies/Institute of Buddhist Studies* 3 (2003): 275–91.
29. Patricia Ebrey. *Confucianism and Family Rituals in Imperial China: A Social History of Writing about Rites.* Princeton: Princeton University Press, 1991.
30. Kim-chong Chong. *Early Confucian Ethics: Concepts and Arguments.* Chicago: Open Court, 2007.
31. Joe Fong. *Complementary Education and Culture in the Global/Local Chinese Community.* South San Francisco: China Books and Periodicals, 2003.
32. Eiichiro Azuma. "Between Two Empires: Race, History, and Transnationalism in Japanese America." New York: Oxford, 2005.
33. Russell Jeung. "Second-Generation Chinese Americans and the Familism of the Nonreligious." In *Sustaining Faith Traditions: Religion, Race, and Ethnicity among the Latino and Asian American Second Generation.* Edited by Carolyn Chen. New York: New York University Press, 2012.
34. Stef Aupers, and Dick Houtman. "Beyond the spiritual supermarket: The social and public significance of new age spirituality." *Journal of Contemporary Religion* 21 (2006): 201–22. [CrossRef]
35. Courtney Bender. *The New Metaphysicals.* Chicago: University of Chicago Press, 2010.

religions

MDPI

Article

An Institutional and Status Analysis of Youth Ministry[1] in the Archdiocese of Detroit

Michael McCallion *, John Ligas and George Seroka

Sacred Heart Major Seminary, 2701 Chicago Blvd., Detroit, MI 48206-1799, USA; jlortho@aol.com (J.L.); gseroka@comcast.net (G.S.)

Academic Editor: Patricia Snell Herzog
Received: 12 January 2016; Accepted: 21 April 2016; Published: 6 May 2016

Abstract: This study finds that a weak institutional infrastructure of youth and young adult (YYA) ministry exists in the Catholic Archdiocese of Detroit (AOD). This helps to explain why there is a disconnect between the Archdiocese proclaiming YYA ministry as a top priority since 1995 and youth ministers self-reporting that they feel like second-class citizens. Moreover, this disconnect is occurring in an increasingly social context in which the current generations of young Catholics are participating less in their faith than previous generations. Interviews with 44 youth ministers and 12 pastors reveal details of this disconnect between archdiocesan *policy* which states YYA ministry is a top priority and the *practices* of the archdiocese which indicate otherwise. Youth ministers are marginalized workers who feel insecure about their employment, causing many to obtain second jobs or routinely search for better employment. The sociology of organization literature, particularly the concepts of decoupling and social status are discussed to help explain this disconnect. Data are interpreted and the conclusions made that ecclesial officials take youth ministry for granted and that a weak institutional infrastructure of youth ministry continues in the AOD.

Keywords: institutional infrastructure; social status; decoupling; marginalized workers; policy *vs.* practices; NONES; lay ministry; youth ministers

---

1. Introduction

Studies have found the Catholic Church to have a weak institutional infrastructure for youth and young adult ministry (YYA). This research investigates a specific case study of the Archdiocese of Detroit (AOD). The purpose of the study is to collect interview data from youth ministers and pastors in order to understand infrastructural issues from their perspective and then analyze the data through the application of social theories. Institutional and social status theories are applied to the case in order to elucidate explanations for the persistence of weak infrastructure, despite stated policy priorities to support and institutionalize youth ministry.

2. Background

2.1. Studies of Religious Participation and Leadership

One of the most relevant insights in extant studies of youth ministry is the assessment that the Catholic Church has a weak institutional infrastructure of YYA ministry compared to other religious

---

[1] Youth ministers are named Coordinators of Youth Ministry in the Archdiocese of Detroit, referring to those paid parish ministers who coordinate a parish ministry for high school teens in the parish—primarily for teens in grades 9 through 12. We use the term 'youth ministers' because it is more commonly used.

denominations [1]. This weak institutional infrastructure may help to explain why many Catholic teens have lower levels of religiosity compared to Protestant teens. As Smith notes:

> Simply put, the U.S. Catholic Church appears in its institutional infrastructure to invest fewer resources into youth ministry and education than do many other Christian traditions and denominations in the United States ([1], p. 216).

Smith and colleagues investigate nationally representative data of youth and find that Catholic teen religiosity is lower than the religiosity of some other religious traditions, such as evangelical Protestantism. In theorizing why this is the case, they identify a weak institutional infrastructure of YYA ministry in the Catholic Church as one possible explanation. In a series of local and more nuanced data, McCallion finds that the conclusions from this national study actually underestimate the extent of the weak institutional infrastructure in Detroit [2,3]. Specifically, the number and percentage of youth ministers in the Archdiocese of Detroit are lower than these national estimates.

Importantly, this weak institutional infrastructural problem has a history that goes back to at least the 1930s in the United States and, some authors believe, was exacerbated by the Church's response to the events of the 1960s. According to Bergler [4,5], the Catholic Church during and after the 1960s lost the strong network of mutually supportive institutions to form young people in the faith, mostly due to the decline of Catholic schools and "has yet to provide an equally effective replacement for its pre-1970 youth-forming institutions" ([4], p. 215). Although the social upheavals of the sixties, Vatican II and the encyclical *Humanae Vitae* often receive blame for this fallout, Bergler notes that "confusion, conflict and collapse in Catholic youth ministries during the 1960s and 1970s also contributed" ([5], p. 216) to the disaffiliation of youth. Bergler's summarized his most telling findings concerning youth ministers when he stated:

> In the late sixties, institutional investment in young people slumped in the Catholic world and has not yet fully recovered. The number of Catholic schools has declined steadily. Catholics were among the last American Christians to hire youth ministers. Catholic youth ministers enjoy lower job satisfaction and support from their fellow Catholics than other fulltime workers in the Catholic church. Catholics adapted quite well to the relatively conservative youth culture of the 1950s, but have not learned how to adapt on a large scale to the newer, more voluntary religious climate ([4], p. 217).

Numerous studies find overall trends of declining youth religious participation [6–12]. For example, Mercadante found that the highest percentage of "nones"—people claiming to have no religious affiliation—is the millennial generation [13]. She describes this trend in saying:

> The results of the extensive General Social Survey shows "nones" at 5 percent in 1972, 7 percent in 1975, 8 percent in 1990, 14 percent in 2000, 18 percent in 2010 and at least 20 percent in 2012. There are now more "nones" in America than mainline Protestants ([13], pp. 1–2).

The author continues by saying that "nones" are largest among Millennials, with trends indicating that their lack of religious participation is not merely a life course phase and can be expected to last as they settle into adulthood. As other studies found, she concludes that the youngest generations are now the mostly religiously unaffiliated of generations tracked to date.

Other studies also found that low youth participation rates have more direct measures of institutional infrastructure. For example, Williams and Davidson found more individualized conceptions of faith among younger generations of Catholics [6]. He argued that the generation of the 1930s and 1940s viewed their faith primarily in institutional terms, whereas the Baby Boom generation generally described their faith as less institutionally based. The generation of the 1970s and 1980s, as the post Vatican II generation, emphasize individualistic views of faith even more than the Vatican II generation did and now, the Millennial generation born since the 1980s represent an individualized conception of faith even more so. The youngest generation, which some call Generation Z, appears to be following this same individualizing pattern [14].

As a result, one major issue confronting religious instiutions is who will fill future leadership roles, as Williams and Davidson suggest:

> Well-documented declines in priestly vocations and religious orders seem even more ominous when listening to the post-Vatican II generation. As the shortage of priests, sisters and brothers suggests a need for greater participation of lay persons in active leadership roles, one is left wondering whether today's young Catholics will be willing to take on such institutional responsibilities ([6], p. 287).

This is especially concerning given that Murnion and DeLambo found that encouragement from church leaders is the best means for engaging youth to consider a vocation in ministry [15]. They stated in their national study of lay ministry that "Nearly 40 percent of all lay ministers were recruited by the pastor or a member of the parish staff" ([15], p. 39). The authors also point out that many laypersons come to the ministry through various church movements, renewal programs and spiritual type experiences. Given the importance of these studies, Murnion and DeLambo are concerned because "the church may be suffering from a decline in spiritual movements that foster both the spiritual life of its members and vocations to the various forms of ministry, ordained and non-ordained" ([15], p. 40). This concern over filling ecclesial institutional positions is related to the weak institutional infrastructure problem, as it forecasts the continual and even weakening lack of institutional support for transmission of the Catholic faith to younger generations. Indeed, these concerns are why one youth minister said: "I don't understand why the bishops don't fund university campus ministry programs to a much greater extent because that is the most likely place where young adults will discover a vocation to the Church whether lay, religious, or clerical" (interview field notes). The situation of future leadership is perhaps even more prescient given the Archdiocese of Detroit has purportedly made youth ministry a major priority.

2.2. History of Youth and Young Adult Ministry in the Archdiocese of Detroit

In 1994, the Archdiocese of Detroit (AOD) resurrected its vicariate structure of 8 to 20 or so parishes engaged in pastoral planning. As early as 1995, YYA ministry[2] surfaced as a top priority in most vicariates. Between the years 1997 and 2000, parishes within these vicariates completed a survey (94,000 responses) asking parishioners what pastoral priorities were most urgent. YYA ministry surfaced again as the number one priority[3]. In 2009, the 16 vicariates were broken down into 40 study groups for more detailed planning and these study groups also named YYA ministry as a top priority.[4]

In 2010, seven Archdiocesan Pastoral Council subcommittees were formed, based on the seven top priorities emerging from years of surveys and vicariate pastoral planning, to flesh out in detail objectives and goals for each priority. After a year of planning the YYA subcommittee formulated their number one objective for Archbishop Vigneron as that of finding monies to train and hire YYA ministers for AOD parishes. Given the results of the work of these subcommittees, it was decided

---

[2] Youth and young adults (YYA) refers to young Catholics in general, both high school youth and those 18 to approximately 35 years of age. In archdiocesan planning, most references are to YYA not just to high school teens or youth ministry. It is important to keep in mind that this research focuses primarily on youth ministry and youth ministers although some sources of data refer to both youth and young adults.

[3] In 1995, the AOD started surveying all parishes to determine what parishioners felt should be the top priorities of the archdiocese (AOD). As parishes in vicariates administered and returned surveys to the AOD over a 3 year period (94,000 responses), youth ministry was the top priority that emerged at the vicariate level (based on the question—"Vicariate level planning allows us to pool our resources with neighboring parishes. What should be our vicariate planning priorities?"—85.4% of parishioners named youth ministry or "programs for teens" as the top priority with young adult ministry or "programs for young adults" close behind at 80.5%). As vicariate planning became known as *Together In Faith* in the early 2000s and then *Together in Faith II* in 2005, "programs for teens and programs for young adults" became more specified as YYA. Moreover, another priority emerged along with YYA ministry as a top priority of the AOD—New Evangelization (NE).

[4] The 40 study group data is housed by the AOD Department of Parish Life and Services. Indeed, most survey data and vicariate data are held by the Department of Parish Life and Services—see AOD website [16].

to conduct another survey of all AOD parishioners about these seven mission priorities. In 2014, a survey was administered and 41,000 responses were gathered. Once again, YYA ministry was ranked a top priority.[5]

During the above diocesan, vicariate and parish planning processes out of which the mission priority of YYA ministry emerged, the specific voices of youth ministers were missing. In the field, anecdotes were heard over and again from parishioners and parish staff about the declining attendance and increasing disaffection of youth from the church. The voices and opinions of youth ministers were needed to better understand the overall picture concerning YYA ministry and if youth ministers perceived a disconnect between the AOD proclaiming YYA ministry a priority and what they actually experienced as youth ministers at the parish level.

Consequently, interviewing youth ministers was the focus of our research beginning in 2014 (44 interviews, see Appendix A for interview protocol). It was also decided to interview priest/pastors about their perceptions of youth ministry and that research began in 2015 (12 interviews have been completed to date, see Appendix B for interview protocol). As the subsequent case study data summarize, these sources of data show the AOD has a weak institutional infrastructure of YYA ministry, meaning that youth ministry positions are not taken for granted as necessary status positions in parishes, and little is being done about it, although diocesan leaders would most likely contest this assertion.

3. Research Methodology

Qualitative interview methods were used to explore how YYA ministry as a top AOD priority has been perceived by youth ministers and priests/pastors. Examples of the questions investigated in this study are: How do youth ministers perceive YYA ministry and how do they feel about those perceptions? Do youth ministers believe the AOD was adequately funding or otherwise resourcing YYA ministry? What obstacles do youth ministers think YYA ministry faces? What would youth ministers tell the archbishop about YYA ministry if they had the opportunity to speak to him one on one? Finally, do youth ministers or pastors perceive a disconnection between YYA ministry being a top priority and little being done about it in practice? Methodologically, collecting qualitative interview data from youth ministers and pastors was important to better understand the situation of YYA ministry from these actual practitioners at the parish level.

Qualitative interviews, therefore, provided youth ministers and pastors a venue through which to "voice" their perceptions and opinions about their ministry. In other words, a goal of qualitative research is to give "voice" to those under study. Marginalized social groups in particular, are given a voice to be heard through qualitative research. Youth ministers are a marginalized group (not all, but most) within the institutional church and more particularly within the realm of lay ecclesial ministry (lay *vs.* ordained). Because of pastors' position of power and less marginalized status within the chuch's institutional infrastructure than youth ministers, it was important to hear if their perceptions about YYA ministry aligned in any way with the perceptions of youth ministers. We maintain therefore, that we have interviewed "real" youth ministers, in "real" parish situations, in "real" time and in the process of doing so have arrived at certain commonalities that youth ministers share regardless of social class, gender, age, or geographic location. After about the 25th interview, the results of this research made clear that youth ministers can be described as a joyful but a beleaguered, marginalized group. The remaining 19 interviews confirmed this description.

---

[5] After the 40 study groups concluded their work, 7 or so mission priorities surfaced and so the Archdiocesan Pastoral Council (APC), which is the lay body that consults and advises the archbishop, broke down into subcommittees based on the 7 seven mission priorities—one of which was YYA ministry. Hence, there was first vicariate planning; second 40 study group planning (vicariates broken down into 40 groups); third APC was broken down into 7 subcommittees to continue pastoral planning. Again, the Department of Parish Life and Services collects and houses these data sources.

Qualitative research is important as well because it allows researchers to "pick-up" or "intuit" interviewees' emotional states or body language [17]. The interview transcriptions do not adequately reveal the intense emotions many interviewees felt about their ministry, especially the lack of support they received. There has been a good deal written about the ability of qualitative research to investigate perceptual and emotional dynamics that fall outside the realm of conscious deliberative and/or discursive processes. In other words, qualitative methods allow researchers to collect, analyze, and present findings about extra-deliberative emotional (non-cognitive) processes and how these same processes shape action. As to this research specifically, attending to the emotional dynamics of the interviewee was as important as what they said. For example, no youth minister directly stated he/she was "beleaguered", but attending to the extra-deliberative processes involved clearly revealed this to be the case. Qualitative research allows access to such non-discursive sources of data.

Finally, quantitative data were collected from AOD surveys, vicariate planning meetings and AOD sub-committee meetings between 1995 and 2014. Two main AOD surveys focused on priority issues of most concern to parishioners, asking them what they believed to be the most important issues facing the parish/church. In addition, an annual survey (1999–2009) of lay ecclesial ministers in the AOD was accessed to gather quantitative data on YYA ministers across the diocese. Another important data source was the 40 study groups created out of the vicariates which were commissioned by the archbishop to discuss and recommend what priorities the AOD should focus on in its pastoral planning.

4. The Archdiocese of Detroit as an Instiutional Case Study

In this section, we present quantitative data showing YYA ministry is a priority in the AOD along with statistics on the number of youth ministers in the AOD over the past 20 years. Secondly, we summarize qualitative interview data from forty-four youth ministers and twelve pastors, revealing taken-for-granted ecclesial processes that perpetuate a weak institutional infrastructure of YYA ministry in the AOD. Finally, the data is analyzed by applying theories drawn from the sociological organizational literature on institutions and social status, toward revealing underlying explanations for the persistence of weak youth ministry infrastructure despite stated priorities.

4.1. Quantitative Data on Youth Ministers

Quantitatively, it helps to first note the number of youth ministers in the AOD and their salaries because these figures suggest, as mentioned earlier, that a weak institutional infrastructure of YYA ministry exists. For example, data in Table 1 shows that the largest number of youth ministers was in the year 2000—the year with the greatest parish response rate—and yet it shows that only 41 percent of parishes have a youth minister.

Table 1 also shows that the number of youth ministers in parishes has not grown substantially in the AOD between 1999 and 2009. For example, in the year 2001 there were 108 professional paid youth ministers in the Archdiocese's 312 parishes, meaning only 39 percent of parishes had a paid youth minister. Moreover, of the 108 youth ministers, 63 or 58.3 percent were part-time. These percentages have remained constant between 1999 and 2006, with the number of all youth ministers, part and full time, declining, growing slightly and then declining again between 1999–2009 (see Table 1). This decline needs to be qualified given the decline in the number of parishes during those same years. Recognizing that parishes have closed throughout all dioceses of the United States, the number of parishes in the AOD has declined from 313 parishes in 1999 to 273 parishes in 2009 (Table 1) to 240 in 2013 (data missing for years 2010–2012), and 226 parishes in 2015 (see AOD website [16]). Keeping these numbers in mind, the *percentage* of parishes with youth ministers has gone up and down as well, with percentages of youth ministers declining since 2006 (Table 1).

Table 1. Youth Minister Trend Data 1999–2009.

Year	Number of Parishes	Number of Parishes Reporting	Percent of Parishes	Youth Ministers	Number of YM if 100% Parishes Reported	Ratio per Parish
1999	313	280	89.5%	112	125	0.40
2000	313	302	96.5%	124	129	0.41
2001	313	280	89.5%	108	121	0.39
2002	313	291	93.0%	104	112	0.36
2003	313	238	76.0%	107	141	0.45
2004	312	214	68.6%	87	127	0.41
2005	310	231	74.5%	119	160	0.52
2006	306	221	72.2%	119	165	0.54
2007	298	243	81.5%	100	123	0.41
2008	282	214	75.9%	88	116	0.41
2009	273	226	82.8%	87	105	0.38

Source: AOD Department of Parish Life and Services.

Table 1 also shows that in 2005 and 2006 there was a spike in the number and percentage of youth ministers after a gradual decline between 1999 and 2004. This is unexplained, other than it had something to do with the high parish response rate during those years. Nevertheless, whether one examines the high or low numbers, both appear low given YYA ministry has been a top priority since 1995. Moreover, youth ministers make up the lowest percentage compared to all lay ecclesial ministers at 10.6 percent (DREs are at 30.7 percent, musicians 30.2 percent, pastoral ministers 11 percent, and Christian Service 10.9 percent). Given these figures, the preferential option for YYA Catholics that Coleman called for in 1990, Hoge and colleagues called for in 2001 [8], and the AOD have been calling for since 1995, has not prompted much ecclesial action from the AOD to increase the institutional infrastructure of YYA ministry with, in particular, more monies and youth ministers, as stipulated by the AOD subcommittee on YYA ministry discussed below.

Moreover, the data in Table 2 show only full-time salaries, revealing that youth ministers are the lowest paid ministers for the year 2009–2010 (section heads are DRE assistants and hence not considered) and received the lowest full-time salaries during the previous decade as well. More revealing still is the fact that the average salary of a youth minister was 20,471 dollars between the years 2000 and 2009—the lowest of all salaried lay ecclesial ministers (data from AOD Dept of Parish Life and Services).

Table 2. Annual Salary of Full-Time Parish Ministers: 2009–2010.

Position	Salary
Music Director	46,002
Pastoral Minister	42,117
Liturgical Musician	41,999
Rite of Christian Initiation of Adults (RCIA Coordinator)	39,000
Director of Religious Education (DRE)	37,960
Christian Service Coordinator	37,325
Liturgy Coordinator	34,048
Youth Minister	32,759
Section Head—Religious Education	28,025
Average Salary All Positions	39,400

Source: AOD Department of Parish Life and Services.

As mentioned previously, the AOD conducted surveys between 1995 and 2014 that consistently identified youth ministry as a top priority.[6] In 2005, however, the 16 Vicariates of the AOD were broken

---

[6] The first archdiocesan wide survey started in 1995 and was administered to vicariates and parishes as each was prepared to take the survey through 1998. It took approximately four years for every parish to conduct the survey—with over 94,000

down into 40 study groups, all of whom reported back to their respective vicariates. This breakdown was done to allow more time for smaller groups of parishioners to delve more deeply into pastoral planning. The 40 study groups identified seven pastoral priorities—again YYA ministry was a top priority (the other six being vocations, Catholic Schools, Lay Leadership, the New Evangelization, Christian Service and Stewardship). Consequently, seven archdiocesan sub-committees were formed based on the seven mission priorities identified by the 40 study groups. After months of discussions, the AOD sub-committee on YYA ministry concluded that its first objective had to be:

> The Archbishop will recognize the limited resources of parishes and locate FUNDING for certified and trained lay ecclesial ministers and vibrant ministry programs, encouraging all stakeholders, especially Pastors, to be well versed in comprehensive ministry to young people and more actively involved in ministry to youth and young adults(August, 2010).[7]

This particular objective (there were 16 objectives total from the YYA subcommittee) was the first objective mentioned because the committee strongly believed that additional monies were necessary if significant changes in this area of the Church's life were to occur. Both youth ministers and pastor interviews show this to be a clarion call of theirs as well, that more monies for salaries and programming are needed for YYA ministry—data we discuss in the next section. We argue these could be considered clarion calls for strengthening the institutional infrastructure of YYA ministry.

4.2. Qualitative Interview Data from Youth Ministers

Of the 44 youth ministers interviewed the majority were white (92.3 percent), female (70 percent), between the ages of 40 to 59 (70 percent), married (71.8 percent) and working in suburban parishes (80 percent). Educationally, 34 percent had master degrees. Both their voices and their non-verbal emotional body language expressed their beleaguered situation and their perception that diocesan Church leadership was not building-up YYA ministry as much as it could.[8]

One of the first questions we asked youth ministers was, "What attracted youth to the youth group or parish?" (see Appendix A) and although the question may seem irrelevant to this study the answers prove otherwise. For example, the first answer most often heard was "other youth" and in combining the response "other youth" with "parish welcomes youth" it became clear that more than 50 percent (50.6 percent) of responses are *relational* in nature. "Social activities" (14.8 percent) and "authentic leadership" (8.6 percent) were the next two most likely responses pertaining to attraction and if combined with the previous answers, shows 74 percent of responses have to do with relationships. The relevancy therefore, is that youth ministers building relationships with teens, parents, and parishioners was essential to having a strong parish youth ministry. Sociologists have long noted the importance of social solidarity for any kind of community building and so it is reasonable that more youth ministers and more financial resources are central to having a more personal relationship-oriented youth ministry, especially given that more than half of youth ministers are part-time. Interestingly, the data also show that programming or content of what occurs in a youth group gathering is secondary. Obviously programming is important, but what mattered most, as many respondents emphasized, was strong, positive relationships with youth ministers, peers and parishioners [18], which is less likely to occur with a weak YYA institutional infrastructure.

---

responses collected. In 2014, another archdiocesan wide survey was administered based on the seven mission priorities that came out of the *Changing Lives Together* pastoral planning process. Over 40,000 responses were collected from this survey. Both surveys showed YYA ministry as a top priority.

7   All of the mission priorities can be found on the AOD website. Also, a pastoral letter from Archbishop Vigneron was mailed to every parishioner in the Archdiocese that listed and explained the seven mission priorities as well as his appreciation to everyone who participated in *Changing Lives Together* (the pastoral planning program).

8   These interviews were conducted during the year 2014. A final report, including a statistical and verbal summary of each and every interview are available through Sacred Heart Major Seminary, Dr. Michael J. McCallion, Director of Catholic Social Analysis. The report carries in its title "Joyful and Beleaugered..."

Another aspect on the relational dimension is the stress and strain described by youth ministers in conducting their ministry—evidence picked-up in their verbal and non-verbal responses. Sociologically, role strain occurs when an individual feels stress in managing the competing obligations of her/his role. Several youth ministers mentioned the strain they experienced in negotiating their pastor's minimalist expectations for the youth ministry program with their own belief that more, not less, time and resources should be devoted to the ministry. Others felt role strain because they incorporated lots of social activities in order to build relationships (a major reason for joining—relational) and yet at the same time felt like they were being judged as not leading a "Catholic" enough program (because, for example, social activities were paramount over catechetical activities). As one youth minister stated:

> "The vocal parents and also the pastor sometimes would complain the teens are not getting doctrine or as they say it—"what it means to be Catholic"—but I am trying to get them to gel as a group, you know, just feel comfortable enough to keep coming to the youth group and that means relationship stuff not catechesis first and foremost. So that is a drag as well—trying to meet everyone's expectations".

It appears from accounts such as this one that role strain developed because of either the pastor's, parents', or peers' expectations and what the youth minister was trying to accomplish in terms of relationship building. Indeed, many of the youth ministers' showed signs of being bodily and emotionally weary while responding to our questions.

Additional data supporting the conclusion that youth ministers are marginalized, was gleaned from responses to the question "What works and what does not work in your ministry". Methodologically, the concern was that this question was really two questions. Consequently, some respondents answered either "what works" or "what does not work" but not both, and therefore the results are not clearly representative of the combination "what works or does not work". Nevertheless, the questions are separated out below for the sake of clarity.

The number-one item mentioned as working was Christian Service (15.8 percent), followed by having a paid youth minister (14.5 percent) and then regular quality youth group meetings (10.5 percent). Talking or teaching or lecturing was not what primarily works. What works is "doing" things together, especially if that "doing" involves helping others—hence Christian service was mentioned most often. One interviewee was quite specific about this:

> "I know catechesis is important but for these teens the best way I can engage them is through Christian service projects, especially if the project is, you know, over a period of time, not just a one-time thing, although one-time things work a little too, but really a long-term project is really good because now you have time to build stronger relationship with them, you know, you are hanging out with them more and not just talking at them".

The data suggests that a potential area through which to establish stronger relations with teens is Christian service. Perhaps in order to justify their positions, several youth ministers were adamant in arguing that this "doing together" with Christian service is going to happen best if there is a paid youth minister on staff to make it happen.

Another interview finding was the fact that some pastors only provided a stipend rather than a salary to their youth minister and moreover, these youth ministers were not members of the parish staff. In one parish, the youth minister received a minimal stipend and did not even know who the parish full-time Director of Music was. Another mentioned an older youth minister receiving such a small stipend that he decided he would give it back to the youth ministry program by buying pizza with it each week they met. These responses were further evidence that youth ministers occupy a second-class citizenship status in the overall field of lay parish ministry.

In the reverse, we also learned from youth ministers what does not work. Youth ministers mentioned an "overemphasis on catechesis" (19 percent) as what most *does not* work. The next largest single category mentioned was "no full-time youth minister" (9 percent). Many respondents mentioned "paid youth minister" in answering the question "what works" and so we believe that is why answering "not having a youth minister" is infrequently mentioned here. It should be noted that in both questions concerning what works and what doesn't work, technology is important but does not play as large a role as relationships. Having a youth minister, doing Christian service together, parents being involved, *etc.*, all have to do with face-to-face or actively engaged relationships—this is what works according to youth ministers. Understanding technology is increasingly important to youth and many youth ministers mentioned its importance in presenting information. One youth minister, for example, said "If I am trying to communicate something, it is best if I put it up on a big screen because I have found that it increases the likelihood of making the topic real and authoritative to them". In addition, several respondents used varied approaches in their ministry which meant that several types of technologies were used each week to maintain and increase the interest of youth. But again, according to youth ministers, if youth are not making regular connections and building relationships with youth ministers and other adults, then the various technologies used were less effective. The belief in youth ministry as essentially relational, along with an emphasis on consistent meeting times, as well as meeting places, with consistent leadership present is what "works".

Another question receiving relevant responses for this study was, "If you had the archbishop's ear, what would you tell him he needs to know about youth ministry?" The primary responses were: Parishes must welcome youth (22 percent), parishes and the AOD need to provide more money and resources to youth ministry (20 percent) and the archbishop needs to provide more support and resources to youth ministry (15 percent). In other words, 57 percent of the responses had to do with receiving more money, resources and support for youth ministry. Indeed, including the item "more presence of church leaders" (10 percent) and "being more pastoral and less judgmental" (6 percent), both of which could be interpreted as "being more supportive", it would be over 70 percent.

The most striking feature about these interviews were the extra-deliberative or extra-discursive or non-verbal responses of the interviewees (data not displayed) and the overwhelming sense among the interviewers regarding how beleaguered, marginalized, yet joyful these youth ministers were because they loved working with youth. In summarizing our additional interview data, our assessment is that youth ministers are beleaguered, regularly seeking better employment and feeling marginalized in their persistent emphasis on the relational dimension of YYA ministry. Their qualitative interview data validate that a weak institutional infrastructure of YYA ministry exists in the AOD for supporting this kind of emotionally intensive, relational youth ministry.

4.3. Qualitative Data from Pastor Interviews

Twelve pastors were interviewed about their perceptions of youth ministry, especially as to why they think so few parishes have a youth minister (see Appendix B). The third question of the interview was "What do you think are some of the obstacles as to why other pastors don't have a youth minister?" Ten out of twelve pastors (83 percent) answered "money!" For example, one pastor said, "The other obstacle, besides seeing it as a need, is the importance of the archdiocese providing more funding if it truly sees it as an integral part of the parish." Another pastor said it bluntly, "Money". And then he went on to say, "the other thing is the older pastors are tired and the young ones don't seem to care". And yet another pastor said, "It's the money. First you hire a musician, then a DRE and then maybe a Christian service coordinator and then you give one of them responsibility for youth ministry."

Other reasons were more along relational lines, especially the issue of priest sexual abuse. One pastor said, "You know, I used to go through the parking lot and the kids would jump all over me and I would play with them, even some of the 7th and 8th graders, but I can't do that anymore because of the sexual abuse stuff. That is why I started 'Hi-fiving' the kids when I walk down the aisle for Mass—it is allowable because the parents are there". Another pastor spoke bluntly: "Pastors are scared of the sex abuse thing," while another said, "Priests are discouraged by the sex abuse thing and of course they see more losing than winning in terms of the youth, you know, winning them over, most don't come and it's discouraging." Another pastor who was more philosophical about the issue believed, "Some pastors just don't know how to speak to youth about truth given their (the youths') highly secular and relativistic views of life. They just don't know how to do it and so they shy away." Given these few responses, were these the sentiments that discouraged them from hiring a youth minister? Perhaps, but the main reason and dominant response was money.

The other main issue in the pastors' responses was the fewer number of teens participating in church or simply the lack of teens in their parish. One pastor said, "You know, they are just busy with high school, they have lots of demands on them from that and so they don't come." Another pastor said, "They have high school and work, they just don't have time." Another pastor was more deliberate saying, "We need more kids to show and so the diocese needs to find funding for parishes to pay youth ministers who have the charisma for ministering to youth to be hired to attract and bring in the youth. It is not just going to happen. We need paid ministers to make it happen." Along similar lines, another pastor said, "Why can't we use the CLT monies (Changing Lives Together—An AOD fundraising campaign) to build a youth room or center at parishes so youth can gather there, have a place they know they can go." Another said, "I need to first find the right person, with the right charisma, you know, someone who can really be with teens and then find the funding, maybe from AOD, but I need to do it NOW but can't without money." Another said the same thing, "Hire a dynamic youth minister and pay him/her a good salary."

Most pastor and youth minister responses did not directly address the issue of a disconnect between policy and practice or of a weak institutional infrastructure of YYA ministry in the AOD, but it is clear from their interviews that they feel underesourced, undersupported and generally marginalized. Consequently, the next section is an attempt to sociologically assess and explain this disconnect between YYA ministry being a top stated priority of the diocese and the practice disconnect. Overall, little seems to be in process for implementing this stated goal. Instead, a weak institutional infrastructure is maintained, allowing the ongoing weak institutional support for youth minsitry to become institutionally normative, taken-for-granted as the way it is.

5. Theoretical Analysis and Discussion

In this section, we provide some theoretically grounded explanations for the disconnect between stated policy and the observed reality of youth ministry practice. We begin by applying two sets of institutional theories: decoupling and backstage organizational processes. Subsequently, we apply social status theories to explain the ongoing marginzalization of youth ministers. These theories are applied in order to examine the presented data on this case study within its broader social context and to reveal the potential social patterns underlying these taken-for-granted trends.

5.1. Institutional Analysis

5.1.1. Decoupling of Policy and Practice

Decoupling refers to the gap between an institution's stated policies and its actual organizational practices. Meyer and Rowan have researched social institutions and found that processes of decoupling are ubiquitous in these settings [19]. Wittberg, for example, found that several Catholic colleges and hospitals decoupled their religious identity from their everyday practices because of pressures from government or other professional stakeholders [20]. As she writes: "Thus, in order to attract the credentialed, high caliber staff and administrators demanded by secular professional standards, a hospital, university, or social agency might downplay its religious identity—while simultaneously emphasizing that identity to alumni, foundations, or denominational supervisors." Wittberg argues, therefore, that "many institutions have responded by decoupling their religious identity from their everyday practices" ([20], p. 151). In other words, decoupling allows organizations to verbally comply symbolically without changing their practices substantially. This appears to be the case with youth ministry in the AOD. The organizational church is giving voice to the importance of youth ministry, raised by so many parishioners via surveys and meetings, but in reality the Church puts little into practice that actually enhances youth ministry. Church leaders, in other words, claim it is a top priority (policy) and then proceed on with other business (practice).

Another explanation for why this disconnect or decoupling exists between YYA policy and practice is that it is not consciously enacted by leadership but exists because of the nature of how things work in large organizations. For example, Pattison's research found that managers/bureaucrats are far from being calm, reflective, systematic planners and instead work "at an unrelenting pace, ... their activities are characterized by brevity, variety and discontinuity and they are strongly oriented to action and dislike reflective activities" ([21], p. 12). Indeed, he argues that "fighting fires is a good way of ensuring ongoing busyness." Of course, this subverts the need to seriously reflect on priorities that have been named via surveys or planning meetings or any other social process the AOD has initiated. Once the policy is written or the report is typed, managers or ecclesial leaders can move on to other business (busyness) because there are many other burning issues to deal with that are more practical and need immediate attention. Pattison questions, therefore, whether an organization's strategic planning is actually strategic:

> Quite apart from the questions of time-scale and proper use of human resources, it is questionable how useful this kind of planning really is. Organizations must have some sense of where they are going and what they are trying to do. The trouble is that the more specific plans are, the more futile often they prove to be. In organizations and the environment around them, so many crucial factors can change so quickly that plans quickly become irrelevant. Like religious faith, much of what strategic planning does is to help people to feel they have some sense of control and direction in the midst of chaotic, unpredictable reality. The planning process allows managers to feel that they are doing something and serves as a ritual activity that brings a sense of efficacy. ([19], pp. 30–31). The only thing that can be safely concluded here is that effective leadership, like being market focused and strategic planning, is an elusive, perhaps longed-for-chimera, a kind of holy grail for managers ([21], p. 32).

Continually naming YYA ministry as a top AOD priority for the last twenty years is a decoupling strategy which allows the institutional church to say, on the one hand, "yes, this is a priority, it is even one of seven mission priorities for the entire diocese and we are working on it," while on the other hand, the AOD goes about devoting its resources to other issues deemed more important and not necessarily doing so consciously or intentionally but because of the nature of how large organizations operate. Some scholars argue therefore that organizations are more *intendedly* rational than actually rational, that is, "more capable of achieving consistent and efficient action than unorganized individuals, but far from synoptically rational" ([22], p. 8). Why then is the stated AOD mission priority of YYA ministry not put into practice? One main reason is because AOD officials consciously or unconsciously participate in institutional decoupling processes.

5.1.2. Backstage Organizational Processes

Another reason, one that is highly correlated with decoupling and the reality that organizations are more intendedly rational than actually rational, is the fact that a whole series of relationships and interactions occur backstage to which ordinary parishioners are not privy and it is in and through these backstage interactions that decisions are actually made. Decisions not based on data that committees have worked hard to compile but on church officials' own backstage cognitive and emotional interactions. Goffman and others have studied these backstage or shadowland interactions and discovered these types of informal interactions often turn an organization this way or that [23]. Taking into account this "shadowland", several theorists have argued that social organizations are "organized anarchies", suggesting that goals and objectives of organizations are always ambiguous and contested and the fulfillment of goals and objectives often depends on who does or does not show up to the meeting. Perhaps this has happened with the YYA ministry—people who have other agendas keep showing up at the meetings and thereby focus attention on priorities other than YYA ministry.

5.1.3. Institutional Analysis Conclusion

Applying these institutional theories leads us to conclude that people, problems, solutions, planning and choices are "loosely coupled, that the definition of a choice may change over the course of deliberations, that most decisions are made by oversight or avoided altogether and that most of them do not solve problems, but simply defer them to another day" ([21], p. 11). Perceiving the AOD as an organized anarchy explains, at least partially, why little has been done to advance YYA ministry. Therefore it would be important to study this "shadowland" of informal relations within the AOD as a next research step. Qualitative methods would be necessary, but exactly how to gain access to this backstage behavior and thinking is another question entirely. It appears, in this case, that under the conditions of ecclesial institutional bureaucracy, the policy of YYA ministry being a priority becomes decoupled from the practice of providing more resources to such ministry. In addition to institutional theories, sociological theories of social status also help to explain why the marginzaliztion of youth workers continues in this case study despite stated priorities.

5.2. Social Status Analysis

5.2.1. The Social Status of Youth Ministry

Another sociological concept that sheds light on the data is the central and popularly known concept of social status. The question of "Why don't pastors hire full-time youth ministers?" quickly reveals that one of the answers is that youth ministers have little social status within the vineyard of lay ecclesial workers. DREs and Musicians have status, youth ministers do not, or have comparatively much less. So why don't pastors hire full-time youth ministers? Because within the institution of the church, youth ministry in general does not have a professional status and more surreptitiously, because a taken-for-granted *inequality* exists perpetuating the degradation of youth ministry. Examining more closely the sociological concept of "social status" will help clarify this ecclesial situation (also, see Appendix D for a case study of a suburban parish and its reluctance to hire a youth minister).

There are three powerful ingredients to social status: resources, power and respect/esteem, therefore the underlying issue of inequality is ever present. For example, comparing DREs to youth ministers clarifies the inequality that exists in that DREs clearly have a higher status than youth ministers (DREs have acquired such status legitimately and without malice to youth ministers). Indeed, many DREs have responsibility for youth ministry and if the DRE is not the youth minister him or herself, the youth minister reports to him/her (the DRE). This is not positive or negative; it is only to say this is the present ecclesial situation. Indeed, DRE's social status has a lot to do with the fact that 80 percent or more of parishes hire a DRE while only 47 percent of parishes hire youth ministers (indeed, there are more business manager types (57 percent) than youth ministers—see AOD Report on Lay Ecclesial Ministers, 2014, Appendix C).

Nevertheless, the question remains as to why does this inequality exists? Of the three ingredients of social status, the primary mechanism behind this inequality is one based on differences in respect/esteem rather than on differences of power or resources—however important these may be. Sociologists are aware that power and resources follow an occupation if respect for such position has been embedded within an organization. In other words, sociologists have long argued that as a micro-motive for behavior, status based on respect is as significant as money and power. Therefore, it is the phenomenon of status inequality based on differences in respect/honor/esteem between lay ecclesial ministers that might shed further light on the issue of the disconnect between YYA ministry being a top priority and little being done about it.

In much of the sociological literature on social status, respect/honor/esteem is the weakest of the three ingredients or variables investigated in predicting social status, but this is an oversight. We often overlook how much people care about being valued by others (society, parish, social group), that is, "respected". I want my son, for example, to have money and resources, but more so I want him to be respected by his peers and others—that he is regarded as an honorable, good man. From this perspective, it becomes even more obvious that youth ministers are not given the respect they deserve in relation to other parish ministries, not because of malice or a veiled disdain for youth ministers, but for reasons associated with social status. There is an unequal distribution of respect amongst lay ecclesial ministers, as there is with the distribution of resources and power, but this inequality is unseen because it is built into the ecclesial structures of dioceses and parishes. Moreover, these hidden social status processes have much to do with why priests exhibit poor youth ministry hiring practices which only perpetuates the weak institutional infrastructure of YYA ministry (again, see Appendix D).

Inequality, in other words, has become a durable ecclesial institutional reality in terms of occupational trajectories among lay ecclesial ministers. The bottom line is that youth ministers are perceived as non-professional or semi-professional at the conscious and unconscious levels by other ecclesial professionals. And consolidation around this "disrespect" definition of the situation amongst pastors and others stabilizes this ecclesial inequality because it transforms the situational control over resources and power into a "status difference" between types of ministries—with DREs ranked diffusely better than youth ministers. As Ridgeway stated in her presidential address to the American Sociological Society: "Status construction studies show that when control over resources in a social setting is correlated with a salient categorical difference (DRE *vs.* YM), people quickly link the appearance of mastery in the situation that the resources and power create with the associated difference between types of people" [24]. In the parishes of the AOD (given the number of youth ministers and their salaries), those in power (pastors and others) have formed a "status belief" (rightly so in many instances) that DREs should receive more resources and power than youth ministers because of their professionalism and ecclesial status earned since Vatican II. Youth ministry and consequently youth ministers have not earned equal status with DREs because of their less formalized professional training and perceived lower status among those in hiring positions. This situational perception by those in power legitimizes this ongoing ecclesial inequality, reinforcing both the weak institutional infrastructure of YYA ministry and the ongoing decoupling of policy and practice.

Conscious or not, these status beliefs fuel social perceptions of difference between DREs and youth ministers. In other words, status processes are now in place that legitimately mobilize the continuing construction of culturally/ecclesially defined social differences on the one hand and on the other hand, high status actors (DREs and Pastors) rely on this difference to justify their channeling less power and resources to youth ministry. This status process then is deeply implicated in the making of obdurate patterns of inequality between various ecclesial ministers based on social status differences.

With this obdurate pattern of inequality now taken for granted via widely shared status beliefs and consequent status differences, these beliefs constitute that difference as an independent dimension of inequality with its own sustained social dynamic. Ridgeway uses the example of gender and says that men have acquired an advantage in resources and power compared to women which fosters the status belief that men are better than women [24]. Once these status beliefs develop they give men the advantage because they are men and *not* because they are richer or more powerful. Even in a situation where men and women are equal in power and resources the man still has more influence. Hence, status beliefs allow an autonomous dynamic to work which maintains inequality. Moreover, this automatic dynamic works at the social relational level—mostly in the arena of self-other expectations and this relational dynamic is examined next by looking at three well documented status social processes, namely, status bias in judgments and behavior, associational preference biases and reactions to status challenges.

5.2.2. Status Biases in Judgment and Behavior

Status biases about a social difference, in this case between youth ministers and DREs, become salient in contexts in which people differ on some social distinction such as mixed-social class or mixed-race. In this case, the social difference becomes salient because of primarily mixed-educational social distinctions. Moreover, the social difference becomes even more salient in contexts in which that social difference is culturally understood to be relevant to the settings' goals—in this case an ecclesial setting that formerly had Catholic schools to handle youth but now does not, except for those who can afford private schooling—which has resulted in most Catholic children and teens needing some kind of religious education. Given Catholic school decline, pastors are expected to provide religious education and so DREs are hired (rightly so). But when it comes to teens there are many perceptions that tend to add up to the fact that teens' high schools dominate their lives and so youth ministry cannot compete and is therefore comparatively insignificant (see pastor interview data). Nevertheless, the thinking goes, "we (the pastor or local parish) have to do something so let's just hire someone part-time or get a volunteer to organize some activities for teens"—status biased thinking.

Moreover, this status bias has become implicitly salient in that this bias has warped people's expectations of what is competent and suitable for youth ministry and these status biases are all the stronger, the more relevant the social difference is perceived to be to the goals of the setting. So the status bias is strong in this case, because the social difference perceived is between "education in faith" (DRE who has credentials) *vs.* having "fun" (youth minister who does not need credentials) in a church context. The social difference is that the DRE is a professional and the YM is not and that has become an embedded bias within the institution. So the status advantaged DRE or musician speaks up to be heard while the status disadvantaged youth minister hesitates to do so given the status bias in place—much like a medical doctor speaks up and the lay person does not. Often in such status bias situations the same idea simply sounds better from the status advantaged person than from the status disadvantaged one. The cumulative result has been the status advantaged is tracked into positions of greater resources and power because of their greater respect/honor or social status (they are simply better).

5.2.3. Associational Preference Biases

Next, this status bias consciously and unconsciously leads to inequalities as to who associates with whom—associational preference bias, the second status concern. As mentioned earlier, our research found youth ministers not attending parish staff meetings or other important parish meetings because youth ministers occupy such low social status. These are experiences of status degradation as Goffman (1963) would state. Associating only with higher status others is necessary but it also feeds into a process of cloning by "actors" from higher status groups. From an organizational perspective, one reason for this cloning has to do with the inherently uncertain conditions of exercising power in organizations. The powerful in the organization tend to favor others similar to themselves and upon whom they feel they can rely [25]. Again, conscious or not, pastors and DREs associate minimally with youth ministers and thereby perpetuate the separation of these status groups and in doing so, maintain power and resources for themselves (pastor and DRE), further exacerbating material and status inequalities between them as well as maintaining the weak institutional infrastructure of YYA ministry.

5.2.4. Status Challenge Biases

Status biases and associational preference biases create and maintain an implicit motive for people of higher status groups to defend their valued sense of group position, according to Ridgeway and others. When lower status groups challenge higher status groups they encounter backlash from higher status group members. Still today, women who seem too dominant in a given social situation are sometimes considered pushy or aggressive, while men saying the same thing are considered competent. Indeed, research shows that much racial prejudice can be understood as a defense of racial group status position. Whereas (1) status bias; and (2) associational preference bias produce relatively unthinking biases in favor of status privilege for those in higher status positions; (3) defense of the status hierarchy bias results in more intentionally hostile actions to constrain lower status individuals who are perceived to go too far. This defensiveness is not necessarily the case in many parishes, so status challenges may be few and far between. But when a pastor is asked (status challenge) about youth ministry he often has a ready answer with "we don't have the money to hire someone but we do have someone part-time helping those teens who do want to gather." Without having to discuss status biases he might harbor about YYA ministry, the pastors can easily decouple policies from practices with respect to YYA ministry at the parish level as can ecclesial hierarchs at the diocesan level.

5.2.5. Social Status Conclusion

These three processes—status biases in judgement and behavior, associational preference biases, and status challenge biases—are culturally influenced interpersonal processes that act as subtle but powerful mechanisms by which exploitations (not having to pay a youth minister or paying them a very low salary) and opportunity hoarding (having one person perform multiple roles, DRE and also youth minister e.g., rather than increasing the division of ecclesial labor within the parish) are accomplished by pastors (high status group). Hence, this status differentiation among ecclesial workers depends on the maintenance of distinctive cultural practices to mark the status boundary, that is, the practice of hiring DREs to be the youth minister or hiring part-time youth minister often with few qualifications (academic degrees), or obtaining a volunteer—all of which maintain the weak institutional infrastructure of YYA ministry.

Our application of these theories leads to our conclusions that, much like gender, race and class have become biases stamped into the structures of society, these ecclesial biases toward YYA ministry are stamped into the ecclesial structures and procedures of employment in the AOD. Having no institutional academic professional degree for YYA ministry as there is for DREs or Musicians is highly problematic from this perspective. The historian Thomas Bergler, mentioned earlier, has delineated the history of the Catholic Church with regards to youth ministry and found it far behind the YYA ministry enhancing efforts of most Protestant denominations—especially in noting Protestant congregations' practices of hiring "youth pastors" (Bergler, 2012, [4]). It behooves the Catholic Church, from what has been said, to consider instituting such a professional degree.

Once Catholic schools started closing in large numbers, the Church did not establish a viable ecclesial infrastructure of YYA ministry which could put into practice, processes of status enhancement for YYA ministry. Instead, processes of status degradation and bias resulted in its absence. Religious education and the role of DRE procured most of the status enhancement processes developed after Vatican II and thereby the requisite power and resources. Consequently, there has only been, for the most part, a part-time effort to build a new ecclesial infrastructure for ministering to, with and for youth. And although this part-time effort is something, it has partly fueled processes of status degradation and status bias in most but not all parishes of the AOD. Because of ecclesial beliefs about YYA ministry's degraded status compared to DREs (structural level—status bias) and the minimal interaction other parish staff have with youth ministers (interpersonal level—associational bias), ecclesial inequality toward YYA ministry is institutionalized into diocesan and parish organizational forms and practices. Despite all diocesan and parish level efforts to enhance YYA ministry (naming it a mission priority), the weak institutional infrastructure of YYA ministry supported by status biases toward such ministry prevent ecclesial leaders from perceiving the social inequalities that persist and seem only to continue to deplete the Church's infrastructure of YYA ministry.

6. Limitations and Future Studies

Despite the strength of this case study data in hearing the perspectives of youth ministers and some pastors regarding their experiences of the archdiocesan priorities, all the data presented in this study are non-representative and self-reported. Such self-reported data rely for their validity on the accuracy of the youth minister perceptions. As highly relationally based youth workers, the youth ministers generally reported intended interventions that rely on relational connections to youth as the ways to form their religiosity. It is worth noting that youth could acquire their religiosity through other, less relationally based approaches. There also could be other ways that the archdiocese could support ministry to youth without supporting youth ministers. However, presuming youth ministry and relational connection to caring adult mentors within the church are the intended change mechanisms, this study raises a number of concerns regarding the successful implementation of these practices.

Future studies should investigate these findings further. For example, studies could compare the approach of this diocese to that of other dioceses, or to that of other religious traditions, especially in order to assess the relative success of approaches that do not rely upon youth ministry. Based on the initial evidence presented in this study, future investigations could seek to collect data from representative samples, especially involving multiple locations. Another fruitful line of inquiry could be to collect data with participating youth to assess the extent to which youth minister perceptions of youth needs align with what their participating youth report. Finally, another approach to future studies could be to collect data on other kinds of religious organizations. Presuming religious youth participate in a number of religious organizations, including para-church groups, it would be important to assess the extent of religious formation they receive from sources outside the archdiocese. These and other studies are revealed to be needed based on the initial contributions of this case study on the weak institutional support for youth ministry in the Archdiocese of Detroit.

7. Conclusions

The church at the archdiocesan level can gather youth and young adults from various parts of the archdiocese (which it is doing as of this writing) and ask them "what they want", but if an ecclesial institutional infrastructure of YYA ministry, a youth minister being paid a just wage, is not operative to implement "what young people want" in any long-term systematic way, then the Church is simply putting the cart before the horse and perpetuating further decoupling processes already in place. As the data shows, what youth want is pastoral care which means to "walk-along-with, to listen to, to hang out with youth and young adults" and when the time is right, to offer solid Catholic catechesis about the Catholic faith. This is unlikely given decoupling processes and status degradation of youth ministry—all of which maintain and perpetuate a weak YYA institutional infrastructure. The findings of this study strongly suggest that the stakes have been raised significantly for the AOD to find realistic and workable measures to strengthen the institutional infrastructure of YYA ministry in the AOD.

Author Contributions: Michael McCallion conceived and designed the research on YYA ministry in the AOD. Michael McCallion did most of the interviewing of YYA ministers and three pastors. John Ligas and George Seroka interviewed most of the pastors and assisted substantially in writing the section on "Pastor Interviews." Michael McCallion wrote the paper with editorial assistance from John Ligas and George Seroka. George Seroka wrote up Appendix D with editorial assistance from John Ligas and Michael McCallion.

Conflicts of Interest: The authors declare no conflict of interest.

Appendix A: Interview Protocol for Youth Ministers (begin January 2014)

INTERVIEW QUESTIONS (This Is Anonymous—names and parish)

1. Are you paid full-time or part-time? *What other responsibilities?*
2. How long have you been in this position? *Have you had other positions?*
3. How would you describe the parish community? I know that is a very general question, but is it liberal, moderate, or conservative politically or theologically? Is it lower class, working class, middle class, or upper class in your estimation?
4. Are you aware that youth and young adults is one of the mission priorities for the AOD?

5. If yes, has it changed anything? *Your ministry perhaps? Your parish?*

6. Does the Parish have a NE or Evangelization Committee: yes___, no___, starting one___, thinking about starting one___, *etc.*

7. If the parish has a NE committee are you/your ministry connected to it? How?

8. What do you make of the NE? Do you like/dislike it? How do you feel about it? Is it effective?

9. Please describe the main activities offered by your ministry? (could dig deeper by asking questions 13 through 16 below or SKIP if already answered in 12):

10. How does the youth group pray? Do they pray a particular devotion?

11. Does your ministry include Christian Service? Any projects monthly or annually?

12. What Catechesis takes place? How often?

13. Socializing? How often? Anything repeated or a regular activity?

14. *OR ask*, What are the opportunities open to youth at the parish?

15. What most attracts youth to the youth group/parish?

16. What works and what has not worked in your ministry here?

17. If your work with youth or young adults was to be *completely* successful, what might that look like to you? Examples? (the ideal)

18. What do leaders & decision makers need to know about your youth or young adults & the program here that they don't already know (have misconceptions about)? If you had the ear of the Bishop what would you tell him!

19. Is there a designated space for the group to meet?

20. What do you find to be inspiration for your work with youth?

21. The social science literature indicates that youth today are more individualistic in their faith lives than previous generations. So my Dad's generation was more committed to the institution of the church than my generation and now today's generation is even less committed to the institutional church. In other words, they tend to do their own thing and not pay much attention to what the Church teaches. Do you tend to agree with that assessment or not? Why?

22. For example, do you know if they give an envelope each week to their parish (or give electronically)? If not, do they give any money? If so, what do they give?

23. Is there anything else you would like to add at this time?

Appendix B: Interview Protocol for Pastors

INTERVIEW QUESTIONS (This is anonymous—names and parish)

1. Do you think high school age kids are attending mass or otherwise engaged in the Church these days and why or why not?

2. If you have or don't have a youth minister here at your parish, why is that so? If not, what are the reasons (barriers) for not having one?

3. What do you think are some of the obstacles as to why other pastors don't have a youth minister (given that about 40% of parishes don't have one)? As you know, youth ministry is one of the mission priorities of the AOD. Has that changed anything here at your parish? Why or why not?

4. Is youth ministry connected to the New Evangelization in anyway at the parish (youth sitting on NE committee for example)?

5. What resources, tools, or training do you feel you need to advance the quality of youth ministry here at your parish?

6. Is there anything else you would like to add?

Appendix C: AOD Paid Lay Ministers 2014–2015

Position	Number	% Laymin	% Parishes
PastoralMinister	74	8%	35%
Director of Religious Education	164	19%	78%
Section Heads	88	10%	42%
Musicians	205	23%	98%
Christian Service Coordinator	72	8%	34%
Youth Ministers	98	11%	47%
Young Adult Minister	5	1%	2%
RCIA Coordinator	31	4%	15%
Worship Coordinator	16	2%	8%
Business Manager	124	14%	59%
Total Paid Lay Ministers	877	100%	

Response Rate: 96% (223 of 233 parishes). Percent of Parishes with Paid Lay Ministers: 94% (210 of 223 reporting parishes). Source: Archdiocese of Detroit: Department of Parish Life and Services

Appendix D: Case Study of a Suburban Parish: Process of Hiring a YYA Minister (2014–2016)

Background and Rationale for pursuing a YYA Minister at this Suburban Parish:

- YYA Ministry has been a top AOD priority since 1995;
- A Survey conducted of AOD Parishioners indicate YYA Ministry is the *number 1 and number 4 priorities* across the Diocese with around 94,000 responses;
- During a review of priorities at the parish in the fall of 2013, Hiring a YYA Minister received the *highest* votes of all of the approximate 100 goals/objectives. *Summary of Activity*:
- Many efforts were made throughout 2014 to approve a YYA Minister position at this parish, but despite the fairly widespread support from the Parish Council, the item was placed on hold pending the appointment of a new pastor;
- In late 2014 and early 2015, the YYA Liaison for the AOD was contacted and provided advice/support. The Vicariate Vicar was also contacted but never returned the calls;
- In early 2015 a conceptual agreement was formulated to share the YYA Minister position with a neighboring parish, including funding. A joint Job Description was developed that completely encompassed all job requirements;
- After a considerable effort and many discussions over several Parish Council Meetings, the position of YYA Minister was approved for the 2015/2016 budget in June of 2015;
- The position was advertised, resumes were reviewed, interviews were conducted during the summer and a selection was made on 8/15/15 (and recommended) to the Pastors;
- The Pastors wanted to meet with the successful candidate but their schedules wouldn't allow for a meeting prior to September 10, and at the meeting, the Pastors asked the candidate to generate a detailed plan and expanded the scope of the position;
- The candidate compiled a detailed plan and submitted it to the two Pastors;
- Subsequent to the detailed plan submittal, the neighboring parish indicated they could not afford the position because collections were down and decided to opt out of the plan.
- Then the initiating parish indicated that they could not afford to fund a full-time position by themselves;
- At the Parish Council Meeting in late October, the recommendation was made to hire the candidate on a part-time basis and the Pastor indicated the candidate agreed to do that with a reduced scope commensurate with the reduced compensation;

- At the Parish Council Meeting on December 9, the YYA Minister had not yet been hired so a recommendation was again made to hire the YYA minister on a part-time basis in January of 2016. 11 members of the Parish Council voted to support this proposal; the remaining 4 members, all paid-staff members, voted against it;
- At the January, 2016 Parish Council Meeting, it was decided to utilize vicariate resources on a limited basis instead of hiring the YYA minister on a part time basis as planned.

References

1. Christian Smith, Kyle Longest, Jonathan Hill, and Karis Christoffersen. *Young Catholic America: Emerging Adults in, Out of, and Gone from the Church*. Oxford: Oxford University Press, 2014.
2. Michael J. McCallion. "Office of Pastoral Resources and Research. Youth Ministry in the Archdiocese of Detroit." *Review of Religious Research* 46 (2005): 423–24.
3. Michael J. McCallion, David R. Maines, and Stephen Wolfel. "Policy as Practice: First Holy Communion as a Contested Situation." *Journal of Contemporary Ethnography* 25 (1996): 300–26. [CrossRef]
4. Thomas. E. Bergler. *The Juvenilization of American Christianity*. Grand Rapids: William B. Eerdmans Publishing Company, 2012.
5. Thomas E. Bergler. "Youth, Christianity, and the Crisis of Civilization, 1930–1945." *Religion and American Culture* 24 (2014): 216. [CrossRef]
6. Andrea S. Williams, and James D. Davidson. "Catholic Conceptions of Faith: A Generational Analysis." *Sociology of Religion* 57 (1996): 273–89. [CrossRef]
7. William Dinges, Dean R. Hoge, Mary Johnson, and Juan L. Gonzales, Jr. "A Faith Loosely Held: The Institutional Allegiance of Young Catholics." *Commonweal*, 17 July 1998.
8. Dean R. Hoge, Willliam D. Dinges, Mary Johnson S.N.D., and Juan L. Gonzales, Jr. *Young Adult Catholics: Religion in the Culture of Choice*. South Bend: University of Notre Dame Press, 2001.
9. Christian Smith, and Melinda Lundquist Denton. *Soul Searching: The Religious and Spiritual Lives of American Teenagers*. Oxford: Oxford University Press, 2005.
10. Christian Smith. *Souls in Transition: The Religious and Spiritual Lives of Emerging Adults*. Oxford: Oxford University Press, 2009.
11. Robert D. Putnam, and David E. Campbell. *American Grace: How Religion Divides and Unites US*. New York: Simon and Schuster, 2010.
12. Robert Wuthnow. *After the Baby Boomers: How Twenty- and Thirty-Somethings Are Shaping the Future of American Religion*. Princeton: Princeton University Press, 2007.
13. Linda A. Mercadante. *Belief Without Borders: Inside the Minds of the Spiritual but not Religious*. Oxford: Oxford University Press, 2014.
14. Patricia Wittberg. *Building Strong Church Communities: A Sociological Overview*. New York: Paulist Press, 2012.
15. Philip J. Murnion, and David DeLambo. *Parishes and Parish Ministries: A Study of Parish Lay Ministry*. New York: National Pastoral Life Center, 1999.
16. Archdiocese of Detroit website. Available online: www.aod.org (accessed on 15 October 2016).
17. Abby Day. "Varieties of Belief over Time: Reflections from a Longitudinal Study of Youth and Belief." *Journal of Contemporary Religion* 28 (2013): 277–93. [CrossRef]
18. Ole Riis, and Linda Woodhead. *A Sociology of Religious Emotion*. Oxford: Oxford University Press, 2010.
19. John W. Meyer, and Brian Rowan. "Institutionalized Organizations: Formal Structure as Myth and Ceremony." *American Journal of Sociology* 83 (1977): 340–63. [CrossRef]
20. Patricia Wittberg. *From Piety to Professionalism—And Back? Transformations of Organized Religious Virtuosity*. New York: Lexington Books, 2006.
21. Stephen Pattison. *The Faith of the Managers: When Management Becomes Religion*. London: Cassell, 1997.
22. N. J. Demerath, III, Peter Dobkin Hall, Terry Schmitt, and Rhys H. Williams, eds. *Sacred Companies: Organizational Aspects of Religion and Religious Aspects of Organizations*. New York: Oxford University Press, 1998.
23. Erving Goffman. *Stigma*. Englewood Cliffs: Prentice-Hall, 1963.

24. Cecilia L. Ridgeway. "Why Status Matters for Inequality." *American Sociological Review* 79 (2014): 1–16. [CrossRef]
25. Robert Jackall. "Morality in Organizations." In *Handbook of the Sociology of Morality*. Edited by Steven Hitlin and Stephen Vaisey. Berlin: Springer, 2011.

![religions logo] *religions*

MDPI

Article

Moral and Cultural Awareness in Emerging Adulthood: Preparing for Multi-Faith Workplaces

Patricia Snell Herzog [1,*], De Andre' T. Beadle [1], Daniel E. Harris [2], Tiffany E. Hood [3] and Sanjana Venugopal [4]

[1] Department of Sociology & Criminal Justice, University of Arkansas, Fayetteville, AR 72701, USA; dbeadle@uark.edu
[2] Department of Management, Sam M. Walton College of Business, University of Arkansas, Fayetteville, AR 72701, USA; dharris@walton.uark.edu
[3] Department of Psychological Science, University of Arkansas, Fayetteville, AR 72701, USA; temiller@uark.edu
[4] Department of Biochemistry, University of Arkansas, Fayetteville, AR 72701, USA; svenugop@uark.edu
* Correspondence: herzog@uark.edu; Tel.: +1-479-575-3779

Academic Editor: John Bartkowski
Received: 29 January 2016; Accepted: 11 April 2016; Published: 15 April 2016

Abstract: The study evaluates a pilot course designed to respond to findings from the National Study of Youth and Religion (NSYR) and similar findings reporting changes in U.S. life course development and religious participation through an intervention based on sociological theories of morality. The purpose of the study is to investigate the impacts of a business course in a public university designed to prepare emerging adults for culturally and religiously diverse workplaces. The intended outcomes are for students to better identify their personal moral values, while also gaining cultural awareness of the moral values in six different value systems: five major world religions and secular humanism. The study response rate was 97 percent (n = 109). Pre- and post-test survey data analyze changes in the reports of students enrolled in the course (primary group) compared to students in similar courses but without an emphasis on morality (controls). Qualitative data include survey short answer questions, personal mission statements, and student essays describing course impacts. Quantitative and qualitative results indicate reported increases in identification of personal moral values and cultural awareness of other moral values, providing initial evidence that the course helps prepare emerging adults for multi-faith workplaces.

Keywords: religion; morality; faith traditions; emerging adulthood; generational changes

1. Introduction

Emerging adulthood is a relatively new stage of life that developed in response to a number of macro-structural changes in the last several decades in the United States [1]. Though many generations have had transitional periods as they discerned adulthood trajectories, emerging adults today now spend a decade or more somewhere between their adolescence and young adulthood. While emerging adulthood can be a time of personal optimism and hope for the future, it is also a period filled with disjointed processes in transitioning to adulthood, turbulence, and moral confusion as young people attempt to establish themselves. Research indicates that many emerging adults have difficulty identifying the moral values that guide their everyday behaviors and instead tend more often make decisions without considerable self-reflection [2,3]. This is especially a problem for workplaces, which rely upon a basis of moral values for ethical decision-making [4].

To respond to this issue, the University of Arkansas Walton College of Business, in partnership with the Tyson Center for Faith in Spirituality in the Workplace, is offering a new course entitled,

"Authentic Leadership in a Multi-Faith Workplace: Remaining True to Yourself in a Professional Kaleidoscope." The goal of the course is to help students of all faith traditions and of no faith tradition to identify their moral values by reflecting on meaning, purpose, and core beliefs, while also learning about other religious and cultural value systems. This is primarily accomplished by exposing students to basic familiarity with the traditions of multiple world religions, represented by five wisdom traditions as well as secular humanism. Specific tasks throughout the semester are dedicated to practicing difficult conversations and writing a personal mission statement that articulates personal moral values as applied to future workplaces. The intended change of this process is to facilitate emerging adults in explicating their moral values toward developing an effective and authentic sense of self, while also learning to respect the plurality of value systems toward becoming culturally aware leaders of multi-faith workplaces.

The purpose of this study was to investigate the impact of the course on facilitating emerging adults in identifying their moral values while also gaining greater cultural awareness. While assessing impact presents a number of challenges, the current study advances knowledge on an intervention designed to respond to known trends by conducting a natural field experiment. Since a laboratory experiment risks external validity, the natural method is preferred, despite its limitations. To control for spurious effects to the extent possible, several methods were undertaken to collect data through a quasi-experimental design: a time one to time two comparison to isolate causal changes within the study duration, a treatment group compared to similar control groups without the primary intervention of interest in order to isolate self-selection effects, and implementation of nationally normed survey measures that allow for nationally representative data to be systematically analyzed for regional subpopulation differences. Despite these controls, a number of limitations remain and are described in the discussion section.

This study investigates the following research questions: Does a course designed to prepare emerging adult college students for multi-faith workplaces appear to develop greater moral and cultural awareness? Upon completion of the course, do students report that they are better able to identify their own moral values and have gained greater awareness of other value systems? Before investigating those questions, the next section summarizes the empirical and theoretical background leading to the creation of this course and to this study designed to evaluate its impacts. To our knowledge, this study is the first of its kind to move beyond description and explanation of existing trends into the relatively uncharted territory of investigating an intervention designed to alter the progression of these trends, at least for the group of participating students. As such, the study is not a replication of well-tested procedures for studying this type of course, of which there are few examples. Instead, we ground the study and its research questions in a rich theoretical and empirical background that indicate the need for this pilot course and a study of its effects. Thus, the next section does not provide a conventional literature review of studies the study parameters, as such is not yet available, and instead describes the theoretical and empirical background leading to the creation of this pilot course, its designed intervention, and this offered approach for its study.

2. Theoretical and Empirical Background

2.1. Religiosity, Spirituality, and Morality in the Workplace

A study of this kind is needed because extant scholarship highlights the importance of studying religiosity as a key aspect of workplace diversity management [5–7]. In reviews of numerous studies, a link is consistently found between religion and spirituality in the workplace and a range of organizational and individual outcomes, such as physical and mental health, creativity, organizational commitment, and ethicality [7,8]. A number of socially desirable outcomes positively associate with workplace spiritual values, including greater employee well-being, lower occupational stress, and decreased employee fatigue [9]. Business leaders who incorporate religious or spiritual practices into their management have lowered stress in handling challenging workplace dynamics [10] and their employees have improved job performance [11].

Of particular importance for organizations is the link to ethical decision-making [12], such that religiosity can offer employees and leaders a shared sense of business ethics [13], acting as a "managerial moral strategy", especially when moral values have been formulated in advance of an ethical decision [14]. Studies find that ethical decision-making is a process that happens through several trainable cognitive strategies that are gained through moral evaluation practice [15] and lead to greater "moral awareness" [16]. In particular, an internalized sense of moral awareness, as compared to interpersonal forms of religiosity, has significant effects on ethical decision-making [17]. This is perhaps related to findings that personal ownership is a necessity for actualizing organizational missions [18]. As such, organizational business ethics often rely upon a set of pre-formulated moral values that are often acquired through religious or spiritual participation.

However, this is a relatively new and underdeveloped area of study that offers more in identifying the importance and calls for future studies than it does in delivering empirical results [19–23]. Further studies are especially needed in this area due to findings that religiosity and spirituality in the workplace can alternatively lead to negative effects [24], such as increased discrimination and marginalization of diverse religions by the dominant workplace religion Thus, it is important to study personal moral awareness that may be based in religious or spiritual traditions while also considering cultural awareness: sensitivity to moral values based in other religious and cultural traditions. Such a dual focus is developed by considering a sociologically informed perspective on the changing role of religiosity in modernity and its resulting social differentiation of moral values [6].

2.2. Modernity, Morality, and Religiosity

To understand modern workplace religious and cultural diversity, it is necessary to consider insights from social theories regarding changes to modern society brought on by industrialization. Historical and contemporary sociology of religion contributes to an understanding of the societal roles of religions within their changing social contexts. Durkheim and similar theories of religion focus on the social impacts of religiosity, viewing religions as representing agreed upon norms of behaviors from a shared sense of morality that is gained from ritualistic practices and can affect social settings such as workplaces [25,26]. From this perspective, moral values are viewed as sets of individually internalized social values that guide decisions about right and wrong in any given situation [27–29]. Thus, moral values reflect an intersection between individual decision making and cultural value systems, as internalized societal guidelines for what is considered to be meaningful, valuable, and important to be and do. These social values guide individual behaviors.

Durkheim [30] theorized that when individuals in a non-diverse religious culture made decisions, they were mostly based on religious moral values that provided societies with a shared sense of right and wrong (mechanical solidarity). However, recent trends indicate that declining participation in religious and other voluntary organizations is likely changing the extent to which young people develop moral values within shared social and cultural contexts (organic solidarity). Based on social theory, we take this to be an indication that cultural conflicts could increase as people from diverse backgrounds encounter multi-faith workplaces and the existence of pluralistic moral values. Yet most workplaces rely upon a shared sense of moral values to undergird ethical decision-making. This raises important questions regarding the changing role of religion in society, and specifically the extent to which religious value systems still provide people with a shared sense of moral values to facilitate workplace cohesion or whether workplace frictions are likely to increase as religious heterogeneity enables greater diversity of moral values.

Additionally, sociologists investigate the changing role of religion and morality in society by examining measures of religious participation and cultural changes over time. For example, results from the National Study of Youth and Religion and other studies provide numerous findings regarding demographic and cultural shifts in religious and civic participation among American young people (e.g., [31–37]). Likewise, in examining changes in religious participation longitudinally within the same cohort of American adolescents as they progressed to early adulthood, we found a net decline. The dominant trend was for stability, with 22.6 percent stable in being highly religiously engaged, 16.5 percent stable in being low-moderate, and 17.4 percent low stable. For 6.9 percent of the sample, there was a tremendous increase in religious engagement over time. However, 9.5 percent evidenced steep decline, and 27.1 percent shallow decline. Combined, Figure 1 shows that this totals to the majority, 57 percent, entering emerging adulthood with the same religious participation they had when in their teenage years, and with nearly seven percent increasing. Yet 37 percent of young Americans enter emerging adulthood less engaged in religious activities than when they were teenagers. This compounds with the already accrued generational declines to reveal a net decline between generations and within the same generation.

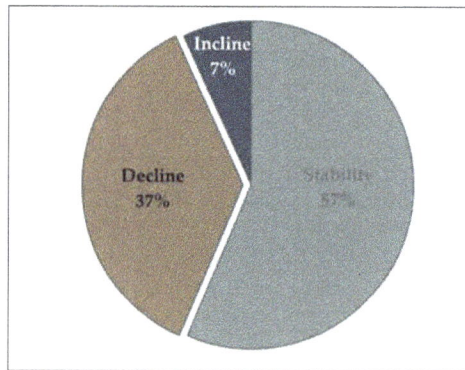

Figure 1. This figure represents the sum of longitudinal trends in religiosity as adolescents entered emerging adulthood, showing net decline. Author calculation based on findings reported in [12].

Likewise, in twenty years of General Social Survey data, Tom Smith finds that younger cohorts have consistently been less likely to vote than older cohorts [36]. However, recent young cohorts show further decline in voting rates relative to previous generations when their same age. Similarly, younger cohorts have consistently been less religious than older cohorts, but recent young cohorts have evidenced declining religiosity relative to prior generations at their same age, especially through attending religious services less often and being less likely to identify as religious. Overall, younger cohorts have the least organizational participation of any kind, have lower rates of social trust, and view other people as less helpful than did prior generations. In summary, sociology has historically identified religious traditions as a primary source for people learning moral values and constructing a shared sense of what is important to be and do, but processes of social differentiation have eroded a shared moral value system, resulting in diversity of moral values learned in different cultural contexts, and increasingly in the American religious landscape a lack of participation in religious value systems.

2.3. Generational Changes and Emerging Adulthood

What accounts for these monumental changes in religious and civic participation? Part of the answer lies in generational changes resulting in a new life stages that is altering the social processes of growing up and establishing adulthood. Arnett [1,38] identifies a number of changes in Western culture that he argues have contributed to the development of a new life stage called "emerging adulthood." During this life stage, the individual has appeared to move beyond adolescence but has not yet reached full adult responsibility. The distinctive feature of emerging adulthood relative to previous generations is that young people today are increasingly taking longer pathways to adulthood [39–42].

The emerging adulthood life stage is described primarily by tremendous variability in transitioning into adult social roles [43].

As a new life stage, emerging adulthood appears to have resulted from four historical changes beginning in the 1960s and 1970s: the technology revolution, the sexual revolution, the women's movement, and the youth movement ([1], p. 3). The technology revolution refers to the advancement of machines to perform manufacturing jobs, resulting in formerly industrialized countries having "shifted from a manufacturing economy to a service economy" ([1], p. 4). The consequence of this shift to a service economy is a greater participation in postsecondary education and training, which contributes to delays in marriage and family formation [44]. Delays in marriage and family formation are also related to the sexual revolution that was facilitated by increased availability of birth control, which also coincided with decreased moral taboos surrounding sexual morality during the 1960s [1]. A third historical change that contributed to the development of the emerging adulthood life stage was the women's movement. Greater opportunities to pursue higher education and have careers, significantly altered the roles and status of women in society [45]. Arnett summarizes the fourth historical change as the youth movement, referring to the time when many youth "denigrated adulthood and exalted being, acting, and feeling young" ([1], p. 6). This movement resulted in a marked cultural shift in how young people view the responsibilities of adulthood, and a lingering desirability to stay young as long as possible. Despite these cultural changes in adulthood transitions, Settersten and Ray find that the twenties are crucial years for making investments that have long-term impacts on adulthood futures [46]. They argue that the delayed pattern is beneficial because it allows young people time to make more strategic choices, and build credentials, skills, and experiences that will ensure stronger and more stable futures.

Regardless of whether delays in life stage development are beneficial for more successful adulthood transitions or whether adulthood is resisted, the central impact of the life stage of emerging adulthood on religiosity is that the delay in adulthood transitions tends to thwart sustained participation in organizational participation of any kind. "Emerging adults are not only less religiously committed and involved than older adults but also tend to be less involved in and committed toward a wide variety of other, nonreligious social and institutional connections, associations, and activities." ([3], p. 92). Scholars find that "life-course events such as marriage, careers, and religious beliefs are "increasingly left to individuals to decide on their own, leaving people to take on new responsibilities for living with the consequences of their actions and decisions, for good and bad" ([47], p. 203; [48]). Thus, studies of emerging adulthood find a number of macro-structural changes that have led to the development of this new life stage and which have also affected religiosity and faith development over the life course.

2.4. Moral Development

Given these significant social changes and alterations in life course progression, how does morality develop as one cognitively and emotionally matures? One of the most notable answers to this question was *Stages of Faith*, in which Fowler identifies seven stages throughout the life cycle that represent a step-wise development in faith that culminates in the ability to reflect upon one's own moral values [49]. In the work of Fowler there is an understanding of moral development from a life stage perspective. Fowler purports that faith and even life is a dynamic, non-static, ongoing process of change and development. Fowler suggested that faith development as a universal human endeavor that deals with *how* a person believes rather than *what* a person believes.

Fowler saw faith development as a process with six marked stages that correspond to increased cognitive capacity. The precursor stage begins with the first two years of life, during which children understand basic concepts such as nurture *versus* neglect. Stage 1, "Intuitive-Projective Faith" is noted by the emergence of imagination and stimulation in response to stories and symbols, which is yet unrestrained by logical thinking. Experiences and images in this stage have long-lasting effects on the life of faith, both positive and negative. This is a stage of self-awareness, called epistemological egocentrism, in which perspective taking has not yet developed. As defined by Fowler, the "Mythic-Literal Faith" of the second stage happens as children become more capable of concrete operational thinking and begin to sort out real from make believe. Children at this stage are most focused on reciprocal fairness and immanent justice.

Beginning in adolescence, stage three is "Synthetic-Conventional Faith" in which social experiences most centrally expand beyond the family, with external social spheres providing sources of authority. New cognitive abilities make mutual perspective-taking possible, enable integration of diverse self-images into a coherent identity, and allow for evaluation of previously taken-for-granted ideas. Feedback from others can be influential in providing positive or negative evaluations of nascent self identities. The fourth stage is "Individuative-Reflective Faith," in which a critical reflection on beliefs, background and values occur. This is when an understanding forms of the self and others as a part of a social system. Fowler define two more stages—"Conjunctive Faith" that focuses on faith paradoxes and "Universalizing Faith" that involves an overcoming of faith paradoxes grounded in oneness with the power of being. However, Fowler reports these latter two stages to be rare, and the changes of the previous section raise questions as to their existence.

While Fowler described this influential theory of faith stages, empirical investigations of the theory have found limited and sometimes conflicting support for this stage-like, linear progression in the way faith develops over time [50]. Moreover, the social changes resulting in emerging adulthood are likely to have altered the developmental process significantly in the three decades since Fowler began studying the life course and faith development. In terms of faith development, the most notable of these is declining religious participation, which makes a singular and universal process of faith development even less likely than it may have been during Fowler's time. While a number of positive social changes have resulted from an increasingly diverse religious landscape in America, one potential issue is that it is less clear how young people are to make meaning of the myriad options available for understanding what is right and wrong to be and do. In this process of social differentiation, there is potential for greater social conflicts to exist, especially in workplaces that often bring together people who may not otherwise be in social contact, thereby increasing the changes of exposure to pluralistic moral values. Moreover, workplaces rely upon ethical decision-making that formerly was based upon moral value systems that were socialized in other social spheres, such as religious congregations. Thus, declining religious participation for younger cohorts implies that moral values are less often meaningfully made within religious contexts.

2.5. Moral and Cultural Awareness

Yet numerous studies find the importance of developing a sense of meaning during life course development, especially through forming a sense of identity [51–55]. Having a faith identity or moral value system relates to a host of positive emerging adult outcomes and appears to be a protective factor during life course development [56–58]. Most notable is that having a sense of personal moral values can give meaning and fill existential voids regarding life purpose, a critical psychological well-being issue. Thus, moral meaning making is an important life process, and developing moral values appears to be an important part of a healthy life course.

However, young people are less likely to enter emerging adulthood with religiously socialized moral values, raising the question: How do emerging adults today learn to identify their moral values? We do not yet know the answers to this question. The limited existing studies in this area are mostly based upon under supported theories that are becoming increasingly outmoded due to their data being collected prior to the changes resulting in the new life stage called emerging adulthood described above. Moreover, the life stage has significantly altered, with religious participation markedly declining. This means that young people in contemporary America are less likely than prior cohorts to participate in meaning-making activities within religious congregations, or within voluntary organizations of any kind. It also means that there is a lack of updated information regarding how emerging adults learn to make meaning of their social experiences by identifying their personal values, but in ways that do not become religiously and culturally hegemonic by respecting the pluralistic milieu of diverse religious and cultural values.

In response to this dearth of updated understandings of emerging adult moral meaning making, this study investigates the piloting of an approach within a large public university to facilitate emerging adults in developing moral reasoning skills for diverse, multi-faith workplaces [16,59–61]. The goal is to raise student moral awareness without culturally hegemony.

3. Methodology

This study collects data on a natural field experiment designed to test whether a college course appeared have its desired impacts. Data were collected in the Fall of 2014 via a survey distributed at the beginning, Time 1, and end of the semester, Time 2, to the primary class and to three control groups of similar leadership classes. The study response rate was 97 percent (n = 109). One quarter of this was the primary class, compared to three quarters in the control classes. T1–T2 pairs total 89 percent of the sample (n = 97). The composition of the class entailed slightly younger females than males (Figure 2a). Two-thirds were business majors, and most of the non-majors were business minors. The vast majority was religious and dominantly Protestant or Catholic (Figure 2b).

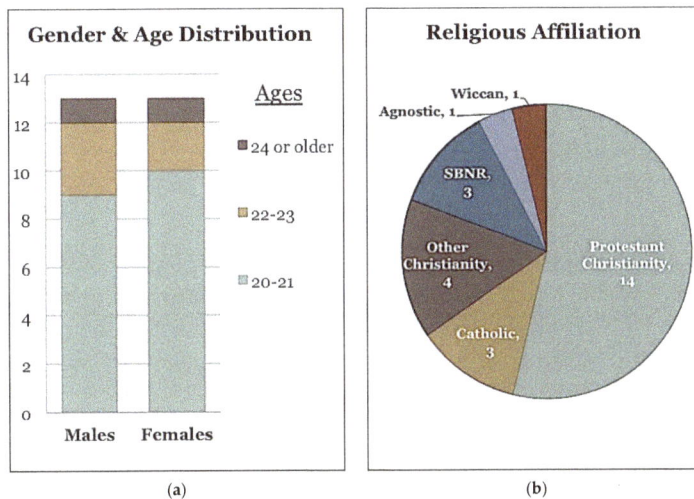

Figure 2. Primary class gender, age, and major at Time 1. (**a**) The primary class represented a slightly greater proportion of female students compared to the control group students. Within the class there was even representation among genders, with female students being slight younger than the male students (y-axis is student counts); (**b**) more than two-thirds of students were Protestant or Catholic.

3.1. National Comparison

To assess potential regional differences in the study, questions from the National Study of Youth and Religion (NSYR) [62] were included on the survey to create benchmarks for comparison to nationally representative data. Such an approach is, to our knowledge, not existent and, therefore, we pilot an approach to using nationally normed data for this purpose. To be clear, this brings the regional location of this one locale study out of the unknown limitations into an empirically known analysis. To do this, respondents were selected from the NSYR Wave 3 survey, when NSYR respondents were the same average ages as the college students in this study. From the larger nationally representative data, a subsample was selected who lived in the South (42 percent), were enrolled in college (51 percent), and were 20 or more years of age (60 percent, sample size is 315 respondents). We then compared results for this group of NSYR respondents to results for the respondents in our study on the measures from the NSYR survey that were also included in this survey to allow such a comparison.

Statistical tests comparing this nationally representative subgroup to the primary and control groups at T1 find a slight overrepresentation of females: 54 percent of primary respondents (n = 14), compared to 46 percent of NSYR respondents (n = 145). Religiously the classes are similar to the NSYR subgroup: classes are 69 percent Protestant (n = 18), 12 percent Catholic (n = 3), zero percent Other, and 19 percent not religious or indeterminate religiosity (n = 5), compared to in NSYR subsample as 68 percent Protestant, 17 percent Catholic, 2 percent Other, and 14 percent not or indeterminate. The largest differences between the nationally representative subsample and classes were on self-reported importance of faith and viewing religion as a private matter. The primary class was significantly more likely to rate faith as very to extremely important, whereas the primary class was significantly less likely to agree that religion is private. Results are displayed in tab:religions-07-00040-t001.

Table 1. Comparison between the primary class, control groups, and subsampled national study on the two measures with most Time 1 self-selection for the primary class.

Importance of Faith	Religion is Private
75%—Primary (n = 26)	21%—Primary (n = 26)
58%—Controls (n = 83)	47%—Controls (n = 83)
56%—National (n = 315)	52%—National (n = 315)

The primary class evidences a self-selection for higher than average importance of faith, with 75 percent rating it very to extremely important, compared to 58 percent with the same rating among the control group classes in the same university and compared to 56 percent in the regional and comparable national subsample. At Time 1, the primary group also evidenced a lower rating for agreeing that religion is a private matter, with only 21 percent of the primary group agreeing, compared to 47 percent of within-university control groups, and 52 percent of national subsample.

3.2. Control Comparison

In addition to the site-specific differences between the classes studied and the nationally representative subsample, there are also some differences between the primary class and control classes. Students in the primary class were statistically significantly more likely than the control groups to disagree at Time 1 that lying is sometimes alright if it is profitable, 76 percent of primary respondents (n = 20) compared to 44 percent of control group respondents (n = 37). Combined with the national differences, there is some evidence of a self-selection effect of emerging adults with statistically significant differences between the control groups and the treatment group, who reported higher importance of faith, greater belief that religion is a public matter, and with more propensities to infuse their morals in the workplace by adhering to their ethical principles even when it comes at a shorter-term personal or organizational cost. Despite these differences, the data of this study present an opportunity to study an intervention effort designed to facilitate emerging adults in becoming more aware of, culturally sensitive to, and better articulators of their moral values and personal missions, especially among those already primed for moral engagement and among a group of relatively committed emerging adults. As such, this course provides a relatively stringent case study for a pilot course among a group of emerging adults known to be particularly non-representative of the average American emerging adult and, therefore, expected to show minimal or no change in their moral and cultural awareness due to their high initial religiosity.

4. Results

The results of the study indicate statistically significant changes over time in student Time 1 to Time 2 quantitative reports of their levels of moral and cultural awareness (as compared to control groups), which they qualitatively attribute to aspects of the intervention course. The largest quantitative changes between Time 1 and Time 2 were in cultural awareness, with the primary class having a statistically significant mean increase of 0.89 as compared to the control groups.

There was also a mean increase of 0.37 in the primary class in their confidence managing conflicts. The primary class also agreed more at Time 2 that they viewed the religion of their youth positively, with a 0.46 mean increase. Thus, primary students most notably gained in their cultural awareness, understanding, and identification of their moral values, positive feelings toward the religion of their youth, and confidence in managing workplace conflicts.

4.1. Control Group Changes

In terms of the qualitative findings, students in the control groups did not evidence significant changes in their open-ended responses regarding their life purpose. For example, one control group student who was unsure of his or her life purpose at Time 1 reported: "I don't really know my purpose in life just yet. But am confident I'll figure it out eventually." At Time 2, this same student responded simply, "I don't know yet." Another student in the control group said this at Time 1, "I believe that I was created by God for the purpose of glorifying him. My beliefs in and about God and myself define my meaning and purpose of everything I do or am." This same student at Time 2 said, "I believe God created me firstly to glorify him in how I respond to the world and its challenges, and to also honor him by loving other people in his name. I am created to be loved by him, and to love him back." A third example comes from a non-religious student who said at Time 1, "Although I feel that life always present[s] uncertainties and questions that cannot be answered, I have a strong sense of my strengths and aspirations." At Time 2, this same student said "I feel like it is my responsibility to be fair and kind to others while bettering myself and striving for success." These form the baseline qualitative comparisons for the following primary class qualitative results.

4.2. Personal Mission Statements

The culminating assignment of the course was the students writing a personal mission statement that they submitted three times through the semester, with revisions based on instructor feedback on prior drafts. This serves as the primary change mechanism, providing students with reflection on all the course content as it relates to them personally. For example, one student wrote:

> [My mission is] being an authentic, genuine and reliable leader that others can admire, look up to and aspire to be. Establish and create a work environment that is welcoming and accepting of all people who come from different backgrounds, experiences and walks of life. Challenge myself to seek opportunities to try or learn something new as often as possible. Vow to surround myself with individuals different from myself, ask questions and search for answers in order to cultivate growth.

Another example of a personal mission statement, and one that evidences a connection between pre-defined moral values and potential changes to ethical decision-making, is:

> To choose the ethical approach by making a personal commitment to honesty and integrity. To find opportunities to use my natural talents such as patience, self-control, sincerity, and logic through my job as a CPA. To strive to be worthy of the respect and admiration of family, friends, and business associates. To find happiness, fulfillment, and value in living.

While the data for this study are collected while students are still in college, the personal mission statements written by students often evidenced the potential for the preparations of this course to impact the kind of work they will do once employed, especially by this student about to graduate:

I will be a positive force in the lives of others by taking time to get to know those who cross my path and helping them in any way that I can. I will not ask anything of anyone that I am not willing to do myself. I have an opportunity to apply these principles in the managerial position I am starting at the end of this month. One of my goals is to advance in my career so that I can touch the lives of as many people as possible. Another goal is to continuously improve myself, and to help others improve themselves.

Many students explicitly religious based moral values in their personal statements, as exampled:

I want my life, as seen by others and my creator, to exemplify the servant leadership, joy, and grace that Jesus showed the world.

In other cases, students who expressed having high levels of religiosity in their survey did not write their personal mission statements in ways that were explicitly religious, as evidenced here:

Honesty—being truthful with others but most importantly myself. Healthy—keeping a healthy mind and body is very important. Humble—having respect for others and never seeing myself as boastful. Transparency—staying open and honest with myself and others Self-knowledge—strive to know who I truly am. PMS: I will strive to create my own path to happiness, not follow others' paths, while surrounding myself with people who sharpen me into a stronger more sophisticated individual, and to one day leave a legacy for my family and children.

These quotes from end of semester personal missions statements exemplify the kind of response that students provided after participating in the course. They evidence moral awareness in personal, especially as compared to the lack of changes in the control group open-ended responses from students also in classes with in-depth discussions and revisions of written work who did not have practice articulating their personal mission statements. These qualitative results mirror quantitative results in Figure 3, providing descriptions of changes that treatment group students reported in their moral awareness and which are not reflected by control group responses.

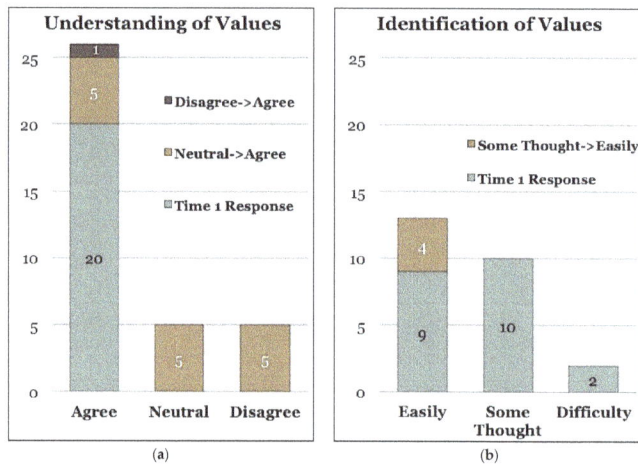

Figure 3. Primary class changes between Time 1 and Time 2. (**a**) Emerging adults in the primary class changed from two-thirds agreeing that they understood their values to all agreeing with this. Twenty percent (n = 5) moved from formerly neutral on this question to agreeing, and four percent (n = 1) changed from disagreeing to agreeing; (**b**) at Time 1, one-third of the class said they could identify their values easily (n = 9), and 16 percent (n = 4) said they could do it with some thought at Time 1 said at Time 2 that they could identify their values easily. The remaining half remained stable in their responses, with 40 percent with some thought (n = 10), and 8 percent with difficulty (n = 2).

4.3. Student Descriptions of Course Impacts

In addition to personal mission statements, students also submitted final essays. In their final course essay, students were asked to describe what, if any, changes this course had on them. Many students expressed that the course helped them gain greater self-awareness, as exemplified by this:

> This class helped me grow as a person. One of the reasons I took this class was to learn about other religions and how to interact with them, be more accepting, and be able to understand where they are coming from.

Additionally exemplified in the above quote, is a recurrent theme of students reporting learning about other religions with which they had minimal or no prior exposure. For example, on student stated:

> I was very interested in the idea of learning more about the world religions and how they hold power over the hearts and minds of so many people. In doing so I had hoped to strengthen my own beliefs as well. I feel as though I have accomplished both of these initiatives. Learning from the many speakers we have had has been incredibly insightful. The Buddhist monk was especially interesting to me. His illustration of Logic and reason as a sort of salvation from the world was incredible. While I disagree with him in this it was an amazing experience to hear from him about his beliefs. I wish that I had more time to talk with him, but I am grateful for the time he provided to us.

Some students explicitly tied these increases in cultural awareness of diverse religions to gains in workplace skills. This student, for instance, describes a new ability for teamwork:

> For strictly religious individuals without this concept, it is difficult to respect others who do not share similar beliefs because these people do not understand that values can be similar for people with different beliefs. I had this problem coming into this class. With this thought, a multi-faith team would rarely accomplish anything. Their conversations would continuous revolve around beliefs that are much less likely to change as opposed to values. Understanding this concept will assist me as an authentic leader with diverse teams.

In describing what particular aspects of the course facilitated changes in their moral awareness, students often described improvements from the process of writing and reflection, such as this:

> The journal posts, especially about the different religions really helped me to write my thoughts down as well as teach me about other religions. I found that I agreed with a lot of the teachings of other religions. I think that Huston Smith's chapter about Hinduism had the biggest impact on me, as well as on my mission. I liked that the Hindu religion taught people to do what they desired and that everything anyone gets is well deserved. I have always believed that what goes around comes around, and this "motto" if you will, helped me to develop my first draft of my mission. I always have and always will want to help others. I want to make the best impression I can on each person I meet and always respect others.

Increases in cultural awareness were alternatively linked to guest speakers from diverse religions:

> Another big part of our class this semester were the guest speakers, and honestly at first I wasn't sure what to expect from these times, but I found myself very enthralled by what they had to say and was propelled with that knowledge...Being familiar with other religions is a great tool to have, to be well rounded instead of ignorant.

Some students described how these increases in cultural awareness improved their emotive skills:

> Hearing about the views and beliefs of people who were raised in different cultures opened my eyes. The two Buddhist speakers relayed the importance of happiness in life and the

potential rewards for having control over our thoughts. Differentiating between feeling angry and admiring feelings of anger rising can make all of the difference in our lives. If I can start to notice when anger or sadness is rising within me, then I can faster take control of those feelings so that I will not be as affected by them.

Others described gains in the cognitive, logical processing skills from the moral awareness efforts:

The lectures helped to define and differentiate between faith, religion and spirituality. In my mind I had always assumed that these ideals were relatively all the same and could be used interchangeably. I had never grasped the true meaning behind these words and what they stood for. Through the lectures I was better able to recognize the differences and understand how I apply each of them to my life. I used to attribute faith to a theistic belief, but I have learned that it is our "overarching, integrating and grounding trust in a center of value and power which enables us to find coherence and meaning."

Relating the different course tasks to each other was described by some students as providing deeper impact through applying the learning into expressed practices. For example:

While practicing difficult conversations, I discovered that having a personal mission statement will really help me in business practice. With these tricky situations, if someone had asked why I believe what I do, I would have never been able to definitively explain. Now, because I have a mission statement, I know how to articulate my values and express why I believe one way or another. The mission statement will help me not only in dealing with difficult conversations, but in my business career as a whole.

In summary, many students described the kind of in-depth changes this course was designed to create, and quite a few were able to explicitly link the content of the course to the kind of workplace leader they want to be after completing the course and graduating. As one student eloquently said:

I will be a more effective leader in a multi-faith workplace when I understand more of my coworkers' culture: it shows that I care about them, and it keeps me from unintentionally offending someone. The speakers were not just supplemental to the reading; they were necessary to my understanding of the different wisdom traditions. The book gave me a good basis, but the speakers allowed me to understand the religion from a personal view and gave me a comfortable place to ask honest questions.

As these quotes evidence, one of the aspects of the course that had the greatest impact was exposure to multiple faiths via speakers who were devout in each of the five wisdom traditions and an ethical secular humanist speaking about how their faith affects them and their workplace behaviors. In response, emerging adults in the class evidence learning more about their own moral values and about the values of other cultures. In-depth reading of essays and personal mission statements reveals that changes need to be understood in reference to different starting positions.

4.4. Understanding Changes Relative to Different Starting Points

The central goal of the primary class was to facilitate emerging adult students in developing moral and cultural awareness. With the sensitizing concepts of moral and cultural awareness, Figure 4 represents a two-dimensional analytical framework that depicts a simplified version of the possible outcomes from combining these two dimensions: low to high moral awareness with low to high cultural awareness. For analytical clarity, each spectrum is represented dichotomously.

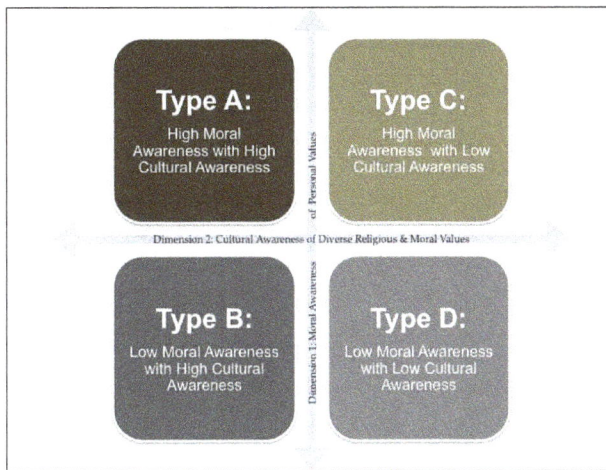

Figure 4. Two-Dimensional Framework of Written Work In-Depth Analysis. Dimension 1: Moral awareness ranging from high (top) to low (bottom) with Dimension 2: Cultural awareness ranging from high recognition of diverse religious and moral values (left) to low cultural awareness (right).

Together these dimensions form four ideal types with quadrants of: Type A—High Moral Awareness and High Cultural Awareness (upper left), Type B—Low Moral Awareness and High Cultural Awareness (lower left), Type C—High Moral Awareness and Low Cultural Awareness (upper right), Type D—Low Moral Awareness and Low Cultural Awareness (lower right).

Employing this typology, student written assignments were coded for ranges from low to high for each of the two dimensions, and students were then given a type coding based on the overall combination and prevalence of each dimension in their written works. In total there were 150 quotes coded for evidence of a relatively high moral awareness, and 69 quotations coded as evidencing low moral awareness. An example of evidence for high moral awareness is: "I will strive to have these values and goals embedded in every aspect of my everyday...I have found my values in my faith, and have designed my goals to come from my values." Another example of high moral awareness is: "I believe in ethics. I believe there are things that are just plain wrong and just plain right, from an ethical standpoint." An example of low moral awareness is: "I make my wagers based on how I feel about my decisions afterwards. I have my own moral compass, and I don't feel that I have to answer to anyone but myself at the end of the day." Another example of low moral awareness is: "There are so many gray areas in ethics, which makes determining what is ethical and what is not difficult." A third example of low moral awareness is: "I am the type of person that accepts the world as it is and goes through life being happy."

Despite cultural awareness evidencing the largest quantitative increase in survey responses, the qualitative instances were sparse, perhaps because the assignments did not directly ask for topics on this. There were 39 instances of high or increasing cultural awareness and 42 quotes of low or absent cultural awareness. An example of cultural awareness is: "In this class I have been able to respect other world religions and the ideas of others more." Another example of gaining cultural awareness is: "Up until this point, I have been naïve and uneducated about the other wisdom traditions that I myself did not identify with...What I have found is that one of the most exciting things for me is learning from people who are different from me." An example of a quote that was lacking a clear impact in increased cultural awareness is: "I knew this class was different than others that I was attending, it was more about learning what you want out of life and...that people have different ways of doing the same things."

Combined, these evidence the presence or absence of each of the two dimensions provided the means for assigning each student a summary code representing their placement within the four quadrants depicted in Figure 4. The result of these codes are displayed in Figure 5, showing that the majority of emerging adults enrolled in this course were Type A, evidencing high moral and high cultural awareness. The next majority was Type C—having high moral awareness but low cultural awareness, followed by Type D—low moral and low cultural awareness. The smallest proportion was Type B—evidencing high cultural awareness with low moral awareness.

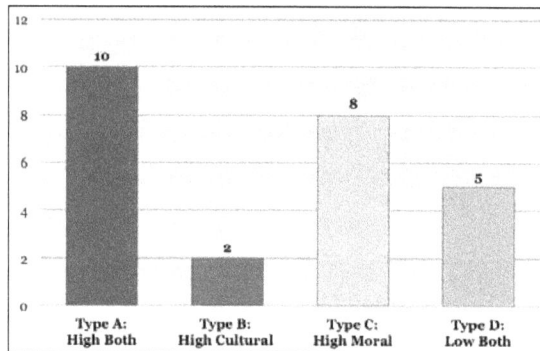

Figure 5. Typology Distribution for 2-Dimensional Framework.

These qualitative findings highlight the importance of understanding change relative to different starting points. For those already articulate about their moral frameworks, the greatest potential for change they experienced in the course is a raising of their cultural awareness. For example, one Type A student reported:

> I've been a Christian for many years, and hearing about other faiths brought me closer to God. I've known about other religions, but they were presented to me as "those people are wrong, but if we know what they believe then we can more easily convert them." This instilled in me an unconscious prejudice towards anyone who follows a different wisdom tradition than I do, and in order to be truly genuine, I've had to overcome that.

In contrast, a student with a similar level of personal moral awareness but with a remaining low level of cultural awareness at the end of the semester—a Type C student—reported:

> As a Christian, a very big part of my life is sharing the truth of Jesus. With that being said, an understanding of what people of other religions believe is a necessary tool if I hope to ever lead anyone to Christ who practices another religion. Being familiar with other religions is a great tool to have.

While these students evidenced a quantitatively similar high level moral awareness, the differences in their cultural awareness made them interpret the meaning of their moral awareness in distinct ways: the Type A student toward respecting different moral values and the Type C toward better conversion to a homogenous set of moral values.

For those generally more culturally aware, the greatest potential for change was becoming clearer about their personal moral values. For example, one Type A student who already reported a high level of cultural awareness described their increase in moral awareness in this way:

> I never really understood the true significance of writing down your values on paper. [Now I see that] it enables me to reflect on what is truly important to me and my life and concretize these values to make them meaningful and representative of who I am. I learned

more about myself than I ever thought I could in such a short amount of time. It has been a satisfying and fulfilling experience that I will take with me through my journey in life.

Alternatively, a Type B student who reported increasing in cultural awareness but did not evidence increases in moral awareness described this somewhat confusing personal mission statement:

> Our set of core values are being respectful, being honestly, being open minded, and being motivated. Being respectful is going to be the main solution to the toxic environment that exist within the team. If each team member has a sense of respect for each other and is able to step back and put their emotions aside to possibly compromise with others then there will be a better atmosphere for everyone to work. Personally being respectful is one of the most important values to have when leading or working with a group because if you do not respect others, then others will not have respect for you.

This quote helps highlight the category of student who has high cultural awareness with low moral awareness, resulting in a desire to have a great deal of respect for different perspectives but seemingly lacking any sort of "moral yardstick" by which to evaluate conflicting views. The implication is that this sort of student would take the path of least resistance in a workplace setting, which is likely to be non-desirable for organizations seeking high levels of moral engagement. Nevertheless, the increase in cultural awareness evidences improvement relative to a student showing low levels of moral and cultural awareness, such as this example:

> Since I came to the first class this semester I knew this class was different than the other ones I was attending, it was more about learning what you want out of life, ways to help you achieve it, and that we as humans all undergo this same process and we need to be respectful towards others and understanding that people have different ways of doing the same things.

This Type D student evidences a minor increase in moral and cultural awareness that may represent a greater level of cultural sensitivity and awareness of possible moral clarity to what existed prior, and which is what the student reported. However, the end result by the conclusion of the course shows a qualitatively distinct meaning that the moral and cultural awareness changes reported for the other types of students, and it remains unclear what if any impact will be had on the ethical decision-making of this student when in their future workplace.

These qualitative examples help elucidate that the quantitative data is useful for describing the average trends in course impacts, especially in order to assess their magnitude as compared to control groups who necessarily did not have these assignments that are part of the intended course change mechanism. However, they also reveal that changes appearing to result from the course need to be understood relative to diverse combination of moral and cultural awareness. In summary, this study provides initial evidence that a pilot college-based course in a business school aids even highly religiously committed emerging adults in gaining greater moral and cultural awareness. As such, this approach offers one way that non-familial adults can support emerging adults in developing moral awareness for ethical decision-making while also gaining cultural awareness of the diversity of religious and other moral values, providing a non-hegemonic intervention in moral development for non-religious social settings, such as public universities.

5. Discussion

Recent studies have found changes occurring in life stage development and in religious participation rates within the U.S. These findings necessarily alter prior theories regarding faith and spiritual development toward moral meaning-making, which have also not been empirically well supported. This study contributes to an updated understanding of moral meaning making, and the contributions of non-familial adults in supporting emerging adults to identify and better articulate their moral frameworks. Ethical decision-making in diverse and multi-faith workplaces rely upon individuals with well-formulated senses of right and wrong that remain culturally inclusive. The results of this study indicate that one possible approach is for public universities to educate students about different orientations for making meaning of ethical actions.

The course intervention appeared to be best at exposing morally inclined students to the existence of other cultural and religious values, helping them to understand their own moral frameworks within a broader cultural milieu. While religious and non-religious students were found in both categories: high and low moral awareness, students who had been exposed to a religious faith but were not currently giving morality conscious attention, either as religious or as being explicitly not religious (e.g., atheist or agnostic), were less likely to have high levels of moral awareness. Rather than inculcating them with specific religious doctrine, this course offers an alternative approach to facilitating students in gaining moral and cultural awareness through exposure to diverse moral value systems, personal reflection, and application to social practices.

One of the primary contributions of the study is the analytical framework specifying distinct combinations of moral and cultural awareness. Its application to the empirical data revealed that quantitative changes in each measure individually do not necessarily represent the same qualitative impact. In other words, a change score of one can represent qualitatively distinct kinds of changes and may not actually represent a shared intensity of change across measures and students. This is because the qualitative findings identify an important intersection between the survey measures, whereby change over time means something qualitatively different for a student entering the course with a high level of moral awareness and low level of cultural awareness than for a student with a moderate level on both or the inverse intersection.

For example, Student 1 had a high level of moral awareness with a low level of cultural awareness (Type C) and described gaining from the course exposure to one specific religious tradition—Islam—which they had low prior exposure to than other religious traditions—e.g., evangelical Protestantism, Catholicism. Their moral values were shaped by evangelical Protestantism, and they had previously understood their values to be superior to those of other religions. However, the course facilitated a personal experience with a devoted Muslim that created a deeper respect for the moral values of that religious tradition, in part from recognizing the similarities to their own moral values and in part from recognizing their differences as understandable given the tenets of the faith tradition from which they were derived. As a result, Student 1 reports no changes over time in their moral awareness and a one-point change in their cultural awareness. Having had prior exposure to some religious traditions, this student does not report a large degree of change as that of a student having global lack of exposure to different religious traditions (Type D) reports, but instead reports a more modest quantitative change referring to knowledge gained on one specific religion that moves toward becoming a Type A.

Alternatively, Student 2 had a low level of moral awareness with a low level of cultural awareness (Type D) and reported a large increase in their cultural awareness with no change in moral awareness. By the end of the course, it is unclear whether they have a pre-defined moral strategy on which to gauge workplace ethical decisions. However, they report a large gain in their cultural awareness and describe that prior to this course they had not had personal experiences with people from different religions. They tended to think morals were self-evident and therefore had not put a great deal of thought into their own moral values. The student describes gaining from the course a realization that different religious traditions support some similar and some distinct moral values, causing the student to think they should do some more reflection to figure out their own sense of morality. While there is no quantitative change detected in the moral values, there is an implication in the qualitative data that this student may eventually gain greater moral awareness, having now gained the cultural awareness to become confused, a therefore think further reflection is needed to gain clarity, making the formerly implicit more explicit.

What these two example students elucidate is that changes relative to only one of the two qualities would miss important changes in the other, and moreover a great deal would be missed by not understanding the intersection of the dimensions and their resulting meanings. This reveals that a one-point change in cultural awareness does not mean a lower impact is had than for a student who reports a three-point change. For example, a one-point change for Student 1 could result in less ethnocentrism, while a three-point change for Student 2 could result in greater introspection. Both are important course impacts, and thus the mixed-methods design of this study was needed to uncover the true sorts of change impacts possible with this intervention approach.

5.1. Limitations

Despite the study strengths in offering an investigation into an updated understanding of moral development that accounts for changing trends in the life course and in declining religious participation, there are two major sets of limitations to this pilot study: its generalizability and external validity. The first set of limitations concerns the generalizability, which is hindered by the small sample size. Moreover, the design of this study allowed for the empirical investigation of potential regional skews, and the sample is found to have greater than average levels of religiosity than nationally representative data on emerging adults. Likewise, the quasi-experimental design allows for a control group comparison, and the course is found to have self-selection biases as represented by higher levels of religiosity in the treatment group at the start of the course (T1).

While these skews represent limitations to the generalizability of the data, they are a strength of the study methodology. Nationally representative studies are costly, resulting in many local studies with smaller sample sizes. However, typically these small sample studies do not include ways of empirically analyzing their potential regional skews. Thus, part of what this study offers is a way to assess and report these skews by asking nationally normed questions and comparing the sampled group results. While it is possible for unknown self-selection or regional biases to remain, these known differences were controlled to the extent possible by assessing the statistical significance of small-sample tests comparing the Time 1 and Time 1-to-Time 2 changes of the three control group classes with the same data in the treatment group. This effectively controls for known self-section biases. The highly religious skew found through these analyses indicates that this pilot study offers an especially stringent design on a group that would be expected to evidence less change in moral and cultural awareness than the average emerging adult. Thus, we think that the results presented here conservatively estimate the extent to which a course such as this can facilitate moral and cultural awareness in a more general population of emerging adults.

A second set of limitations concern the external validity of the study. For one, there is a relatively short duration between Time 1 and Time 2, without data on the extent to which reported changes will last for longer periods of time and especially after students' transition to workplaces. Second, the study findings rely upon self-reported data, both in quantitative survey measures and in written descriptions of course impacts. As such, all findings are dependent upon student truthfulness and self-awareness. At the same time, the fact that many students reported having low levels of the intended outcomes of the course indicates that students were not inclined to only give socially desirable answers, and the unique study design provides a way to learn from low self-awareness evidenced in qualitative responses. Additionally, observer evaluations of student moral and cultural awareness could be even more limited than relying on self reports.

With these limitations in mind, we offer this pilot study as a way to assess course impact within the bounds of a single semester and to assess the regionally-specific and self-selection skews inherent in any non-nationally representative study conducted at a single or multiple universities.

5.2. Future Studies

This pilot study provides initial evidence of the success of this course in creating short-term changes in the intended outcomes. Rather than assuming the course is successful, drawing upon anecdotal evidence, or relying upon student evaluations that mostly assess course enjoyment, this study systematically investigates student changes using multiple methods that intentionally limit and reasonably control for self-selection biases and regional skews. Given the initial evidence of this study, we suggest that future studies implement a similar design that draws upon nationally normed data, compares treatment results to comparable controls groups, and assesses change using quantitative survey measures, written work, and qualitative descriptions of change impacts. If the same design were implemented at multiple universities, the results could be tallied across locales into a highly affordable study with greater generalizability.

Moreover, the results of this study provide an analytical framework with initial qualitative support of its usefulness in understanding student changes. We suggest that future studies also apply this framework to quantitative data by plotting students into the categories at Time 1 and then assessing their changes over time relative to the distinct positions learned about in this study. To do so would require a larger sample size in order to have large enough groups of students in each category at the start of the study to representatively asses their multiple forms of changes. This study provides initial evidence that such an approach would be worthwhile to conduct.

This pilot study also provides evidence for the utility of studies that considerably upscale this study: by collecting data outside the bounds of a course and on nationally representative samples, tracking students over time, adding observer collected data, and linking workplace behaviors to earlier preparation strategies. Given the clear increases in both moral and cultural awareness evidenced in this modest study, we believe all such efforts would be efficacious and likely yield even more marked results than those found in this pilot study.

Acknowledgments: The authors are grateful to the University of Arkansas Tyson Center for Faith and Spirituality in the Workplace and Department of Sociology and Criminal Justice for funding student research assistance, as well as to the National Study of Youth and Religion for use of selected survey questions and comparison data. We also wish to thank Andre Delbecq for insights on the project at various stages.

Author Contributions: Patricia Snell Herzog in the Department of Sociology and Criminal Justice, primarily authored this paper, designed and programmed the survey, developed the theoretical framework, conducted the quantitative analyses, and supervised student research assistants in qualitative coding and literature reviewing. De Andre' T. Beadle in the Department of Sociology and Criminal Justice, wrote first drafts of portions of the literature review and conducted the qualitative coding. Daniel E. Harris in the Department of Management in the Sam M. Walton College of Business, designed the primary course in the study, recruited instructors for the control group courses, taught the primary class, and collected and provided feedback on personal mission statements and final course essays. Tiffany E. Hood, undergraduate student in the Department of Psychological Sciences, conducted portions of the qualitative coding and gathered relevant studies for the literature review. Sanjana Venugopal in the Department of Biochemistry, conducted portions of the qualitative coding.

Conflicts of Interest: The authors declare no conflict of interest.

Abbreviations:

NSYR National Study of Youth and Religion

References

1. Arnett, Jeffrey J. *Emerging Adulthood: The Winding Road from the Late Teens through the Twenties*, 2nd ed. New York: Oxford University Press, 2015.

2. Arum, Richard, and Josipa Roksa. *Aspiring Adults Adrift: Tentative Transitions of College Graduates*. Chicago: University of Chicago Press, 2014.

3. Smith, Christian, and Patricia Snell. *Souls in Transition: The Religious and Spiritual Lives of Emerging Adults*. New York: Oxford University Press, 2009.

4. Moore, Celia. "Moral Disengagement in Processes of Organizational Corruption." *Journal of Business Ethics* 80 (2008): 129–39. [CrossRef]

5. Duffy, Ryan D., Laura Reid, and Bryan J. Dik. "Spirituality, Religion, and Career Development: Implications for the Workplace." *Journal of Management, Spirituality and Religion* 7 (2010): 209–21. [CrossRef]

6. Schaeffer, Charles B., and Jacqueline S. Mattis. "Diversity, Religiosity, and Spirituality in the Workplace." *Journal of Management, Spirituality & Religion* 9 (2012): 317–33. [CrossRef]

7. Day, Nancy E. "Religion in the Workplace: Correlates and Consequences of Individual Behavior." *Journal of Management, Spirituality & Religion* 2 (2005): 104–35. [CrossRef]

8. Benefiel, Margaret, Louis W. Fry, and David Geigle. "Spirituality and Religion in the Workplace: History, Theory, and Research." *Psychology of Religion and Spirituality* 6 (2014): 175–87. [CrossRef]
9. Arnetz, Bengt B., Matthew Ventimiglia, Pamela Beech, Valerie DeMarinis, Johan Lökk, and Judith E. Arnetz. "Spiritual Values and Practices in the Workplace and Employee Stress and Mental Well-Being." *Journal of Management, Spirituality & Religion* 10 (2013): 271–81. [CrossRef]
10. Delbecq, André L. "The Impact of Meditation Practices in the Daily Life of Silicon Valley Leaders." In *Contemplative Practices in Action: Spirituality, Meditation, and Health*. Goleta: ABC-CLIO, 2010, pp. 183–204.
11. Vandenberghe, Christian. "Workplace Spirituality and Organizational Commitment: An Integrative Model." *Journal of Management, Spirituality & Religion* 8 (2011): 211–32. [CrossRef]
12. Fernando, Mario, and Brad Jackson. "The Influence of Religion-Based Workplace Spirituality on Business Leaders' Decision-Making: An Inter-Faith Study." 2006. Available online: http://ro.uow.edu.au/commpa pers/165 (accessed on 10 October 2015).
13. Vitell, Scott J. "The Role of Religiosity in Business and Consumer Ethics: A Review of the Literature." *Journal of Business Ethics* 90 (2009): 155–67. [CrossRef]
14. Soule, Edward. "Managerial Moral Strategies—In Search of a Few Good Principles." *Academy of Management Review* 27 (2002): 114–24.
15. Thiel, Chase E., Zhanna Bagdasarov, Lauren Harkrider, James F. Johnson, and Michael D. Mumford. "Leader Ethical Decision-Making in Organizations: Strategies for Sensemaking." *Journal of Business Ethics* 107 (2012): 49–64. [CrossRef]
16. VanSandt, Craig V., Jon M. Shepard, and Stephen M. Zappe. "An Examination of the Relationship between Ethical Work Climate and Moral Awareness." *Journal of Business Ethics* 68 (2006): 409–32. [CrossRef]
17. Kum-Lung, Choe, and Lau Teck-Chai. "Attitude towards Business Ethics: Examining the Influence of Religiosity, Gender and Education Levels." *International Journal of Marketing Studies* 2 (2010): 225–32. [CrossRef]
18. Darbi, William Phanuel Kofi. "Of Mission and Vision Statements and Their Potential Impact on Employee Behaviour and Attitudes: The Case of A Public But Profit-Oriented Tertiary Institution." *International Journal of Business and Social Science* 3 (2012): 95–109.
19. Bandsuch, Mark R., and Gerald F. Cavanagh. "Integrating Spirituality into the Workplace: Theory & Practice." *Journal of Management, Spirituality and Religion* 2 (2005): 221–54.
20. Bowman, Timothy James. "An Ideal Type of Spiritually Informed Organizations: A Sociological Model." *Journal of Management, Spirituality and Religion* 5 (2008): 293–320. [CrossRef]
21. Brotheridge, Céleste M., and Raymond T. Lee. "Hands to Work, Heart to God: Religiosity and Organizational Behavior." *Journal of Management, Spirituality and Religion* 4 (2007): 287–309. [CrossRef]
22. Probst, Tahira M., and Paul Strand. "Perceiving and Responding to Job Insecurity: A Workplace Spirituality Perspective." *Journal of Management, Spirituality and Religion* 7 (2010): 135–56. [CrossRef]
23. Saks, Alan M. "Workplace Spirituality and Employee Engagement." *Journal of Management, Spirituality and Religion* 8 (2011): 317–40. [CrossRef]
24. Chaston, Jacqui, and Marjolein Lips-Wiersma. "When Spirituality Meets Hierarchy: Leader Spirituality as a Double-Edged Sword." *Journal of Management, Spirituality and Religion* 12 (2015): 111–28. [CrossRef]
25. Groen, Janet. "Spirituality within a Religious Workplace: Is it So Different?" *Journal of Management, Spririituality, and Religion* 4 (2007): 310–25. [CrossRef]
26. Robertson, Roland. "Individualism, Societalism, Worldliness Universalism: Thematizing Theoretical." *Sociology of Religion* 38 (1977): 281–308.
27. Seidman, Steven. "Modernity and the Problem of Meaning: The Durkheimian Tradition." *Sociology of Religion* 46 (1985): 109–30. [CrossRef]
28. Schafer, Markus H. "Ambiguity, Religion, and Relational Context: Competing Influences on Moral Attitudes?" *Sociological Perspectives* 54 (2011): 59–81. [CrossRef]
29. Husted, Bryan W., and David B. Allen. "Toward a Model of Cross-Cultural Business Ethics: The Impact of Individualism and Collectivism on the Ethical Decision-Making Process." *Journal of Business Ethics* 82 (2008): 293–305. [CrossRef]
30. Durkheim, Emile, and Karen Fields, trans. *The Elementary Forms of Religious Life*. New York: Free Press, 1995.
31. Pearce, Lisa D., and Melinda Lundquist Denton. *A Faith of Their Own: Stability and Change in the Religiosity of America's Adolescents*. New York: Oxford University Press, 2011.

32. Smith, Christian, Kari Christoffersen, Hilary Davidson, and Patricia Snell Herzog. *Lost in Transition: The Dark Side of Emerging Adulthood*. New York: Oxford University Press, 2011.

33. Dean, Kenda Creasy. *Almost Christian: What the Faith of Our Teenagers Is Telling the American Church*. New York: Oxford University Press, 2010.

34. Smith, Christian, and Melina Lundquist Denton. *Soul Searching: The Religious and Spiritual Lives of American Teenagers*. New York: Oxford University Press, 2009.

35. Smith, Tom. "Generation Gaps in Attitudes and Values from the 1970s to the 1990s." In *On the Frontier of Adulthood: Theory, Research, and Public Policy*. Edited by Richard A. Settersten, Jr., Frank F. Furstenberg and Rubén G. Rumbaut. Chicago: University of Chicago Press, 2005, pp. 177–224.

36. Wuthnow, Robert. *After the Baby Boomers: How Twenty- and Thirty-Somethings Are Shaping the Future of American Religion*. Princeton: Princeton University Press, 2010.

37. Wuthnow, Robert. *America and the Challenges of Religious Diversity*. Princeton: Princeton University Press, 2007.

38. Arnett, Jeffrey J. "Emerging Adulthood: What Is It, and What Is It Good For?" *Child Development Perspectives* 1 (2007): 68–73. [CrossRef]

39. Waters, Mary C., Patrick J. Carr, Maria J. Kefalas, and Jennifer Holdaway, eds. *Coming of Age in America: The Transition to Adulthood in the Twenty-First Century*. Berkeley: University of California Press, 2011.

40. Hartmann, Douglas, and Teresa Toguchi Swartz. "The New Adulthood? The Transition to Adulthood from the Perspective of Transitioning Young Adults." *Advances in Life Course Research, Constructing Adulthood Agency and Subjectivity in Adolescence and Adulthood* 11 (2006): 253–86. [CrossRef]

41. Bynner, John. "Rethinking the Youth Phase of the Life-Course: The Case for Emerging Adulthood?" *Journal of Youth Studies* 8 (2005): 367–84. [CrossRef]

42. Cote, James E. *Arrested Adulthood: The Changing Nature of Maturity and Identity*. New York: NYU Press, 2000.

43. Osgood, Wayne D., Gretchen Ruth, Jacquelynne S. Eccles, Janis E. Jacobs, and Bonnie L. Barber. "Six Paths to Adulthood: Fast Starters, Parents without Careers, Educated Partners, Educated Singles, Working Singles, and Slow Starters." In *On the Frontier of Adulthood: Theory, Research, and Public Policy*. Edited by Richard A. Settersten, Frank F. Furstenberg and Rubén G. Rumbaut. Chicago: University of Chicago Press, 2005, pp. 320–55.

44. Cherlin, Andrew J. "The Deinstitutionalization of American Marriage." *Journal of Marriage and Family* 66 (2004): 848–61. [CrossRef]

45. Domina, Thurston, and Josipa Roksa. "Should Mom Go Back to School? Post-Natal Educational Attainment and Parenting Practices." *Social Science Research* 41 (2012): 695–708. [CrossRef] [PubMed]

46. Settersten, Richard, and Barbara E. Ray. *Not Quite Adults: Why 20-Somethings Are Choosing a Slower Path to Adulthood, and Why It's Good for Everyone*. New York: Bantam, 2010.

47. Schwartz, Seth J., Byron L. Zamboanga, Koen Luyckx, Alan Meca, and Rachel A. Ritchie. "Identity in Emerging Adulthood Reviewing the Field and Looking Forward." *Emerging Adulthood* 1 (2013): 96–113. [CrossRef]

48. Beck, Ulrich. *Risk Society: Towards a New Modernity*. Thousand Oaks: SAGE, 1992.

49. Fowler, James W. *Stages of Faith: The Psychology of Human Development and the Quest for Meaning*. San Francisco: HarperOne, 1995.

50. Parker, Stephen. "Research in Fowler's Faith Development Theory: A Review Article." *Review of Religious Research* 51 (2010): 233–52.

51. Barry, Carolyn McNamara, and Mona M. Abo-Zena, eds. *Emerging Adults' Religiousness and Spirituality: Meaning-Making in an Age of Transition*. New York: Oxford University Press, 2014.

52. Mayseless, Ofra, and Einat Keren. "Finding a Meaningful Life as a Developmental Task in Emerging Adulthood the Domains of Love and Work across Cultures." *Emerging Adulthood* 2 (2014): 63–73. [CrossRef]

53. Kimball, Cynthia, Kaye Cook, Chris Boyatzis, and Kathleen Leonard. "Meaning Making in Emerging Adults' Faith Narratives: Identity, Attachment, and Religious Orientation." *Journal of Psychology and Christianity* 32 (2013): 221–33.

54. Good, Marie, and Teena Willoughby. "Adolescence as a Sensitive Period for Spiritual Development." *Child Development Perspectives* 2 (2008): 32–37. [CrossRef]

55. Barry, Carolyn McNamara, and Larry J. Nelson. "The Role of Religion in the Transition to Adulthood for Young Emerging Adults." *Journal of Youth and Adolescence* 34 (2005): 245–55. [CrossRef]

56. Jung, Jong Hyun. "Sense of Divine Involvement and Sense of Meaning in Life: Religious Tradition as a Contingency." *Journal for the Scientific Study of Religion* 54 (2015): 119–33. [CrossRef]

57. Barkin, Samuel H., Lisa Miller, and Suniya S. Luthar. "Filling the Void: Spiritual Development among Adolescents of the Affluent." *Journal of Religion and Health* 54 (2015): 844–61. [CrossRef] [PubMed]

58. Madge, Nicola, Peter Hemming, and Kevin Stenson. *Youth on Religion: The Development, Negotiation and Impact of Faith and Non-Faith Identity*. New York: Routledge, 2014.

59. Astin, Helen S., and Anthony Lising Antonio. "The Impact of College on Character Development." *New Directions for Institutional Research* 122 (2004): 55–64. [CrossRef]

60. Weber, James, and David Wasieleski. "Investigating Influences on Managers' Moral Reasoning the Impact of Context and Personal and Organizational Factors." *Business & Society* 40 (2014): 79–110. [CrossRef]

61. Godwin, Lindsey N. "Examining the Impact of Moral Imagination on Organizational Decision Making." *Business & Society* 54 (2015): 254–78. [CrossRef]

62. National Study of Youth and Religion. Available online: http://youthandreligion.nd.edu/ (accessed on 12 June 2015).

religions   MDPI

Article

Charitable Sporting Events as a Context for Building Adolescent Generosity: Examining the Role of Religiousness and Spirituality

Nathaniel A. Fernandez *, Sarah A. Schnitker and Benjamin J. Houltberg

School of Psychology, Fuller Theological Seminary, 135 N Oakland Ave, Pasadena, CA 91182, USA;
sschnitker@fuller.edu (S.A.S.); bhoultberg@fuller.edu (B.J.H.)
* Correspondence: nathanielfernandez@fuller.edu; Tel.: +1-626-765-5479

Academic Editor: Patricia Snell Herzog
Received: 23 January 2016; Accepted: 15 March 2016; Published: 21 March 2016

Abstract: Previous research demonstrates an association between religiousness, spirituality, and generosity in adolescents, but few studies have tested the mechanisms by which religion might facilitate the development of generosity in real-world contexts. In this paper, a theoretical model is presented describing the potential mechanisms by which engagement in transformational contexts (_i.e._, participating in charity marathon training) may lead to the development of generosity in adolescents. Participation in charity sporting events is theorized to increase generosity through both higher-order mechanisms, such as sanctification and the development of transcendent identity, and lower-order mechanisms, such as increased entitativity, positive emotions, and dissonance reduction. An empirical strategy for testing the model is presented; suggested methods for inquiry are longitudinal mixed method designs incorporating observations, questionnaires, and qualitative interviewing. Additionally, a case study of ongoing research on adolescents running with Team World Vision is described as an application of the model to an actual research context.

Keywords: generosity; religion; spirituality; adolescents; sport

1. Introduction

The effects of religiousness on the development of generosity is a topic of great interest to scientists and practitioners alike, but methodological and research design constraints of previous studies limit conclusions that can be made from the extant literature. There is ample evidence that religiosity is a factor in predicting at least certain kinds of generosity in adults (_i.e._, in-group generosity [1]), but this evidence is somewhat controversial, with small effects found in meta-analyses [2]. Moreover, fewer empirical studies have looked at spirituality and generosity in children and adolescents (compared to adults), and most studies with children and adolescents have established correlational associations rather than testing causal mechanisms of change. However, information on _how_ the ways that adolescents make meaning of their spiritual and religious convictions in real-world contexts affect the development of generosity is an important line of research. This is especially true as changing social norms and ever-developing technology and social media continue to shape upcoming generations in new ways [3].

Generosity in adolescents has been defined as the "'work' that persons engage and through which they expend themselves in order to increase the good of the other" ([4], p. 1). We conceptualize generosity as encompassing the giving of both more objective resources (e.g., money, labor, time), as well as more subjective resources (e.g., attention, emotions, energy), but we distinguish generosity from other attributes such as empathy or compassion, which more primarily involve emotional reactions to others and do not necessitate a social exchange in conceptual definitions (though generous giving is a common outcome) [5].

Several studies have examined associations between religiousness/spirituality and generosity in adolescent populations [6–8]. However, many of these studies tend to focus more generally on connections between religiosity and generosity without testing the possible mechanisms for these effects. For instance, James and Fine found that adolescent participants coded as having a more coherent spirituality or sense of purpose (as opposed to an ambiguous spirituality) scored higher on measures of all six "Cs" of positive youth development (*i.e.*, Competence, Confidence, Character, Connection, Caring/Compassion, and Contribution), with higher scores on the Contribution factor indicating higher levels of generosity [9]. Similarly, Spiewak and Sherrod found that generosity was correlated with religious beliefs, spiritual transcendence, and religious practices in a cross-sectional sample of adolescents and emerging adults [10], and Bussing, Kerksieck, Günther, and Baumann found that spirituality and religiousness were correlated with generative altruism in adolescents and emerging adults [11]. Although these are important contributions to the literature in establishing empirical relations between religion, spirituality, and generosity, they do not address causal processes or the directionality of effects.

Additionally, much of the research on this topic that does address causation and mechanisms focuses on laboratory tasks that assess generosity and religiosity outside their ecological contexts [12]. These studies provide important information about causal processes, but there is a need for more studies aimed at real-world applicability, especially to those who are interested in considering how to foster religiosity and generosity. This is especially true for adolescent populations because researchers have demonstrated that the religiousness and spirituality of adolescents is often highly interpersonal and affected by social and cultural context [13]. In order to develop insight into how religious and spiritual variables affect the development of generosity in adolescents, it is important to study the phenomena as they are occurring in the real world.

One possible avenue for research to explore is the effects of major generosity-building contexts that young people are engaged in, such as charity sporting events. A broad array of charity walks, tournaments, races, fun runs, and the like are put on every year by all kinds of organizations. A Google search for "charity sporting events" yields millions of hits. These kinds of programs are also popular with adolescents because the events require more time engagement than direct monetary engagement on the part of the participant. Feldman demonstrated that donations of time and money are interchangeable, and adolescents are more likely to have excess time than money available for charity [14]. From a positive youth development perspective [15], adolescents' participation in these sporting events are likely major developmental assets in terms of their ability to promote positive developmental outcomes. However, how do these potential assets function to increase both religiosity and generosity? Moreover, how do events that are tied to religious organizations or activate spirituality have, perhaps, a greater potential to build adolescent generosity?

To address these questions, our research team has constructed a theoretical model to understand the various mechanisms by which participation sporting events affect spirituality and generosity, and we are in the process of conducting a study that examines adolescent religiousness, generosity, and key mediating/moderating variables in a real-world context. Although results of the study will not be presented in this paper, we will use our study design as a case study to illustrate the processes of change in our theoretical model and to depict the type of study design for which we are advocating. The study follows a group of adolescents over the course of their participation in a charity marathon or half marathon with a religious nonprofit organization dedicated to the cause of providing clean water initiatives to the developing world. Using a mixed method approach, we are gathering longitudinal questionnaire data and in-depth qualitative interviews from participants, as well as objective outcomes, such as race performance and money raised by participants. Participants are tracked from the point at which they sign up for training through two months post-race. Our study is an example of a design that can address previously stated gaps in the literature by gathering specific information to test mechanisms of change across time and by studying religiosity and generosity in an ecologically valid way within the actual experiences of adolescents in the real world rather than in laboratory conditions. As this research is ongoing, we present here our proposed theoretical model and rationale, with a focus on the predisposing factors that might lead adolescents to participate in these kinds of events and the mechanisms that might produce subsequent increases in religiosity and generosity. Our hope is that this theoretical model will guide other teams seeking to examine faith and generosity in youth. We present our model (Figure 1) piece by piece, explaining the rationale for proposed pathways, starting with factors predisposing adolescents to participate in charity marathon events and moving on to those processes that may be activated by participation.

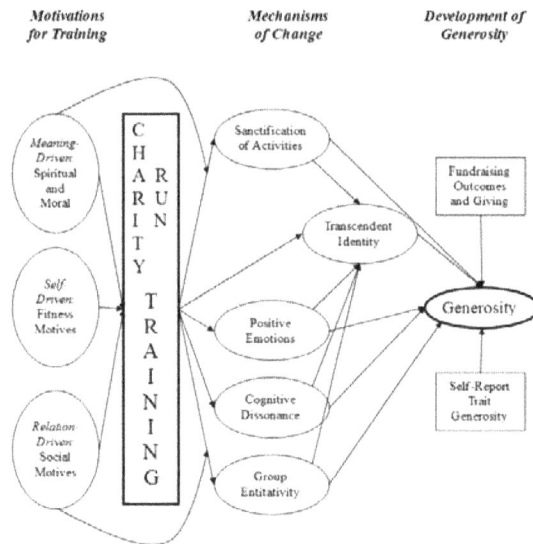

Figure 1. Theoretical model predicting generosity in the context of marathon participation.

2. Theoretical Model

2.1. Predisposing Factors

We begin with a discussion of those factors included in our model that predispose participants to join charity marathons. Charity sporting events have a broad appeal. Bennet, Mousley, Kitchin, and Ali-Choudhury examined the motivating factors for participation in charity sporting events and identified four major motivations: personal involvement with the good causes supported, opportunities to lead a healthy lifestyle, involvement in the sport in question, and a desire to mix socially with other attendees [16]. Out of these broad categories, adolescents may be particularly influenced by the opportunity that these events present to spend time socially with their peers, as peer influences are especially important in this developmental period [17]. Additionally, adolescents are typically more physically active than their adult counterparts [18], which makes the opportunity to stay physically fit and to participate in a marathon all the more appealing. This suggests that participants do not exclusively join such events out of a sense of moral duty to support the cause. Instead, youth participate in such activities for a broad variety of reasons. Youth who may not begin training for a charity run with explicit moral or spiritual motivations may still be afforded the opportunity to grow morally and spiritually as part of the experience. However, some youth do engage in running charity events primarily for the moral or transcendent purposes behind the event. Caprara, Alessandri, and Eisenberg showed that self-transcendent motivations in emerging adulthood are a predictor of engagement in prosocial behaviors, such as volunteering and charitable giving [19]. Specifically, they noted the presence of a value system that transcends the self-predicted empathic self-efficacy—the belief in an individual's ability to affect change for others and to help people beyond themselves. These findings suggest that self-transcendent motivation may be a key factor that enhances the positive impact of participating in charity sporting events and may lead to further participation.

In addition to these factors generally contributing to participation in charity marathons, there are religious and spiritual factors that may contribute to participation in charity events generally and religiously affiliated charity marathons in particular. Indeed, religion is often a primary context for self-transcendence in adolescents, and therefore, it is closely related to other forms of self-transcendence that are not specifically religious. In addition, religious persons are more likely to give of their time and energy to religiously affiliated groups [1]. Religious communities may foster a spirit of volunteerism and civic engagement. Caputo showed that parental religious affiliation significantly predicted youth volunteer behavior [20]. Beyerlein and Hipp showed that in some congregations religious participation resulted in increased civic engagement [21]. This seems to indicate that religious youth, especially those who are in religious communities modeling and promoting civic engagement, may have specifically religious motives to participate in charity marathons beyond the broadly social, moral, and fitness reasons which provide an incentive for all participants.

As can be seen in our model (Figure 1), all the motivations for engaging in active philanthropy are expected to contribute to adolescents' pursuing participation in charity marathons, and certain motivations are also expected to moderate the effects of the specific psychological processes activated by training. Moral and religious motivations for training are expected to moderate the effect of training on goal sanctification, such that those with higher religious and moral motivations will be more likely to sanctify the run, charitable goal, and fund-raising. Social motivations, meanwhile, are expected to moderate the effect of training on group entitativity (e.g., belongingness to and cohesiveness in the group) such that those with higher social motivation to participate will be more influenced by group processes inherent in the training. The rationale behind these proposed moderations will be explained presently in the discussion of each mechanism.

2.2. Specific Mechanisms Active in Training

These predisposing factors will increase adolescents' likelihood of becoming a participant in a charity sporting event, but how might that participation affect their generosity? And, more specifically, what are the particular mechanisms that will drive any change? As previously mentioned, a goal of our research is to better define the pathways that lead from participation in a charity marathon to a change in a person's generosity going forward. As seen in the figure, we propose that once adolescents join a charity marathon, whatever the predisposing reasons that are present, a series of psychological processes will be activated by their participation. We propose that these mechanisms will have unique effects upon participants, all leading to the eventual increase in generosity as shown. We have divided these mechanisms up into two groups: the "higher-order" spiritual and identity-based processes that may be particularly active in the context of charity sporting events and the "lower-order" mechanisms that are more universal social psychological processes.

2.3. Higher-Order Mechanisms

2.3.1. Sanctification

In this study, we are defining spirituality through the lens of sanctification. Sanctification is the psychological process by which people perceive or actively construe aspects of life as having a spiritual character or significance [22]. As previously mentioned, a variety of active philanthropy groups are religiously affiliated, and it is likely that many runners engage in charity runs and the like for religious and spiritual reasons. For individuals engaged in a training context with spiritual overtones, the process of sanctification may be a mechanism of change. Numerous studies have found that participants invest more effort into sanctified goals and derive greater satisfaction from achieving them. For instance, Pargament and Mahoney found that goal sanctification was positively correlated with effort invested, perceived support, and anticipation of success [22]. Additionally, Emmons, Cheung, and Tehrani found that participants with higher theistic strivings had higher goal instrumentality, which is a measure of how much the pursuit of one goal facilitates the pursuit of other goals in a person's goal system [23]. Even activities and goals that may not appear explicitly spiritual can be sanctified. For instance, people commonly imbue parenting or work with spiritual significance. In the case of training for a charity race, a person might find themselves sanctifying the charitable aim of the race and imbuing their fund-raising activity with the same spiritual significance.

Although sanctification is related to religiousness, it is a distinct psychological process. Pargament and Mahoney found that sanctification was correlated with church attendance and self-reported religiosity, but sanctification was uniquely associated with self-reports of meaning and purpose in life even after controlling for general religiousness [22]. Although we expect that participants in explicitly religious charities will sanctify their engagement, this research suggests it is possible that participants in non-religiously-affiliated charity work may also sanctify their participation, deriving meaning and purpose from their participation.

This sanctification of the charitable mission of the event would influence runners to view fund-raising goals as highly salient. Mahoney and colleagues showed that the more highly goals were sanctified, the more time and energy participants exerted on them on a daily basis. In the case of charity marathons, runners who sanctify the activity may exert increased time and effort expended on the charitable cause, which could then increase in generosity more broadly [24].

Team World Vision (TWV), the charity specifically investigated in our study, provides an example of how this mechanism would work in the real world. TWV is an arm of World Vision International specifically tasked with using charity running events to produce funds. A religious institution, World Vision describes itself as "a Christian humanitarian organization dedicated to working with children, families, and their communities worldwide to reach their full potential by tackling the causes of poverty and injustice... Motivated by our faith in Jesus Christ, we serve alongside the poor and oppressed as a demonstration of God's unconditional love for all people" [25]. Participants who take part in a marathon with TWV are inundated with this messaging. Through participation over months of training, it is likely that runners will be influenced by this message and may even come to share in this outlook to a lesser or greater extent. As some participants take on this worldview, they will likely begin to sanctify the process of fund-raising, which is hypothesized to increase effort expended pursuing this goal. This in turn is hypothesized to increase subsequent generosity not only in the context of TWV events but also in the broader context of charity programs that pursue similar aims. Further, as depicted in Figure 1, spiritual and religious motivations are likely to strengthen the positive relationship between engaging with TWV and goal sanctification. Thus, we expect that training with TWV will engage many young people to sanctify goals—whether or not they have initial spiritual motives. Of course, some runners may be completely immune to the spiritual message of the group, but most will be influenced by it to some extent. However, we would anticipate that the sanctification process would be stronger in young people who have a propensity to invest a spiritual or self-transcendent meaning in participation because these young people are already oriented toward spiritual meaning.

2.3.2. Identity

The second higher-order mechanism that we include in our model is identity development. As noted above, part of the way sanctification seems to affect goal achievement is through its relationship to increased meaning and purpose in life, or in other words, a meaningful identity. Identity development is a primary developmental task of adolescence [26], and identity has been linked to volunteering and prosocial behavior. For instance, Crocetti, Erentaitė, and Žukauskienė showed that varying identity styles were related to frequency of volunteering [27]. Similarly, Furrow,

King, and White showed that personal meaning was related to prosocial personality, and spiritual identity was also related to these constructs [28].

McAdams and Pals argue for three levels of personality, including basic tendencies or traits, contextualized middle-level units called characteristic adaptations, and personal identity narratives [29]. McCrae and Costa argue for a similar three-level system, though using different terminology [30]. Narrative identity specifically is conceptualized by McAdams and Pals as the dynamic life story that an individual uses to make sense of the particular series of events that occur in one's life [29]. Bauer, McAdams, and Pals argue that narrative identity is tied to eudaimonic well-being outcomes [31]. Eudaimonia, a word borrowed from the tradition of Aristotelian ethics, refers to the cultivation of the objectively good life and the highest expression of character and virtue. Within this framework, the development of generosity is an aspect of eudaimonic well-being because it is connected to meaningful personal growth and the cultivation of character strengths.

Bauer, McAdams, and Pals assert that the process of constructing a narrative identity involves fitting the seemingly random series of events in one's life into a coherent narrative by drawing on themes, symbols, plot devices, and so forth which are typically gleaned from the cultural context [31]. Narratives that interpret life events into the overall frameworks of growth stories are associated with greater well-being, especially eudaimonic well-being. Indeed, McAdams showed that participants who scored high on generativity measures had redemptive narrative identities that drew heavily on their participation in religious communities, spiritual activities, and civic engagement [32]. The study demonstrates that when people situate their narrative identity within the framework of a system that transcends self-goals, they experience greater eudaimonic well-being and virtue development. This likely occurs because transcending self-goals taps in to community ideals and narrative tropes of purpose in life. As participants engage in charity marathons with self-transcendent missions—especially religiously affiliated charities that emphasize transcendent meaning—they may be more likely to construct narrative identities that promote the development of generosity.

Referring again to TWV as a concrete example, the self-transcendent religious narratives of TWV can serve as a rich cultural resource for participants and can provide narrative frameworks and devices through which TWV runners can view the events in their life in terms of a growth narrative. As participants incorporate these self-transcendent narratives into their own identities, it is likely that they will develop a firmer sense of self and an identity that increases eudaimonic well-being. Prosocial engagement and character, including generosity, are likely to be a major part of the narrative identities that the participants construct, and their inclusion as central components of identity are hypothesized to engender more generous giving of time and money. As participants then act out this new identity in fundraising and running for charity, the incorporation of generosity into identity may become solidified.

2.4. Lower-Order Mechanisms

As mentioned, both increased sanctification and increased identity development are higher-order factors that are activated by participation in charity marathons. A number of other mechanisms are also included in our model. These mechanisms are more basic psychological processes, but nonetheless, they are hypothesized to serve as key pathways by which marathon training may increase generosity. These lower-order mechanisms include increased entitativity, cognitive dissonance, and increased positive emotion.

2.4.1. Increased Entitativity

The first lower-order mechanism presented in the model is increased group entitativity. Entitativity is a sense of belongingness to a group and perceiving that group as a single cohesive entity [33]. In a group with high entitativity, members feel like they are highly connected to each other and to the goals of the group; whereas in a group with low entitativity, members feel less connected and more individual. The intensive group training in which participants engage during preparation to run a marathon affords them the opportunity to form strong in-group bonds. Additionally, team leaders have the opportunity to exert additional influence on participants; previous research shows that coach leadership and relationship variables contribute to increased group cohesion [34]. This increase in group belongingness is likely to have the effect of increasing subsequent generosity. Bernhard, Fischbacher, and Fehr suggest that there is a basic human tendency towards parochial altruism—or giving to one's own social group—on the basis of anthropological research [35]. For instance, members of university groups that promote strong in-group ties, such as fraternities, sororities, and athletic teams, are more likely to give to their universities after graduation [36,37]. Thus, people with strong group ties are more willing to give to what is considered central to the group's identity.

The increased group cohesion may play an additional role beyond the simple promotion of belongingness. Research has shown that there is a tendency for people in a group to adapt their giving practices to be more similar to those of others in their group [38]. Those participants who are drawn to participate in a charity run event for religious or moral reasons likely already participate in charitable giving at a higher rate than their peers. Additionally, the team captains and program employees participating alongside new runners are likely to be exemplars of charitable giving and intentionally fostering group norms of generosity. Thus, it is hypothesized that a group effect will emerge by which the group exerts pressure on those who are participating in the event to be generous. For those who started out less generous, the positive group norm should influence them to become more generous.

Moreover, strong moral norms in combination with high group cohesion present the possibility that behaviors are undertaken in order to increase reputation within the group. This is the main principle behind costly signaling theory, which maintains that a person might be motivated to undertake a costly behavior (such as participating in a marathon or raising a large amount of money for a charitable cause) in order to signal they were sincerely committed to a group. A recent study on costly signaling theory of religion used the innovative method of examining the longevity of religious communes as a function of the costliness of their membership [39]. They found that groups with more stringent entry requirements lasted longer than more permissive groups because groups with higher entry costs typically promote a greater feeling of belongingness and commitment to the group. In the context of charity marathons, those participants who want to demonstrate their commitment to the group for social approval are incentivized to engage in generous acts of fund-raising, which leads to higher levels of generosity. Although generosity due to group belongingness factors may initially increase because of external motivations, it is hypothesized that over time the group norms become internalized through cognitive dissonance processes (see below) and as the group's identity becomes central to the self. Thus, entitativity will not only change generous behavior within the race team context, but it will also change generosity outside the context to the extent that group norms are internalized by the individual.

Referring back to our model and case example, TWV marathon runners will experience this increased group entitativity as they engage in the grueling process of training for a marathon. The high level of camaraderie will be a positive experience for most participants, and they will come to identify strongly with the group. As participants identify strongly with their TWV teams, they will be motivated to become more generous in giving to TWV. This increase in giving will be primarily driven by loyalty to the group, peer influence, and the desire to earn social standing through generous acts. These influences will help participants to develop generous habits, which may internalize over time. As shown in the diagram, these group processes should be particularly influential for those participants choosing to engage in the marathon for social reasons, as they will be more invested in group belongingness and social connections the training provides.

2.4.2. Positive Emotionality in Marathon Participation

The next lower-order mechanism is positive emotionality. Participating in charity marathons is an enjoyable activity for many, which is likely why charity sporting events are so popular. How might an increase in positive emotionality experienced from participating in a charity run relate to increased generosity? According to the broaden-and-build theory of positive emotions, positive emotions increase peoples' behavioral repertoires and expand their openness to new possibilities in the environment, which they are likely to explore [40]. In essence, positive emotions open people up to take risks and form new experiences. This then would likely increase subsequent generosity as participants in a good mood spread that good mood through generosity. Previous studies have supported this premise, demonstrating that inducing positive emotions like gratitude can increase giving in the laboratory [41].

A variety of factors are likely to underlie the enjoyability of charity marathon participation. In part, marathon training, though difficult, is enjoyable because of the effects of physical activity on positive emotions. Fox showed physical activity was such a reliable means to increase positive emotions and regulate negative emotions that he suggested it should be considered a viable treatment for depression and anxiety [42]. In a review of physical activity research, Penedo and Dahn highlighted the positive effects of physical activity on a variety of mood outcomes in addition to the physical health benefits it conveyed [43].

Beyond the positive effects of physical activation, participating in charity marathons also has higher-order psychological effects that are linked to increased positive affect. The goal sanctification that charity marathons engender has been associated with positive emotional outcomes. Tix and Frazier found that goal sanctification was associated with decreased anxiety, hostility, and depression [44]. Similarly, Pargament and Mahoney found that participants derived a greater degree of meaning and life satisfaction from sanctified goals compared to self or materially oriented goals [22]. In general, the pursuit of sanctified goals leads to better emotional outcomes for all involved.

In addition to these benefits there are many emotional benefits associated with giving itself. Thotis showed that volunteering was associated with greater meaning and purpose in life, which in turn was related to greater well-being [45]. Hallam and colleagues found that adolescents who participated in activities meant to benefit others demonstrated greater emotional competence in young adulthood, and this emotional competence reduced the risk of developing adult anxiety and depression [46]. Aknin *et al.*, presented a series of studies suggesting that the positive experience of giving to others is a cultural universal [47], and imaging studies provide evidence that giving behaviors produced similar brain activation as receiving a reward [48].

With these factors and perhaps others contributing to the enjoyability of charity sporting event participation, runners' positive emotions will likely be strongly elevated by their participation in the charity activities. Referring back to the broaden-and-build theory, this increase in positive emotionality will predict a subsequent increase in prosocial behaviors as participants broaden their social networks and build upon their experience. What is more, there is evidence that an upward, "virtuous" cycle whereby giving produces happiness, which produces greater giving, and so forth can be activated [49].

In applying our model to the case study of training for TWV marathons, participants join for a variety of reasons and goals for their training experience. The experience likely fulfills these desires (*i.e.*, providing an opportunity for participants to demonstrate their religious and moral convictions, providing physical activity outlets, and providing social interaction with peers), which likely increases positive emotions. The benefits of training described above are also likely to then induce positive emotions, which prompt them to give more generously of their time and money.

2.4.3. Dissonance Reduction

A final major contributing factor to the effects of participating in charity sporting events on change in generosity is the process of value system change facilitated though dissonance reduction. The idea of attitude change through cognitive dissonance (the mental stress associated with a contradiction between belief/attitudes and behavior) has been a vital part of social psychology since the theory was proposed [50]. The theory maintains that when people experience dissonance, they will change either their beliefs/attitudes or their behaviors to bring the two into alignment.

It is likely that a large number of people participating in charity marathons do not sanctify the goals of the charity or situate their narrative identities within a self-transcendent framework. As previously stated, many participants are joining marathons for social, health, and sporting reasons rather than moral or spiritual reasons. However, participating in a marathon is a huge commitment. According to Running USA, only 541,000 people finished a marathon in 2014 [51], and newspapers such as the *Huffington Post* have published satirical articles highlighting reasons not to run marathons [52]. All participants training for a marathon will experiences difficulties and challenges in training. Though training leads to positive emotions, it also involves hardships and a large amount of effort. This means that participants who train for more self-focused reasons will likely feel dissonance as they expend a high degree of energy to train for an event supporting a charity for which they may not have that much investment.

In order to alleviate this dissonance, participants will either need to alter their behavior or their attitudes. Thus, participants who feel dissonance but who choose to persist in running the marathon will naturally increase their commitment to the charitable cause promoted by the organization (*i.e.*, changing their attitudes to align with their behavior). Increased fund-raising and generosity would then follow this increased commitment to avoid additional dissonance. The increased commitment may also lead to a sanctification of the goals of the charity and to using these goals as an organizer of the participants' personality, the two higher-order mechanisms we previously discussed. In turn, this increase in sanctification and identity development could lead to increased generosity, as previously outlined. Research on disaster responses to the 2004 Red Cross tsunami relief supports this supposition; it found that people are more likely to contribute to causes when they felt dissonance, and that the contributions helped to restore psychological equilibrium [53].

In the case of TWV, marathon participants join the marathon for a variety of reasons. Regardless of why they joined, however, they spend 18 weeks training for an intense 26.2-mile race, which is grueling both mentally and physically. This is hypothesized to create a high amount of dissonance for those who do not initially believe in the cause or value generosity, as a discrepancy will likely arise between their attitudes and behaviors. Participants making costly signals of group membership by being particularly generous may experience dissonance if they find themselves giving heavily of time and money to a cause for which they do not have initially high levels of commitment. Participants may continue to train because they like the positive emotions it brings or the group entitativity experience, but they may also need to justify their actions rationally in order to reduce dissonance. For some participants, this may lead them to modify their value system in order to reduce dissonance. In order to do this, they will likely incorporate the sanctified pursuit of the clean water initiatives supported by TWV into their own motivational frameworks and use the self-transcendent mission of the TWV project as an organizing tool for their personalities. Thus, they may become more generous people as they adopt the prosocial agenda of TWV.

3. Discussion

3.1. Summary

In summary, we have proposed a model for understanding the role of various psycho-spiritual processes in explaining how adolescents' participation in charity sporting events fosters generosity. Adolescents are motivated by a variety of social, physical, and religious/moral reasons to participate in charity sporting events. These events may or may not be religiously affiliated, but they are all inherently self-transcendent in their focus on charitable giving to others. Charity sporting events are theorized to serve as a developmental asset for building generosity through at least five interrelated higher- and lower-order mechanisms. First, charity organizers promote the sanctification of the charitable cause, which increases participants' drive to accomplish self-transcendent goals, which may increase their generosity. Second, organizers also provide a self-transcendent identity context for participants. Participants are able to view their identity and purpose in life as being tied to something greater than themselves, which increases eudaimonic well-being, including generosity. The conditions of these particular types of events further promote generosity beyond these mechanisms through a series of lower-order mechanisms. Namely, increased group entitativity motivates adolescents to conform their ideals and generous behaviors to the norm of the group, which is likely more self-transcendent and generosity-promoting than a typical sample of nonparticipants. Additionally, participation in training has the capacity to produce a variety of positive emotions, which may increase the likelihood of future generosity as participants broaden and build their experience; ultimately, this may trigger a virtuous cycle of positive emotion and generosity. Lastly, participants are placed in high-demand situations that require a great deal of effort expenditure, promoting a dissonance reaction that may be resolved by an increased commitment to generosity.

3.2. Methodological Challenges

There are a variety of methodological challenges inherent in a project such as this. First, measurement of generosity, the key outcome, is complicated in adolescents. Adolescents typically have few financial resources to contribute to an organization despite their desires to give, so dependence upon actual giving is problematic in assessment. Moreover, measuring generosity in terms of financial resources contributed to charitable causes is confounded by socioeconomic status. However, relying on other indicators of generosity has challenges because questionnaire data has inherent self-report bias and measuring volunteer time committed is difficult in this context because all participants are dedicating a majority of their free time to the training for the marathon itself. Therefore, multiple generosity indicators are needed to try to gain a complete picture of the phenomenon as it occurs in this and other real-world contexts. In the study we conduct, we assess both self-reported change in generosity as well as fund-raising outcomes (quantified as both total dollars raised and number of donors). We encourage research teams to employ multiple measures of generosity that capture behaviors in addition to self-assessments.

Measurement issues also exist in assessing what motivates participants to engage in charity marathon training because this is not a very often studied area. Similarly, the measurement of spirituality and religiosity is always challenging, but it is especially so in adolescent populations where there is a high degree of volatility in identity and belief systems. However, it is this very developmental plasticity that makes studying the development of generosity in this context so fruitful. In order to account for these difficulties, we propose that researchers adopt a mixed method design. For example, in the TWV case study we describe, we combine observable behavioral data with quantitative self-reports and semi-structured qualitative interviews in order to try to develop a more ecologically valid picture of these processes as they unfold.

Finally, testing the model we propose requires longitudinal assessment. It is essential to measure motives for training before training begins, the mechanisms of change during the training, and generosity after the race is complete. Moreover, several of the mechanisms proposed imply that the race experience would lead to changes in identity and generosity that last beyond the training experience. Thus, a post-race follow-up several months after the event is finished allows for a full test of the model.

4. Conclusions

This proposed theoretical model and suggestions for research design are important because they aim to address gaps in areas of existing research related to the development of adolescent spirituality, religiousness, and generosity. We propose a study protocol that uses a rich mixed method design to assess adolescent experiences of religious charity marathon participation by utilizing multiple sources of information including surveys, interviews, and fund-raising. We hope others will follow our example by employing designs that ensure ecological validity by studying the development of generosity and religiosity in context and observing the developmental processes at work through activities in which adolescents are already participating. Although laboratory studies are valuable, we strongly encourage researchers to also engage in studies with such generalizability. However, just because research takes place in the field does not mean researchers should desist in examining specific mechanisms of change. In our proposed theory and case study, we aim to test specific mechanisms that may explain the link between religiosity and generosity rather than studying the link more broadly with less depth.

As this research is ongoing, the theoretical model described is yet untested. However, we hope that it can serve as a stimulus for other researchers who might be interested in this topic to consider investigating this relatively under-studied area and to continue to develop a knowledge base for understanding how religious charity sporting events and other transformational contexts may impact adolescent positive development.

Acknowledgments: This publication was made possible through the support of a grant from the John Templeton Foundation. The opinions expressed in this publication are those of the authors and do not necessarily reflect the views of the John Templeton Foundation.

Author Contributions: Nathaniel Fernandez (N.F.), Sarah Schnitker (S.S.), and Benjamin Houltberg (B.H.) were all involved in the conceptual development of the theoretical model. Nathaniel Fernandez wrote the first draft of the paper. Sarah Schnitker wrote extensive revisions of the paper. Benjamin Houltberg made additional modifications to the manuscript. Sarah Schnitker procured the grant supporting this work and originally designed the TWV case study described. Benjamin Houltberg oversees the execution of the TWV case study and its ongoing revision.

Conflicts of Interest: The authors declare no conflict of interest.

References

1. Bekkers, René, and Pamala Wiepking. "Who gives? A literature review of predictors of charitable giving part one: Religion, education, age and socialization." *Voluntary Sector Review* 2 (2011): 337–65. [CrossRef]
2. Galen, Luke W. "Does religious belief promote prosociality? A critical examination." *Psychological Bulletin* 138 (2012): 876–906. [CrossRef] [PubMed]
3. Lenhart, Amanda, Kristen Purcell, Aaron Smith, and Kathryn Zickuhr. *Social Media & Mobile Internet Use among Teens and Young Adults. Millennials.* Washington: Pew Internet & American Life Project, 2010.
4. Smith, Christian, and Jonathan P. Hill. "Toward the measurement of Interpersonal Generosity (IG): An IG scale conceptualized, tested, and validated." 2009. Available online: https://generosityresearch.nd.edu/assets/13798/ig_paper_smith_hill_rev.pdf (accessed on 21 January 2016).
5. Davis, Mark H. "Measuring individual difference in empathy: Evidence for a multidimensional approach." *Journal of Personality and Social Psychology* 44 (1983): 113–26. [CrossRef]
6. Benson, Peter L. "Emerging themes in research on adolescent spiritual and religious development." *Applied Developmental Science* 8 (2004): 47–50. [CrossRef]
7. Büssing, Arndt, Axel Föller-Mancini, Jennifer Gidley, and Peter Heusser. "Aspects of spirituality in adolescents." *International Journal of Children's Spirituality* 15 (2010): 25–44. [CrossRef]
8. Warren, Alberts, Amy Eva, Richard M. Lerner, and Erin Phelps, eds. *Thriving and Spirituality among Youth: Research Perspectives and Future Possibilities.* Hoboken: John Wiley & Sons, 2012.
9. James, Anthony G., and Mark A. Fine. "Relations between youths' conceptions of spirituality and their developmental outcomes." *Journal of Adolescence* 43 (2015): 171–80. [CrossRef] [PubMed]
10. Spiewak, Gabriel S., and Lonnie R. Sherrod. "The shared pathways of religious/spiritual engagement and positive youth development." In *Thriving and Spirituality among Youth: Research Perspectives and Future Possibilities.* Edited by Amy Eva Alberts Warren, Richard M. Lerner and Erin Phelps. Hoboken: John Wiley & Sons, 2012, pp. 167–81.
11. Büssing, Arndt, Philipp Kerksieck, Andreas Günther, and Klaus Baumann. "Altruism in adolescents and young adults: Validation of an instrument to measure generative altruism with structural equation modeling." *International Journal of Children's Spirituality* 18 (2013): 335–50. [CrossRef]
12. Shariff, Azim F., and Ara Norenzayan. "God is watching you: Priming God concepts increases prosocial behavior in an anonymous economic game." *Psychological Science* 18 (2007): 803–9. [CrossRef] [PubMed]
13. Desrosiers, Alethea, Brien S. Kelley, and Lisa Miller. "Parent and peer relationships and relational spirituality in adolescents and young adults." *Psychology of Religion and Spirituality* 3 (2011): 39–54. [CrossRef]

14. Feldman, Naomi E. "Time is money: Choosing between charitable activities." *American Economic Journal: Economic Policy* 2 (2010): 103–30. [CrossRef]

15. Benson, Peter L., Peter C. Scales, Stephen F. Hamilton, and Arturo Sesma. *Positive Youth Development: Theory, Research, and Applications.* Hoboken: John Wiley & Sons, 2006.

16. Bennett, Roger, Wendy Mousley, Paul James Kitchin, and Rehnuma Ali-Choudhury. "Motivations for participating in charity-affiliated sporting events." *Journal of Customer Behavior* 6 (2007): 155–78. [CrossRef]

17. Gardner, Margo, and Laurence Steinberg. "Peer influence on risk taking, risk preference, and risky decision making in adolescence and adulthood: An experimental study." *Developmental Psychology* 41 (2005): 625–35. [CrossRef] [PubMed]

18. Caspersen, Carl J., Mark A. Pereira, and Katy M. Curran. "Changes in physical activity patterns in the United States, by sex and cross-sectional age." *Medicine and Science in Sports Exercise* 32 (2000): 1601–9. [CrossRef]

19. Caprara, Gian V., Guido Alessandri, and Nancy Eisenberg. "Prosociality: The contribution of traits, values, and self-efficacy beliefs." *Journal of Personality and Social Psychology* 102 (2012): 1289–303. [CrossRef] [PubMed]

20. Caputo, Richard K. "Religious capital and intergenerational transmission of volunteering as correlates of civic engagement." *Nonprofit and Voluntary Sector Quarterly* 38 (2009): 983–1002. [CrossRef]

21. Beyerlein, Kraig, and John R. Hipp. "From pews to participation: The effect of congregation activity and context on bridging civic engagement." *Social Problems* 53 (2006): 97–117. [CrossRef]

22. Pargament, Kenneth I., and Annette M. Mahoney. "Sacred matters: Sanctification as a vital topic for the psychology of religion." *The International Journal for the Psychology of Religion* 15 (2005): 179–262. [CrossRef]

23. Emmons, Robert A., Chi Cheung, and Keivan Tehrani. "Assessing spirituality through personal goals: Implications for research on religion and subjective well-being." *Social Indicators Research* 45 (1998): 391–422. [CrossRef]

24. Mahoney, Annette, Kenneth I. Pargament, Brenda Cole, Tracey Jewell, Gina M. Magyar, Nalini Tarakeshwar, and Russell Phillips. "A higher purpose: The sanctification of strivings in a community sample." *The International Journal for the Psychology of Religion* 15 (2005): 239–62. [CrossRef]

25. World Vision. "Who We Are." 2015. Available online: http://www.worldvision.org/about-us/who-we-are (accessed on 21 January 2016).

26. Erikson, Erik H. *Identity: Youth and Crisis.* New York: WW Norton, 1968.

27. Crocetti, Elisabetta, Rasa Erentaitė, and Rita Žukauskienė. "Identity styles, positive youth development, and civic engagement in adolescence." *Journal of Youth and Adolescence* 43 (2014): 1818–28. [CrossRef] [PubMed]

28. Furrow, James L., Pamela E. King, and Krystal White. "Religion and positive youth development: Identity, meaning, and prosocial concerns." *Applied Developmental Science* 8 (2004): 17–26. [CrossRef]

29. McAdams, Dan P., and Jennifer Lilgendahl Pals. "A new big five: Fundamental principles for an integrative science of personality." *American Psychologist* 61 (2006): 208–17. [CrossRef] [PubMed]

30. McCrae, Robert R., and Paul T. Costa. "The five-factor theory of personality." In *Handbook of Personality: Theory and Research.* Edited by Oliver P. John, Richard W. Robins and Lawrence A. Pervin. New York: Guilford, 2008, pp. 159–81.

31. Bauer, Jack J., Dan P. McAdams, and Jennifer L. Pals. "Narrative identity and eudaimonic well-being." *Journal of Happiness Studies* 9 (2008): 81–104. [CrossRef]

32. McAdams, Dan P. "Generativity in midlife." In *Handbook of Midlife Development.* Edited by Margie E. Lachman. New York: Wiley, 2001, pp. 395–443.

33. Lickel, Brian, David L. Hamilton, Grazyna Wieczorkowska, Amy Lewis, Steven J. Sherman, and A. Neville Uhles. "Varieties of groups and the perception of group entitativity." *Journal of Personality and Social Psychology* 78 (2000): 223–46. [CrossRef] [PubMed]

34. Jowett, Sophia, and Victoria Chaundy. "An investigation into the impact of coach leadership and coach-athlete relationship on group cohesion." *Group Dynamics, Theory, Research, and Practice* 8 (2004): 302–14. [CrossRef]

35. Bernhard, Helen, Urs Fischbacher, and Ernst Fehr. "Parochial altruism in humans." *Nature* 442 (2006): 912–15. [CrossRef] [PubMed]

36. Harrison, William B., Shannon K. Mitchell, and Steven P. Peterson. "Alumni donations and colleges' development expenditures: Does spending matter? " *The American Journal of Economics and Sociology* 54 (1995): 397–413. [CrossRef]

37. Marr, Kelly A., Charles H. Mullin, and John J. Siegfried. "Undergraduate financial aid and subsequent alumni giving behavior." *The Quarterly Review of Economics and Finance* 45 (2005): 123–43. [CrossRef]
38. Wu, Shih-Ying, Jr-Tsung Huang, and An-Pang Kao. "An analysis of the peer effects in charitable giving: The case of Taiwan." *Journal of Family and Economic Issues* 25 (2004): 483–505. [CrossRef]
39. Sosis, Richard, and Eric R. Bressler. "Cooperation and commune longevity: A test of the costly signaling theory of religion." *Cross-Cultural Research* 37 (2003): 211–39. [CrossRef]
40. Fredrickson, Barbara L. "The role of positive emotions in positive psychology: The broaden-and-build theory of positive emotions." *American Psychologist* 56 (2001): 218–26. [CrossRef] [PubMed]
41. DeSteno, David, Monica Y. Bartlett, Jolie Baumann, Lisa A. Williams, and Leah Dickens. "Gratitude as moral sentiment: Emotion-guided cooperation in economic exchange." *Emotion* 10 (2010): 289–93. [CrossRef] [PubMed]
42. Fox, Kenneth R. "The influence of physical activity on mental well-being." *Public Health Nutrition* 2 (1999): 411–18. [CrossRef] [PubMed]
43. Penedo, Frank J., and Jason R. Dahn. "Exercise and well-being: A review of mental and physical health benefits associated with physical activity." *Current Opinion in Psychiatry* 18 (2005): 189–93. [CrossRef] [PubMed]
44. Tix, Andrew P., and Patricia A. Frazier. "Mediation and moderation of the relationship between intrinsic religiousness and mental health." *Personality and Social Psychology Bulletin* 31 (2005): 295–306. [CrossRef] [PubMed]
45. Thotis, Peggy A. "Role-identity salience, purpose and meaning in life, and well-being among volunteers." *Social Psychology Quarterly* 75 (2012): 360–84. [CrossRef]
46. Hallam, William T., Craig A. Olsson, Meredith O'Connor, Mary Hawkins, John W. Toumbourou, Glenn Bowes, Rob McGee, and Ann Sanson. "Association between adolescent eudaimonic behaviours and emotional competence in young adulthood." *Journal of Happiness Studies* 15 (2014): 1165–77. [CrossRef]
47. Aknin, Laura B., Christopher P. Barrington-Leigh, Elizabeth W. Dunn, John F. Helliwell, Justine Burns, Robert Biswas-Diener, Imelda Kemeza, Paul Nyende, and Michael I. Norton. "Prosocial spending and well-being: Cross-cultural evidence for a psychological universal." *Journal of Personality and Social Psychology* 104 (2015): 635–52. [CrossRef] [PubMed]
48. Harbaugh, William T., Ulrich Mayr, and Daniel R. Burghart. "Neural responses to taxation and voluntary giving reveal motives for charitable donations." *Science* 316 (2007): 1622–24. [CrossRef] [PubMed]
49. Aknin, Laura B., Elizabeth W. Dunn, and Michael I. Norton. "Happiness runs in a circular motion: Evidence for a positive feedback loop between prosocial spending and happiness." *Journal of Happiness Studies* 13 (2012): 347–55. [CrossRef]
50. Festinger, Leon. *A Theory of Cognitive Dissonance*. Palo AltoStanford: Stanford University Press, 1957.
51. Running USA. "2014 Annual Marathon Report." 2014. Available online: http://www.runningusa.org/index.cfm?fuseaction=news.details&ArticleId=332 (accessed on 21 January 2016).
52. Klein, Sarah. "26 Reasons not to Run a Marathon." *The Huffington Post*, 2013. Available online: http://www.huffingtonpost.com/2013/10/29/why-not-shouldnt-run-marathon_n_4171186.html (accessed on 21 January 2016).
53. Waters, Richard D. "Examining the role of cognitive dissonance in crisis fundraising." *Public Relations Review* 35 (2009): 139–43. [CrossRef]

religions

MDPI

Article

Secular Volunteerism among Texan Emerging Adults: Exploring Pathways of Childhood and Adulthood Religiosity

Reed T. DeAngelis *, Gabriel A. Acevedo and Xiaohe Xu

Department of Sociology, University of Texas at San Antonio, One UTSA Circle, San Antonio, TX 78249, USA; gabriel.acevedo@utsa.edu (G.A.A.); xiaohe.xu@utsa.edu (X.X.)
* Correspondence: Reed.DeAngelis@utsa.edu; Tel.: +1-210-410-7550

Academic Editor: Patricia Snell Herzog
Received: 31 January 2016; Accepted: 2 June 2016; Published: 13 June 2016

Abstract: Prior research suggests that religiosity, especially public religious participation, is related to greater volunteerism. However, less is known about religious transmission across the life course, in particular whether and how religiosity in childhood is linked to later life volunteerism. This study investigates a sample of emerging adults in South Texas ($n = 701$) with a high percent of Hispanic Americans (53 percent). Specifically, we examine pathways of childhood and emerging adulthood religiosity leading to secular volunteerism. Findings indicate that both childhood and emerging adulthood religiosity are associated with greater volunteerism, but the effects of childhood religiosity on emerging adulthood volunteerism are mediated through emerging adulthood religiosity. These findings provide further confirmation of the importance of childhood religiosity only insofar as religiousness persists into adulthood. In other words, we find that it is emerging adulthood religiosity that transmits childhood religiosity into greater secular volunteerism in later life. Furthermore, emerging adulthood public religiosity has the most robust direct effects on volunteerism.

Keywords: emerging adulthood; volunteerism; religious transmission; social learning theory; Hispanic Americans; race and ethnicity

1. Introduction

This study investigates the relationship between volunteerism and religiosity for a sample of emerging adults in South Texas. Grounded in theories of social learning, this study also suggests two potential mechanisms for the volunteerism and religiosity relationship. The first expectation is derived from emerging adulthood studies, from the psychological process described as "recentering" [1], which implies that childhood religiosity will affect later life volunteerism insofar as childhood religious socialization is internalized as an individualized aspect of emerging adult identity, *i.e.*, private religiosity. This expectation is contrary to sociological studies finding forms of social participation are central [2,3], *i.e.*, public religiosity. Thus, this study investigates volunteerism as it relates to life course public and private religiosity.

We contribute to the literature on volunteerism by examining the relationship between religiosity and civic engagement among a sample of emerging adults attending a large public university in South Texas. For our study, emerging adults are operationalized as young adults between the ages of 18 and 29. We explore how emerging adult volunteering is associated with multiple domains of religiosity, net of socio-demographic controls. The high proportion of Hispanic Americans in South Texas also enables an examination of potential racial and ethnic differences in religious transmission across the life course. Based on extant studies finding that African and Asian Americans have high rates of religious transmission across the life course [4,5], we investigate whether these trends also hold in predominantly Hispanic populations.

Particularly noteworthy, however, is that our study measures two key dimensions of religiousness: (a) public and private forms of religiosity during emerging adulthood; and (b) public and private forms of religiosity during childhood. Theoretically, we draw from work that has conceptualized processes of religious socialization and internalization as "drivers" of civic engagement, as well as social learning theories across the life course. To contextualize our analysis, we first offer an overview of the literature on civic engagement with emphasis on work that has addressed linkages between volunteerism, religion, and emerging adulthood. We also discuss the theoretical frameworks which inform our study. Within this theoretical and empirical context, we subsequently propose an analytical framework with testable hypotheses. We then empirically test our hypotheses and close with a discussion of the implications of this study for understanding emerging adult volunteerism and propose avenues of future research.

2. Theoretical and Empirical Context of Emerging Adult Volunteerism and Religiosity

2.1. Volunteerism

Civic engagement involves the desire and capacity of individuals to volunteer their resources to various activities accepted as beneficial to common objectives and goals. Some scholars have suggested that civic engagement is a central element of democratic societies, and one that was identified as early as the 18th century in Alexis de Tocqueville's classic *Democracy in America* [6].

Putnam and colleagues, for instance, have amassed a considerable body of empirical research that, following in de Tocqueville's footsteps, demonstrates how volunteer participation is a keystone of vibrant democratic societies [7–10]. However, critics have questioned Putnam on the grounds that his data is either inaccurate and omits considerable evidence of continuing civic engagement in democratic states [11], or that Putnam fails to account for the changing nature of present-day volunteer activities [12].

Consequently, more recent work has shifted the focus away from broad generalizations linking volunteer participation to macro level social processes such as political systems and culture. Instead, this line of inquiry has explored individual level predictors that may explain propensities to engage in civic volunteering [13]. These studies draw from individual level data to assess relationships between such factors as gender [14–16], race/ethnicity [17,18], socioeconomic status [19,20], educational attainment [21–23] or intersections of these characteristics and propensities to participate in volunteerism [24,25].

Moreover, studies of the life course have shown a positive relationship between age and formal volunteerism—a rather intuitive finding when one considers the greater levels of financial autonomy and spare time that most Americans accumulate as they age [13,17,26,27]. There is also a less developed but growing body of work focused primarily on civic engagement among emerging adults [18,28,29]. However, to date, little work explores possible relationships between volunteerism and religiosity among emerging adults.

2.2. Volunteerism and Religiosity

Thus far, one common thread appearing in social scientific research on civic engagement has been the role of religiosity in fostering prosocial behaviors such as volunteering and charitable giving [30–32]. The general consensus is that religiosity motivates and bolsters civic engagement in the form of religious volunteerism and charitable giving [32–34]. Furthermore, findings in this body of work indicate that religiosity also fosters secular volunteerism [35]. Our theoretical arguments are based on the assumption that religious investments, in the form of learned religious norms and practices, can foster both competencies and propensities for civic engagement [36]. It is not surprising that studies of religion have specifically focused on linkages between religion and volunteerism in the United States, a society characterized by both high rates of volunteerism and charitable contributions to religious organizations [37]. The general research finding confirms this pattern, namely, there is a positive association between religion and volunteerism [36], while being careful not to generalize to all forms of religiousness [38].

Similar to extant scholarship, we argue that what has been less clearly conceptualized in volunteerism research is the distinction between public (e.g., attending religious services) and private religiosity (e.g., prayer, reading scripture, *etc.*) [39] and how these distinct forms of religiosity might affect volunteering behaviors [40]. Considerable attention has been given to private forms of religiosity, through a focus on beliefs and psychological dispositions in motivating volunteerism [26,41]. These studies have converged around a series of core insights that are particularly relevant for our study. First, scholars working from a rational choice framework tend to argue that prosocial behaviors are motivated by self-interest over altruistic tendencies [42–44]. This body of work has been criticized on both theoretical [45,46] and empirical [47,48] grounds. Second, a parallel line of work has found positive correlations between psychological wellbeing and volunteerism [49,50]. Finally, research has also explored religious belief as a motivating factor in volunteer activities [38,51–53]. This work has repeatedly identified a positive association between religious belief and proclivities to volunteer. While approaching volunteerism from distinct methodological, theoretical, and conceptual avenues, these studies tend to emphasize personal, internalized psychological processes as shaping prosocial and volunteer activities.

In contradistinction, another line of scholarship has taken a less cognitive approach by focusing primarily on public, social, and structural religiosity factors, such as religious participation. Lim and MacGregor, for instance, suggested spillover effects of association with religious communities, whereby even non-religious individuals who reported more friendships with religious individuals displayed a greater propensity to volunteer in both religious and secular organizations [54]. Johnston, drawing from longitudinal data, presented similar findings that reinforced the idea that immersion into religious communities promoted volunteerism over the life course [52]. Furthermore, this religious spillover effect was present irrespective of psychological dispositions. Taken together, these studies represent a body of scholarship that has assessed multifaceted linkages between religion and volunteerism and highlighted moderating factors such as race-ethnicity [24], health and well-being [41,55], age [56], and gender [29,57]. From these studies, we incorporate an emphasis on public, extra-individual, and social processes as shaping prosocial and volunteer activities [58].

Combined, we apply the insights of extant studies through a focus on both the personal, individualized forms and the public, social forms of religiosity, as related to volunteerism.

2.3. Social Learning Theory: The Impact of Childhood Socialization

Previous studies investigating rates of volunteerism have focused on both personal and public forms of religiosity as related to charitable behaviors [13,32,53]. Related to these studies, we are particularly interested in how childhood religious socialization relates to later life volunteerism. A plausible theoretical mechanism has been proposed by Bandura's social learning theory [59], which suggests that behavior is acquired through observation and emulation of others in social situations. Applied to childhood socialization, social learning theory has been employed to explain processes by which children learn to model their behaviors based on interaction with parents [60,61].

One strand of this research has considered general altruistic behaviors that are (a) transmitted through processes of family socialization (*i.e.*, intergenerational transmission); and (b) translated to service provision in volunteer settings [62,63]. In terms of specific volunteering behaviors, a parallel body of work has considered the parental transmission of prosocial behaviors that enhance propensities to become civically engaged. Results drawing from both cross-sectional and panel data support the central tenets of social learning theory and suggest that parents serve as role models who can motivate prosocial volunteer behaviors in both religious and secular settings [64,65].

However, it is also important to note the determinants of family socialization, which include material resources like income, accumulated wealth, and neighborhood quality. For example, some of the empirical studies have emphasized the substantial impediments and challenges to civic engagement experienced by low-income families [66,67]. However, results of longitudinal research presented by Lichter and colleagues [68] indicate that lower propensities to volunteer among the economically disadvantaged are offset by socioemotional stability and positive life experiences. While these studies raise important questions for research on the impediments and resources that motivate volunteerism, the current study takes additional determinants into consideration, namely, the role of religion as a possible antecedent of civic engagement.

Growing attention has been paid to "emerging adulthood" (e.g., a new life stage between 18 and 29 years of age) [69–71]. As related to volunteerism, one major study found that increased family and community ties during adolescence predicted an increased rate of civic engagement during emerging adulthood [72]. Echoing Bandura's social learning theory, researchers have noted that unique familial and community environments shape adolescents' and young adults' civic identities [73,74]. To summarize, these studies have established positive linkages between various dimensions of religiosity, ranging from public religious participation to private religious devotion, and civic engagement during adolescence or emerging adulthood [4,5,75–79].

Despite the fact that there has been a growing body of research linking religiosity with volunteerism across the life course, the empirical research on the linkage between childhood religious socialization and propensities to volunteer during emerging adulthood is scant and often indirect [79,80]. Applying social learning theories to this study implies two potentials for the volunteerism and religiosity relationship. The first expectation is derived from emerging adulthood studies, from the psychological process described as "recentering" [3], which implies that childhood religiosity will affect later life volunteerism insofar as childhood religious socialization is internalized as an individualized aspect of emerging adult identity, *i.e.*, private religiosity. This expectation is contrary to sociological studies finding forms of social participation are central [4,5], *i.e.*, public religiosity. Thus, this study takes a social learning approach to investigating life course volunteerism as it relates to public and private religiosity in childhood and emerging adulthood.

3. Conceptual Models: Religious Socialization, Life Course Religiosity, and Volunteerism

Based on the discussion above, we propose two conceptual models assessing empirical relationships between childhood religious socialization, emerging adult private and public religiosity, and civic volunteerism. In these models, we develop two competing hypotheses. The first is that childhood religiosity will foster emerging adult civic volunteerism through private forms of emerging adult religiosity. We represent this first conceptual model in Figure 1 and propose that the effects of childhood religiosity on emerging adult volunteerism are mediated through emerging adult private religiosity.

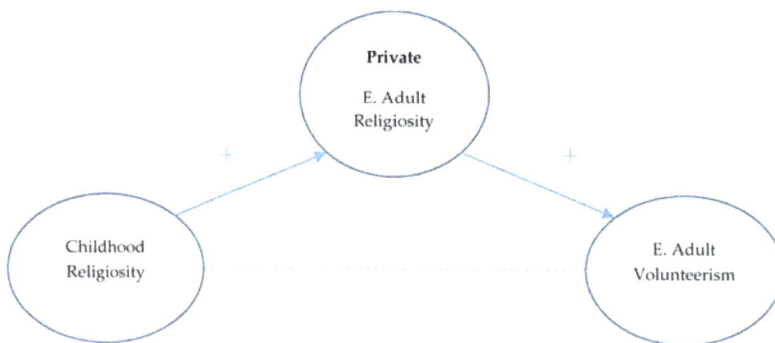

Figure 1. Mediating effects of *private* emerging adult religiosity on rates of volunteerism.

In contrast, we propose a second conceptual model in Figure 2 that is also based upon extant literature but with a different theorized expectation. In this alternative hypothesis, we propose that childhood religiosity is also indirectly associated with emerging adult volunteerism through emerging adult religiosity. However, in this model we propose instead that it is mediated through public, social forms of religiosity. Stated differently, childhood religiosity can be translated into emerging adult volunteerism only when childhood religiosity is transmitted into public forms of religiosity during emerging adulthood.

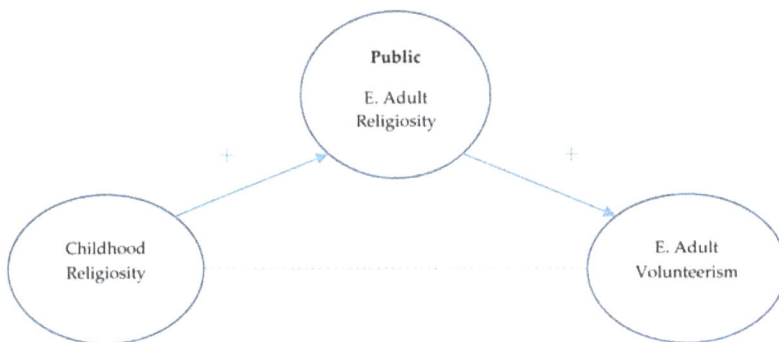

Figure 2. Mediating effects of *public* emerging adult religiosity on rates of volunteerism.

4. Research Methods

4.1. Data Collection

The current study analyzes survey data collected from undergraduate students enrolled at the University of Texas at San Antonio (UTSA), a Hispanic-serving, public university located in South Texas. After receiving appropriate human subjects institutional review board (IRB) approvals, students across several colleges completed the self-administered questionnaire on paper before class lectures throughout the 2015 academic year. Students did not receive compensation from either the research team or their professors for completing the survey. Although the data limit the generalizability of our findings, these limitations are somewhat offset by the fact UTSA is characterized by a diverse and nontraditional student body. For instance, two-thirds of the UTSA student population is made up of international students and students from underrepresented minority groups. In addition to the traditional college student age bracket of 18 to 22 years, over one-third of the UTSA student population is aged 23 years and older [81]. In our view the general demographic profile of the UTSA student body provides a unique opportunity to examine the patterns of voluntaristic behavior among less advantaged, college attending emerging adults.

4.2. Secular Volunteerism Measure

Emerging adult secular volunteerism was measured via responses to the following survey question, which was subsequently followed by a list of various types of organizations for which one could volunteer: "Over the past 12 months, about how many *weeks* did you spend doing unpaid volunteer work for the following groups/organizations?" Response categories were ordinal and ranged from "0 weeks" = 0, "1–10 weeks" = 1, "11–20 weeks" = 2, "21–30 weeks" = 3, "31–40 weeks" = 4, and "41 + weeks" = 5. The list of organizations included: (a) health (hospital, hospice, nursing home, mental health unit, clinic, *etc.*); (b) educational (elementary school, library, tutoring organization, *etc.*); (c) human service (day car, foster care, meals on wheels, homeless shelter, Red Cross, United Way, women's shelter, family counseling center, *etc.*); (d) animal welfare/environmental (SPCA, Humane Society, Animal Defense League, Highway Clean-Up, community beautification program, *etc.*); (e) arts and humanities (museum, cultural/ethnic group, public television/radio, *etc.*); (f) political (political parties, political campaigns, nonpartisan political groups, *etc.*); (g) youth development (boy/girl scouts, 4-H club, Little League, Big Brothers/Sisters); (h) one-day/short-term service (Day of Caring, Make a Difference Day, MLK Day, Earth Day, *etc.*); and (i) other. Because the majority of respondents volunteered minimally (*i.e.*, 1–10 weeks in the past year), if at all, the dependent variable was dichotomized such that 1 = volunteered in the past year, and 0 = did not volunteer in the past year.

4.3. Religiosity Measures

Emerging adult religiosity was assessed through the following measures. Respondents were asked to give their religious affiliation via the following question: "What is your religious preference? Is it Protestant, Catholic, Jewish, some other religion, or no religion?" They were then provided a list of denominations to choose from, which included Baptist, Southern Baptist, Catholic, Episcopalian, Jewish, Latter Day Saint, Lutheran, Methodist, Muslim, Pentecostal, Hindu, Buddhist, none, and other. A follow-up question then listed 14 specific Protestant denominations one could belong to. Respondents' choices were then dummy-coded into four separate variables based on the denominational categories found by Steensland and colleagues [82]. These were Catholic, Conservative Protestant, Mainline Protestant (=1), and other/no religion (=0) as the reference category. Descriptive statistics based on the study sample are displayed in Table 1.

Table 1. Sample characteristics (*n* = 701).

Variables	%	Mean	Range	SD
Dependent Variable				
Volunteered in Past Year	69	-	0, 1	-
Religious Variables				
Public Religiosity	-	2.13	0, 8	2.10
Private Religiosity	-	0.88	0, 4	0.86
Childhood Public Religiosity	-	5.62	0, 12	3.72
Childhood Private Religiosity	-	7.92	0, 16	4.86
Catholic	39	-	0, 1	-
Conservative Protestant	23	-	0, 1	-
Mainline Protestant	10	-	0, 1	-
Other/None (reference)	28	-	0, 1	-
Covariates				
Female	61	-	0, 1	-
Male (reference)	39	-	0, 1	-
Age	-	21.54	18, 29	2.44
Married or Cohabitating	17	-	0, 1	-
Single (reference)	81	-	0, 1	-
Employed	59	-	0, 1	-
Unemployed (reference)	42	-	0, 1	-
White (reference)	21	-	0, 1	-
Hispanic	53	-	0, 1	-
Black	15	-	0, 1	-
Other race	11	-	0, 1	-
GPA	-	3.52	0, 6	1.43
Parents' Education	-	11.39	0, 16	3.37
Family Social Class	-	1.69	0, 3	0.71
Year at UTSA	-	2.50	1, 4	1.14
Fulltime Student	93	-	0, 1	-

Emerging adult public religiosity was gauged by responses to two separate questions measuring the frequency of religious attendance at both regular religious services as well as additional church activities outside of regular services. Respondents were asked, "Apart from religious events like weddings, funerals, and baptisms, about how often do you attend religious services (Church, Mosque, Synagogue, *etc.*)?" and "About how often do you take part in the activities and organizations of a church or place of worship other than attending regular services?" Responses ranged from 0 = Never to 4 = Several times a week. The two items were then summed together to create an index variable (α = 0.786).

Emerging adult private religiosity was indicated by responses to four survey questions measuring frequencies of prayer, reading religious scripture by oneself or with a small group, watching/listening to religious programs on the television/internet/radio, and reading religious material other than scripture. Responses were also coded from 0 = Never to 4 = Several times a week. The four items were then averaged to create an index variable (α = 0.780).

Childhood religiosity was also measured via two separate index variables measuring both the private (α = 0.890) and public (α = 0.860) dimensions. For the private dimension of childhood religiosity, respondents were instructed to signify how often they participated in the following religious activities while growing up: (a) receiving religious instruction at home; (b) praying before meals; (c) reading scripture or other religious material; and (d) praying before bedtime. For the public dimension of childhood religiosity, respondents were asked how often they (a) attended church/religious services; (b) attended religious youth groups; and (c) attended "Bible camp" (e.g., religious retreats, religious summer camps, *etc.*). For both dimensions, responses ranged in values from 0 = Never to 4 = A great deal and were then summed to create two index variables.

4.4. Control Measures

Our analyses include a series of standard control variables. These include gender (dummy coded with 1 = female and 0 = male); year of age (in years); marital status (dummy coded with 1 = married/cohabiting and 0 = single); employment status (dummy coded with 1 = employed and 0 = unemployed); race/ethnicity (dummy coded into Hispanic, African American, and other, with white as the reference category); grade point average (ordinal ranging from 0 = Below 1.5 to 6 = Above 4.0); mother's and father's educational attainment (ordinal ranging from 0 = none to 8 = graduate school and beyond); family social class (ordinal, 0 = lower class, 1 = working class, 2 = middle class, 3 = upper class); year of study at UTSA (ordinal, 1 = freshman, 2 = sophomore, 3 = junior, 4 = senior); student enrollment status (dummy coded with 1 = full time and 0 = part time).

4.5. Analytical Strategies

For our outcome measure, we estimate binary logistic regression models with multiple imputation to predict odds of past year secular volunteerism. Our first set of regression models, Models 1–5 in Table 2, examine the direct and independent effects of religious factors on volunteering net of socio-demographic variables. Our second set of models employ structural equation modeling (SEM) to estimate potential mediating effects between religious factors on volunteering (Table 3). Each model includes the effects of two main religious predictors with statistical controls. These models allow for the evaluation of mediation of childhood religiosity and emerging adult volunteerism through two different forms of emerging adult religiosity: public and private. To further investigate these potential mediating effects, we conducted path analysis of direct and indirect effects in accordance with previous literature [83,84]. These results are displayed in Table 4.

5. Results

Table 2 presents results of binary logistic regression models predicting odds of past year secular volunteering. Across Models 1–4, results clearly indicate statistically significant and positive associations between all the religious measures and odds of emerging adult volunteerism. However, two findings are particularly noteworthy. First, emerging adult public religiosity is the only religious dimension to maintain statistical significance in Model 5, once all the other religious measures are included simultaneously. Substantively, this model indicates that a one unit increase in public religiosity predicts significantly greater odds of past year secular volunteerism by a factor of 1.240 or 24 percent, even after controlling for sociodemographic variables and religious covariates. Second, the measures of childhood religiosity are no longer statistically significantly related to emerging adult volunteerism in Model 5, which suggests potential mediation effects of emerging adulthood religiosity. Next we turn to the results of Table 3.

Table 2. Binary logistic regression models predicting odds of past year secular volunteerism.

Variables	(1)	(2)	(3)	(4)	(5)
Religious Variables					
Public religiosity	1.268 ***	-	-	-	1.253 **
Private religiosity	-	1.473 **	-	-	0.999
Childhood public religiosity	-	-	1.107 **	-	1.033
Childhood private religiosity	-	-	-	1.052 **	0.989
Sociodemographic/Control Variables					
Female	1.691 **	1.649 **	1.620 **	1.649 **	1.661 **
Age	0.925	0.926	0.959	0.933	0.959
Married or Cohabitating	1.185	1.110	1.084	1.143	1.129
Employed	1.495 *	1.444	1.287	1.439	1.363
Hispanic	1.082	1.082	1.225	1.068	1.221
Black	0.947	0.880	0.937	0.841	1.029
Other race	2.008	2.126	2.054	2.252	1.854
GPA	1.079	1.090	1.065	1.089	1.082
Parents' education	1.035	1.028	1.019	1.019	1.036
Family social class	0.886	0.918	0.913	0.911	0.889
Year at UTSA	0.812	0.789 *	0.757 **	0.782 *	0.768 *
Full-time student	0.511	0.541	0.656	0.562	0.614
Catholic	0.853	0.929	0.927	0.941	0.848
Mainline Protestant	0.888	0.897	0.871	0.906	0.857
Conservative Protestant	1.046	1.171	1.360	1.320	1.025
Likelihood ratio χ^2	68.39 ***	54.87 ***	45.06 ***	50.83 ***	63.61 ***
df	16	16	16	16	19
n	701	701	701	701	701

$* p < 0.05; ** p < 0.01; *** p < 0.001.$

Table 3. Direct effects of emerging adulthood religiosity in logistic regression models using SEM [a].

Variables	(1)	(2)	(3)	(4)
Religious Variables				
Public religiosity	1.247 ***	1.261 ***	-	-
Private religiosity	-	-	1.358 *	1.367 *
Childhood public religiosity	1.024	-	1.051	-
Childhood private religiosity	-	1.006	-	1.026
Sociodemographic/Control Variables				
Female	1.655 **	1.572 **	1.572 **	1.611 **
Age	0.959	0.951	0.951	0.955
Married or Cohabitating	1.130	1.078	1.076	1.067
Employed	1.365	1.311	1.301	1.313
Hispanic	1.215	1.222	1.221	1.180
Black	1.004	0.919	0.936	0.844
Other race	1.854	1.987	1.985	1.906
GPA	1.082	1.073	1.074	1.075
Parents' education	1.035	1.025	1.026	1.025
Family social class	0.893	0.922	0.920	0.932
Year at UTSA	0.766 *	0.759 *	0.762 *	0.753 *
Full-time student	0.618	0.645	0.648	0.649
Catholic	0.845	0.895	0.910	0.908
Mainline Protestant	0.858	0.855	0.857	0.879
Conservative Protestant	1.019	1.122	1.126	1.166
df	17	17	17	17
n	701	701	701	701

[a] Odds coefficients reported; $* p < 0.05; ** p < 0.01; *** p < 0.001.$

Following previous methodological strategies and findings on volunteerism [84,85], we highlight the mediating effects of emerging adulthood public and private religiosity using SEM. Table 4 features unstandardized direct, indirect and total effects of path decomposition analysis. As seen in Table 4, emerging adult public religiosity significantly mediates the effects of childhood religiosity and adult private religiosity. This is indicated by the fact that the direct effects are statistically insignificant while indirect effects are highly statistically significant in the path models. These results confirm our prior observation that both public and private emerging adult religiosity mediate the relationship between childhood religiosity and emerging adult volunteerism, and public emerging adult religiosity has the most direct and robust effect.

Table 4. Path analysis of mediation effects using SEM.

Variables	Direct Effect	Indirect Effect	Total Effect
Mediator: Public Religiosity			
Private Religiosity	−0.001	0.186 ***	0.185 **
Childhood Public Religiosity	0.046	0.108 ***	0.155 **
Childhood Private Religiosity	0.016	0.121 ***	0.137 **
Mediator: Private Religiosity			
Childhood Public Religiosity	0.050	0.101 ***	0.151 **
Childhood Private Religiosity	0.067	0.066 ***	0.133 **

* $p < 0.05$; ** $p < 0.01$; *** $p < 0.001$.

We close this section by briefly emphasizing some noteworthy effects of control measures. First, we find no significant effects of race-ethnicity or religious affiliation on emerging adult volunteerism. Next, we observe that female students show higher odds of volunteering in the past year compared with their male counterparts. Finally, year at UTSA decreases odds of past year volunteerism. This could be due to increasing academic and non-academic obligations.

6. Discussion and Conclusions

Our analysis contributes to the growing literature exploring linkages between religious factors and civic engagement. Whereas previous work has often focused on civic engagement in later stages of life, we focus on volunteerism during the formative years of emerging adulthood. Young adults in higher educational settings are often faced with a series of competing interests that motivate and modify behavioral choices in the absence of direct parental supervision. Moreover, it is at this stage of the life course that young adults can go through a process of re-centering wherein they explore their religious identity and formulate and solidify their own religious beliefs in addition to or independent of their familial religious traditions [3]. At the most general level, our results support existing findings that religiosity is related to prosocial behaviors among emerging adults. In addition, our results extend previous scholarship in two important ways.

First, while this study surmises the important role of childhood religious socialization on civic engagement, our findings suggest that religious upbringings are important insofar as they are translated to emerging adult religiosity. As we surmised, childhood religious socialization is positively associated with both forms of emerging adult religiosity. This confirms prior research finding that religious engagement during childhood influences levels of religiosity in later life [1,2]. Our results reinforce this general association and are consistent with social learning theory, which explicates the impact of childhood experiences on later behavioral outcomes. However, unlike prior studies we do not find any distinguishable differences by race and ethnicity.

Second, our study shows a more robust direct effect of public religiosity in emerging adulthood than private religiosity. This means that while internalized religious factors, such as individualized religious devotions, are predictive of civic engagement, it is the social expression of religiosity, such as religious participation, that is most unwaveringly linked with propensities to volunteer among emerging adults attending a large public university in South Texas. This finding is also consistent with previous work that underscores the importance of religious social capital as a pathway to volunteering [86,87]. We view this result as potentially explained by recent studies suggesting that emerging adults who regularly engage in religious activities with fellow congregants are provided additional opportunities to volunteer in secular civic activities. As such, these religious associations and friendship ties developed among regular congregants can motivate emerging adults to volunteer with anticipated socio-religious rewards. Furthermore, within a higher education setting, there might be an institutional "cross-pollination" in that student organizations typically cooperate and share volunteer opportunities with one another. Therefore, students who do not attend religious activities may be unaware that these additional volunteer opportunities exist. Additionally, as multiple studies have shown, religious organizations may promote specific skills and competencies (e.g., public speaking, fundraising strategies, and leadership capabilities) that can be translated to success in secular settings [88,89].

6.1. Interpreting Mediation of Childhood Religiosity

Given that our study finds emerging adult religiosity mediates the relationship between childhood religiosity and emerging adult volunteerism, this raises the question: What can explain the prominence of adulthood religiosity over childhood socialization? To answer this question, we suggest two plausible mechanisms.

First, students might abandon or become less committed to religious activities while in college [90,91]. In this case, students will no longer be embedded in religious communities and, consequently, may no longer be exposed to volunteer opportunities. On the other hand, students might be introduced to new religious organizations upon entering college. This is particularly likely considering the institutional context where our data collection took place. Our study site is characterized by the presence of strong, active religious student organizations and visible on-campus proselytizing efforts. It is therefore quite likely that less religious and non-affiliated students would be presented with religious options when choosing from various on-campus organizational opportunities. In short, this line of reasoning suggests that the university setting may be a unique case in which emerging adults encounter a diverse marketplace of ideas, organizations and alternate worldviews that may at times conflict with childhood religious socialization [92,93].

Secondly, there is reason to suspect that childhood religious socialization is a product of family dynamics. Stated simply, parents often make religious choices on behalf of their children who are then expected to participate irrespective of personal desires. Once becoming adults, individuals begin to voluntarily make personal choices that include either opting in or out of one's familial religious traditions. Therefore, childhood religious experiences should only matter to the extent that they are carried over into emerging adulthood. When these experiences do carry over, we should expect this to result in continued religiosity and increased civic engagement.

6.2. Conclusions

To summarize, our study findings resonate primarily with two theoretical perspectives. First of all, the strong association between childhood and emerging adulthood religiosity confirms many of the central tenets of social learning theory. As implied by the path analysis in Table 4, the greater the level of childhood religious socialization, the greater the level of emerging adulthood religiosity. As social learning theorists have argued, the behavioral and attitudinal patterns established in childhood carry over into adulthood and shape outcomes in later life. Second, emerging adult involvement in religious services and activities is the most robust factor mediating involvement with volunteer organizations. In essence, religious participation can be seen as a property of social structure external to individual cognition, which helps shape personal religiosity.

6.3. Limitations and Future Studies

Future theoretical work would gain from attempts to synthesize both structural and psychological perspectives, as this paper has done. Although our study contributes to the scholarship on emerging adulthood, religiosity and civic engagement, it is important to acknowledge several limitations. First, our study is limited by a lack of specific indicators of religious salience and other forms of subjective religiosity. While we recognize this as a study limitation, we suggest that this could pave the way for future research. Second, because our study utilized a cross-sectional design, we are unable to establish causal relationships between various religious factors and volunteerism. Moreover, though our childhood religiosity was gauged via a series of retrospective questions, we caution readers to refrain from drawing strict causal conclusions without panel data. Third, our study does not contain qualitative information from in depth interviews; as such, future research should employ mixed methods to better examine and understand motivations, either religious or secular, for volunteering. Fourth, future research could explore if the religiosity-civic engagement link, as we uncovered in the present study, exists for emerging adults who have either (1) never attended college; or (2) currently hold college degrees but juggle competing commitments such as careers and family life. Finally, previous studies indicate that parental volunteering and volunteering during grade school are also significant predictors of emerging adulthood volunteerism [94]. Future studies should consider including these measures as additional predictors of adulthood volunteerism.

In closing, we are mindful of the fact that college students represent a distinct minority population among all American young adults. Therefore, the motivations to volunteer may be distinct from individuals at different stages of the life course. On the one hand, college students may be concerned with more utilitarian aspects of volunteerism, such as accumulating experiences that may translate to later employment skills and competencies, or as a means to strengthen one's future employment resume. On the other hand, college students have been shown to often hold more idealistic views regarding social issues and perceived injustices. For these reasons, examining patterns of volunteerism among emerging adults can greatly enhance the body of scholarship on civic engagement. Our study is a small step in this direction.

Author Contributions: Reed DeAngelis collected original survey data and co-authored the initial draft with Gabriel Acevedo. Xiaohe Xu performed additional statistical analyses and substantially revised the original manuscript.

Conflicts of Interest: The authors declare no conflict of interest.

References

1. Jennifer L. Tanner. "Recentering During Emerging Adulthood: A Critical Turning Point in Life Span Human Development." In *Emerging Adults in Aermica: Coming of Age in the 21st Century*. Edited by Jeffrey J. Arnett and Jennifer L. Tanner. Washington: American Psychological Association, 2006.
2. Christian Smith, and Patricia Snell. *Souls in Transition: The Religious and Spiritual Lives of Emerging Adults*. New York: Oxford University Press, 2009.
3. Jonathan P. Hill, and Kevin R. Den Dulk. "Religion, Volunteering, and Educational Setting: The Effect of Youth Schooling Type on Civic Engagement." *Journal for the Scientific Study of Religion* 52 (2013): 179–97. [CrossRef]
4. Neal Krause, and Christopher G. Ellison. "Parental Religious Socialization Practices and Self-Esteem in Late Life." *Review of Religious Research* 49 (2007): 109–27.
5. Jerry Z. Park, and Elaine Howard Ecklund. "Negotiating Continuity: Family and Religious Socialization for Second-Generation Asian Americans." *The Sociological Quarterly* 48 (2007): 93–118. [CrossRef]
6. Alexis de Tocqueville. (1885) 1989. *Democracy in America*. New York: Harper Collins.
7. Gerald Gamm, and Robert D. Putnam. "The growth of voluntary associations in America, 1840–1940." *Journal of Interdisciplinary History* 29 (1999): 511–57. [CrossRef]
8. Robert D. Putnam. "Bowling Alone: America's Declining Social Capital." *Journal of Democracy* 6 (1995): 65–78. [CrossRef]

9. Robert D. Putnam. "Tuning In, Tuning Out: The Strange Disappearance of Social Capital in America." *Ps-Political Science & Politics* 28 (1995): 664–83. [CrossRef]
10. Robert D. Putnam. *Bowling Alone: The Collapse and Revival of American Community*. New York: Simon & Schuster, 2000.
11. Dietlind Stolle, and Marc Hooghe. "Review article: Inaccurate, exceptional, one-sided or irrelevant? The debate about the alleged decline of social capital and civic engagement in western societies." *British Journal of Political Science* 35 (2005): 149–67. [CrossRef]
12. Russell J. Dalton. "Citizenship norms and the expansion of political participation." *Political Studies* 56 (2008): 76–98. [CrossRef]
13. John Wilson. "Volunteering." *Annual Review of Sociology* 26 (2000): 215–40. [CrossRef]
14. Paul A. Djupe, Anand E. Sokhey, and Christopher P. Gilbert. "Present but Not Accounted for? Gender Differences in Civic Resource Acquisition." *American Journal of Political Science* 51 (2007): 906–20. [CrossRef]
15. Jill E. Fuller. "Equality in Cyberdemocracy? Gauging Gender Gaps in On-line Civic Participation." *Social Science Quarterly* 85 (2004): 938–57. [CrossRef]
16. Michael A. Lewis, and Eri Noguchi. "The Female Corp of Volunteers: How Gender and Labor Supply Interact to Affect Civic Participation." *Race, Gender & Class* 13 (2006): 255–67.
17. Ian A. Gutierrez, and Jacqueline S. Mattis. "Factors Predicting Volunteer Engagement among Urban-Residing African American Women." *Journal of Black Studies* 45 (2014): 599–619. [CrossRef]
18. Belinda C. Lum, and Michelle M. Jacob. "University-Community Engagement, Axes of Difference & Dismantling Race, Gender, and Class Oppression." *Race, Gender & Class* 19 (2012): 309–24.
19. Jan E. Mutchler, Jeffrey A. Burr, and Francis G. Caro. "From paid worker to volunteer: Leaving the paid workforce and volunteering in later life." *Social Forces* 81 (2003): 1267–93. [CrossRef]
20. Shu-Chun Chang, Chen-Ling Fang, Yi-Chang Ling, and Bi-Kun Tsai. "Effects of Socioeconomic Status on Leisure Volunteering Constraint: A Structural Equation Model." *Social Behavior & Personality: An International Journal* 39 (2011): 477–89. [CrossRef]
21. David H. Smith. "Determinants of Voluntary Association Participation and Volunteering: A Literature Review." *Nonprofit and Voluntary Sector Quarterly* 23 (1994): 243–63. [CrossRef]
22. Norman H. Nie, Jane Junn, and Kenneth Stehlik-Barry. *Education and Democratic Citizenship in America*. Chicago: University of Chicago Press, 1996.
23. Maurice Gesthuizen, and Peer Scheepers. "Educational Differences in Volunteering in Cross-National Perspective: Individual Contextual Explanations." *Nonprofit and Voluntary Sector Quarterly* 41 (2012): 58–81. [CrossRef]
24. Marc A. Musick, John Wilson, and William B. Bynum. "Race and Formal Volunteering: The Differential Effects of Class and Religion." *Social Forces* 78 (2000): 1539–70. [CrossRef]
25. David H. Smith, and Burt R. Baldwin. "Parental Socialization, Socioeconomic Status, and Volunteer Organization Participation." *Journal of Voluntary Action Research* 3 (1974): 59–66.
26. Susan Eckstein. "Community as Gift-Giving: Collectivistic Roots of Volunteerism." *American Sociological Review* 66 (2001): 829–51. [CrossRef]
27. Sally K. Gallagher. "Doing Their Share: Comparing Patterns of Help Given by Older and Younger Adults." *Journal of Marriage and Family* 56 (1994): 567–78. [CrossRef]
28. Cassie L. Barnhardt, Jessica E. Sheets, and Kira Pasquesi. "You Expect What? Students' Perceptions as Resources in Acquiring Commitments and Capacities for Civic Engagement." *Research in Higher Education* 56 (2015): 622–44. [CrossRef]
29. Elizabeth Weiss Ozorak. "Love of God and Neighbor: Religion and Volunteer Service among College Students." *Review of Religious Research* 44 (2003): 285–99. [CrossRef]
30. Kraig Beyerlein, and John R. Hipp. "From Pews to Participation: The Effect of Congregation Activity and Context on Bridging Civic Engagement." *Social Problems* 53 (2006): 97–117. [CrossRef]
31. Kraig Beyerlein, and David Sikkink. "Sorrow and Solidarity: Why Americans Volunteered for 9/11 Relief Efforts." *Social Problems* 55 (2008): 190–215. [CrossRef]
32. John Wilson, and Marc Musick. "Who Cares? Toward an Integrated Theory of Volunteer Work." *American Sociological Review* 62 (1997): 694–713. [CrossRef]
33. Pui-Yan Lam. "As the Flocks Gather: How Religion Affects Voluntary Association Participation." *Journal for the Scientific Study of Religion* 41 (2002): 405–22. [CrossRef]

34. Valerie A. Lewis, Carol A. MacGregor, and Robert D. Putnam. "Religion, Networks, and Neighborliness: The Impact of Religious Social Networks on Civic Engagement." *Social Science Research* 42 (2013): 331–46. [CrossRef] [PubMed]

35. Elton F. Jackson, Mark D. Bachmeier, James R. Wood, and Elizabeth A. Craft. "Volunteering and Charitable Giving: Do Religious and Associational Ties Promote Helping Behavior? " *Nonprofit and Voluntary Sector Quarterly* 24 (1995): 59–78.

36. Jerry Z. Park, and Christian Smith. "'To Whom Much Has Been Given...': Religious Capital and Community Voluntarism among Churchgoing Protestants." *Journal for the Scientific Study of Religion* 39 (2000): 272–86. [CrossRef]

37. Brett G. Scharffs. "Volunteerism, Charitable Giving, and Religion: The U.S. Example." *Review of Faith & International Affairs* 7 (2009): 61–67. [CrossRef]

38. John Wilson, and Thomas Janoski. "The Contribution of Religion to Volunteer Work." *Sociology of Religion* 56 (1995): 137–52. [CrossRef]

39. Gabriel A. Acevedo. "Collective Rituals or Private Practice in Texas? Assessing the Impact of Religious Factors on Mental Health." *Review of Religious Research* 52 (2010): 188–206.

40. Pamela Paxton, Nicholas E. Reith, and Jennifer L. Glanville. "Volunteering and the Dimensions of Religiosity: A Cross-National Analysis." *Review of Religious Research* 56 (2014): 597–625. [CrossRef]

41. Marc A. Musick, and John Wilson. "Volunteering and depression: The role of psychological and social resources in different age groups." *Social Science & Medicine* 56 (2003): 259–69. [CrossRef]

42. Warren B. Hrung. "After-Life Consumption and Charitable Giving." *The American Journal of Economics and Sociology* 63 (2004): 731–45. [CrossRef]

43. Jonathan Rosborough. "A Theory of Congregational Giving." *Journal of Public Economic Theory* 17 (2015): 270–95. [CrossRef]

44. David Horton Smith. "Altruism, Volunteers, and Volunteerism." *Nonprofit and Voluntary Sector Quarterly* 10 (1981): 21–36. [CrossRef]

45. Steve Bruce. "Religion and Rational Choice: A Critique of Economic Explanations of Religious Behavior." *Sociology of Religion* 54 (1993): 193–205. [CrossRef]

46. Mark Chaves. "On the Rational Choice Approach to Religion." *Journal for the Scientific Study of Religion* 34 (1995): 98–104. [CrossRef]

47. Lionel Prouteau, and François-Charles Wolff. "On the relational motive for volunteer work." *Journal of Economic Psychology* 29 (2008): 314–35. [CrossRef]

48. Lynette S. Unger. "Altruism as a motivation to volunteer." *Journal of Economic Psychology* 12 (1991): 71–100. [CrossRef]

49. Zandra N. Quiles, and Jane Bybee. "Chronic and Predispositional Guilt: Relations to Mental Health, Prosocial Behavior, and Religiosity." *Journal of Personality Assessment* 69 (1997): 104–26. [CrossRef] [PubMed]

50. Peggy A. Thoits, and Lyndi N. Hewitt. "Volunteer Work and Well-Being." *Journal of Health and Social Behavior* 42 (2001): 115–31. [CrossRef] [PubMed]

51. Nancy T. Ammerman. "Religious narratives, community service, and everyday public life." In *Taking Faith Seriously*. Edited by Mary Jo Bane, Brent Coffin and Richard Higgins. Cambridge: Harvard University Press, 2005, pp. 146–74.

52. Joseph B. Johnston. "Religion and Volunteering Over the Adult Life Course." *Journal for the Scientific Study of Religion* 52 (2013): 733–52. [CrossRef]

53. Marc A. Musick, and John Wilson. *Volunteers: A Social Profile.* Bloomington: Indiana University Press, 2008.

54. Chaeyoon Lim, and Carol Ann MacGregor. "Religion and Volunteering in Context: Disentangling the Contextual Effects of Religion on Voluntary Behavior." *American Sociological Review* 77 (2012): 747–79. [CrossRef]

55. Francesca Borgonovi. "Doing well by doing good. The relationship between formal volunteering and self-reported health and happiness." *Social Science & Medicine* 66 (2008): 2321–34. [CrossRef] [PubMed]

56. Lona H. Choi. "Factors Affecting Volunteerism among Older Adults." *Journal of Applied Gerontology* 22 (2003): 179–96. [CrossRef]

57. Barbara R. McIntosh, and Nicholas L. Danigelis. "Race, gender, and the relevance of productive activity for elders' affect." *The Journals of Gerontology Series B: Psychological Sciences and Social Sciences* 50 (1995): S229–39. [CrossRef]

58. John Wilson, and Marc Musick. "The Contribution of Social Resources to Volunteering." *Social Science Quarterly* 79 (1998): 799–814.

59. Albert Bandura. *Social Learning Theory*. Englewood Cliffs: Prentice-Hall, 1977.

60. Thomas G. O'Connor, Carla Matias, Annabel Futh, Grace Tantam, and Stephen Scott. "Social Learning Theory Parenting Intervention Promotes Attachment-Based Caregiving in Young Children: Randomized Clinical Trial." *Journal of Clinical Child & Adolescent Psychology* 42 (2013): 358–70. [CrossRef] [PubMed]

61. Ronald L. Simons, Les B. Whitbeck, Rand D. Conger, and Katherine J. Conger. "Parenting factors, social skills, and value commitments as precursors to school failure, involvement with deviant peers, and delinquent behavior." *Journal of Youth and Adolescence* 20 (1991): 645–64. [CrossRef] [PubMed]

62. E. Gil Clary, and Jude Miller. "Socialization and Situational Influences on Sustained Altruism." *Child Development* 57 (1986): 1358–69. [CrossRef] [PubMed]

63. Michela Lenzi, Alessio Vieno, Massimo Santinello, Maury Nation, and Adam Voight. "The Role Played by the Family in Shaping Early and Middle Adolescent Civic Responsibility." *The Journal of Early Adolescence* 34 (2014): 251–78. [CrossRef]

64. Rene Bekkers. "Intergenerational Transmission of Volunteering." *Acta Sociologica* 50 (2007): 99–114. [CrossRef]

65. Sarah Mustillo, John Wilson, and Scott M. Lynch. "Legacy Volunteering: A Test of Two Theories of Intergenerational Transmission." *Journal of Marriage and Family* 66 (2004): 530–41. [CrossRef]

66. Amanda Moore McBride, Margaret S. Sherraden, and Suzanne Pritzker. "Civic Engagement among Low-Income and Low-Wealth Families: In Their Words." *Family Relations* 55 (2006): 152–62. [CrossRef]

67. Fengyan Tang. "What Resources Are Needed for Volunteerism? A Life Course Perspective." *Journal of Applied Gerontology* 25 (2006): 375–90. [CrossRef]

68. Daniel T. Lichter, Michael J. Shanahan, and Erica L. Gardner. "Helping Others?: The Effects of Childhood Poverty and Family Instability on Prosocial Behavior." *Youth & Society* 34 (2002): 89–119. [CrossRef]

69. Jeffrey J. Arnett. "Emerging Adulthood: A Theory of Development from the Late Teens through the Twenties." *American Psychologist* 55 (2000): 469–85. [CrossRef] [PubMed]

70. Jeffrey J. Arnett. *Emerging Adulthood: The Winding Road from the Late Teens through the Twenties*. New York: Oxford University Press, 2006.

71. Manfred H. M. van Dulmen. "Emerging Adulthood—The Journal." *Emerging Adulthood* 1 (2013): 3–4. [CrossRef]

72. Naomi N. Duke, Carol L. Skay, Sandra L. Pettingell, and Iris W. Borowsky. "From Adolescent Connections to Social Capital: Predictors of Civic Engagement in Young Adulthood." *Journal of Adolescent Health* 44 (2009): 161–68. [CrossRef] [PubMed]

73. Richard M. Clerkin, Sharon R. Paynter, and Jami Kathleen Taylor. "Public Service Motivation in Undergraduate Giving and Volunteering Decisions." *American Review of Public Administration* 39 (2009): 675–98. [CrossRef]

74. James Youniss, Jeffrey A. McLellan, and Miranda Yates. "Religion, community service, and identity in American youth." *Journal of Adolescence* 22 (1999): 243–53. [CrossRef] [PubMed]

75. Christian Smith. "Religious Participation and Network Closure among American Adolescents." *Journal for the Scientific Study of Religion* 42 (2003): 259–67. [CrossRef]

76. Christian Smith, and Melissa Denton. *Soul Searching: The Religious and Spiritual Lives of American Teenagers*. New York: Oxford University Press, 2005.

77. Kathryn A. Johnson, Adam B. Cohen, and Morris A. Okun. "Intrinsic Religiosity and Volunteering During Emerging Adulthood: A Comparison of Mormons with Catholics and Non-Catholic Christians." *Journal for the Scientific Study of Religion* 52 (2013): 842–51. [CrossRef]

78. Edmund Forst, and Rose Marie Healy. "Correlations among Religion, Commitment, And Volunteer Participation." *Psychological Reports* 69 (1991): 1224. [CrossRef]

79. Troy Gibson. "Religion and civic engagement among America's youth." *The Social Science Journal* 45 (2008): 504–14. [CrossRef]

80. Richard K. Caputo. "Religious Capital and Intergenerational Transmission of Volunteering as Correlates of Civic Engagement." *Nonprofit and Voluntary Sector Quarterly* 38 (2009): 983–1002. [CrossRef]

81. University of Texas at San Antonio. "The University of Texas at San Antonio Fall Semester 2015 Student Profile: Census Day—Preliminary Paid Report." 2015. Available online: http://www.utsa.edu/registrar/enrollment.html (accessed on 3 December 2015).

82. Brian Streensland, Jerry Z. Park, Mark D. Regnerus, Lynn D. Robinson, W. Bradford Wilcox, and Robert D. Woodberry. "The measure of American religion: Toward improving the state of the art." *Social Forces* 79 (2000): 291–318. [CrossRef]

83. Meredith McGinly, Sharon Lipperman-Kreda, Hilary F. Byrnes, and Gustavo Carlo. "Parental, social and dispositional pathways to Israeli adloescents' volunteering." *Journal of Applied Developmental Psychology* 31 (2010): 386–93. [CrossRef]

84. Amanda Shantz, Tina Saksida, and Kerstin Alfes. "Dedicating time to volunteering: Values, engagement, and commitment to beneficiaries." *Applied Psychology* 63 (2014): 671–97. [CrossRef]

85. Joonmo Son, and John Wilson. "Using Normative Theory to Explain the Effect of Religion and Education on Volunteering." *Sociological Perspectives* 55 (2012): 473–99.

86. Kevin F. Forbes, and Ernest M. Zampelli. "Volunteerism: The Influences of Social, Religious, and Human Capital." *Nonprofit and Voluntary Sector Quarterly* 43 (2014): 227–53. [CrossRef]

87. Stephen M. Merino. "Religious Social Networks and Volunteering: Examining Recruitment via Close Ties." *Review of Religious Research* 55 (2013): 509–27. [CrossRef]

88. Lisa A. Keister. "Religion and Wealth: The Role of Religious Affiliation and Participation in Early Adult Asset Accumulation." *Social Forces* 82 (2003): 175–207. [CrossRef]

89. Christian Smith. "Theorizing Religious Effects among American Adolescents." *Journal for the Scientific Study of Religion* 42 (2003): 17–30. [CrossRef]

90. David Caplovitz, and Fred Sherrow. *The Religious Drop-outs: Apostasy among College Graduates.* Beverly Hills: Sage, 1977.

91. Jonathan P. Hill. "Higher Education as Moral Community: Institutional Influences on Religious Participation During College." *Journal for the Scientific Study of Religion* 48 (2009): 515–34. [CrossRef]

92. Philip F. Jacob. *Changing Values in College.* New York: Wiley, 1958.

93. Kenneth A. Feldman, and Theodore M. Newcomb. *The Impact of College on Students.* Piscataway: Transaction Publishers, 1969.

94. Thomas Janoski, and John Wilson. "Pathways to Voluntarism: Family Socialization and Status Transmission Models." *Social Forces* 74 (1995): 271–92. [CrossRef]

MDPI

Article

Intergenerational Transmission of Religious Giving: Instilling Giving Habits across the Life Course

Patricia Snell Herzog [1,*] and Scott Mitchell [2]

[1] Department of Sociology & Criminal Justice, 210 Old Main Building, University of Arkansas, Fayetteville, AR 72701, USA
[2] Business Intelligence, Performics, Chicago, IL 60601-3713, USA; smitche60@gmail.com
* Correspondence: herzog@uark.edu; Tel.: +1-479-575-3779

Academic Editor: John P. Bartkowski
Received: 1 February 2016; Accepted: 12 July 2016; Published: 16 July 2016

Abstract: This paper investigates the research question: How do religious youth learn to give? While it is likely that youth learn religious financial giving from a variety of different sources, this investigation focuses primarily on how parents teach giving to their children. Supplementary data are also analyzed on the frequency in which youth hear extra-familial calls to give within their religious congregations. In focusing on parental transmission, the analysis identifies a number of approaches that parents report using to teach their children religious financial giving. It also investigates thoughts and feelings about religious financial giving by the children of these parents as a means of assessing the potential impacts of parental methods. Additionally, congregation member reflections on how they learned to give provide insights on giving as a process that develops across the life course, often instilled in childhood, but not appearing behaviorally until adulthood. As such, this paper contributes to a life course understanding of religious giving and has implications for giving across generations.

Keywords: financial giving; prosociality; life course development; youth; parents

1. Transmission of Prosociality

Many religious faiths call adherents to serve others [1]. Given the congregational structure of religious institutions in the U.S. [2], transmission of religious giving is central to the continuation of religious organizations across generations. The need to better understand this process is underscored by recent trends indicating declines in religious participation across generations [3–5].

A study of American religious congregants reported that an overwhelming majority of respondents cited their parental upbringing as one of their primary explanations for their current giving, saying that they give to the church because that is what their parents raised them to do [6]. A number of pastors interviewed also reported the important role of parents in cultivating giving. These pastors attributed the dearth of giving in their congregations to parents not teaching their children to give. This research indicates that parents play a central role in cultivating giving, with both givers and pastors citing parental teaching as an important socializing agent that helps to explaining giving. However, it remained unanswered how it is that parents pass on an inclination to prosocial behaviors, especially giving.

Reviewing numerous studies on the transmission of prosociality, giving scholars find that modeling desired behaviors is key in their actualization [7]. In focusing on the transmission of giving time resources across generations, two primary methods that parents used to increase prosocial behavior in their children were identified: Rewarding prosocial behavior in children with parental approval and a process of "value internalization," whereby children learn to value what they see valued by parents. Providing initial evidence on transmission of prosociality through role modeling of giving time resources, these findings raise questions as to how learning to give financial resources may be similar to or different from transmission of giving time. In a study specifically examining the transmission of financial giving across generation, researchers find a strong relationship between the religious giving of parents and the religious giving of their children as grown adults [8]. Based on developmental psychology studies, these researchers outline a number of mechanisms by which parents teach financial giving, finding that role modeling is effective in increasing giving in children.

Combined, these studies indicate that parental role modeling is an important part of the transmission of giving across generations. They also indicate remaining questions in need of study. For example, a thorough review of extant studies on parental teaching of prosocial behaviors finds that the majority of investigations are social psychological experiments [9]. They identify and outline a host of different mechanisms in these studies but also note that the experimental nature of this research imposes significant limitations. Experimental research can only measure the effects of these methods within the laboratory setting, which can be limited in its external validity, giving little indication of the actual extent of particular methods. In particular, scholars observe that these experiments did not use the child's actual parents when testing the aforementioned methods. They also observe that this experimental research cannot report on the prevalence with which these methods are used outside the laboratory, noting that laboratory-observed behaviors may not be practiced at home. It also remains unknown whether these methods transmit into adulthood prosocial behaviors.

This study contributes to extant knowledge on transmission of giving by examining data collected in natural settings. Based on calls for needed research in prior studies, this investigation links parental teaching of giving with data collected from the children of those parents. By using an interview format to gather data about religious and charitable giving from both parents and their children, this study reports on the prevalence of various teaching methods and analyzes the thoughts, feelings, and actual giving practices of both adult and youth congregation members. In a third contribution, the data provide a concurrent reflection by adults of how they learned to give, providing some insights into the long-term effects of parental teaching methods after transitioning into adulthood. In so doing, this study contributes a needed balance to experimental methods by providing qualitative, meaningful, relational, and life course data on transmitting religious giving.

2. Data and Methods

Data analyzed are from the Northern Indiana Congregation Study (NICS). NICS was a collaborative, mixed-methods research project that collected data in five phases, beginning in 2007 and concluding in 2009. The first phase consisted of phone surveys conducted with all congregations located in three mid-sized contiguous cities with a response rate of 98.9 percent ($n = 269$). Next, U.S. Census data was linked to the congregational survey data by postal codes. Third, in-person interviews were conducted with a stratified quota sample of youth ministers from these congregations ($n = 42$) [10]. The fourth phase entailed a continuation of the project via content analysis and participant observations with four religious congregations selected to represent each of four aggregated Christian denominational categories defined by as mainline Protestant, evangelical Protestant, black Protestant, and Catholic [11]. Religious worship services, youth groups, Bible studies, confirmation classes, Sunday schools, and other congregational meetings were observed throughout the course of a year. A total of 229 discrete events were observed with a total of 724 recorded pages in field notes in each of the congregations (EP: 83 events and 311 pages, MP: 62 events and 162 pages, BP: 13 events and 34 pages, CA: 71 events and 217 pages). Content analysis included online and printed materials.

The fifth phase of the study, upon which this investigation most heavily draws, consisted of additional in-person interviews with congregation members, youth participants, and parents of youth participants ($n = 233$) with a response rate of 87.6 percent. Youth participants were all adolescents and spanned the range between middle school or high school seniors. They were stratified quota sampled across a range of time involved in the youth group, frequency of attendance, perceived race and ethnicities, perceived socioeconomic status, and perceived engagement in youth activities. Parents were selected to match interviews with participating youth who were interviewed for this study.

Congregation members were selected from a list provided by each congregation in which individuals were categorized by their giving and participation levels.

The interviews lasted an average of an hour in length and were recorded and later transcribed for analysis. At the evangelical Protestant church, a total of 84 interviews were completed with an 89.4 percent response rate. Interviews were conducted with one pastor, one youth minister, two financial officers, 35 congregation members, 26 participating youth, and 19 parents of the participating youth. Interviews at the mainline Protestant church were conducted with a total of 70 respondents with a 90.9 percent response rate. The interviews consisted of one with the pastor, one with the youth minister, two with financial officers, 30 with congregation members, 23 with participating youth, and 13 with parents of participating youth. At the black Protestant church, a total of 20 interviews were completed with a 90.9 percent response rate. These interviews consisted of one youth minister, 12 participating youth, and 7 parents of participating youth.[1]

For this analysis, we focus especially on interview questions that asked parents how they taught their children about giving. Responses were organized into a typology of teaching methods and were coded for subsequent analysis. Parents were also coded as teaching children with low, medium, or high intensity, measured in terms of their described frequency for engaging in giving teaching with their children. The children of these parents were asked questions on their thoughts, feelings, and practices regarding religious and charitable financial giving. Their responses are categorized into most noted themes as described below. Congregation members were also asked a set of questions that investigated how they taught their children to give to the church and how the congregation members themselves learned to give. We draw in particular on these retrospective accounts of learning to give as a primary benefit of qualitative interviews that allow a life course perspective on giving as a dynamic process that unfolds over time. While recollection is not perfect, we give credit to their life course assessment.

3. Findings from Parent Interviews

In the following sections we report emergent themes from religiously involved adults and youth in-depth interviews on: the methods parents employ for teaching their children to give, youth thoughts and feelings about giving, and adult congregation participant reflections on learning to give. In this first section of results, findings from parent interviews revealed a variety of different methods employed in teaching their children to be givers, which are summarized below. In so doing, this paper offers an exploratory analysis of the meaningful categories that are operative across generations in everyday social settings and without the artificial controls of laboratory settings or with assumptions made across research studies investigating adults or youth but without parent-child links and among different people experiencing the same social context.

3.1. Modeling Giving

One of the prevalent methods for parents teaching their children to give was through modeling giving. Modeling giving was mainly discussed in terms of parental behaviors at Sunday services. As one parent described: "Every week, they see us go to church. They see us write out a check, put it in an envelope, and put it in the [plate]; so [we] model giving." Nearly one-half of all parents interviewed spoke about using this "teach by example" method, a notably high amount considering that modeling was not directly asked about during the interviews.

However, some caveats are important to mention. First, modeling seemed to be mentioned in some cases when parents may not have actually done anything intentional to teach about giving. For example, one parent stated, "They see us put money in the collection plate, but you know what, we are guilty of not really discussing that as they were growing up." Due to the social desirability of

---

[1] Catholic parish interviews were also conducted but are not included in this analysis due to a number of differences between the Catholic parish and the three Protestant parishes [12].

wanting to be both a generous person and a good parent who teaches children appropriately, it could be that asking parents directly about giving provoked parents to affirmatively describe themselves as having taught their children about giving and referred to indirect "osmosis" type approaches as their hope that prosocial giving messages were transmitting across generations. In summary, it seemed to us that some parents mentioned modeling through indirect example as an alternative to admitting that they had not done anything explicit to teach their children to give. This possibility is supported by the fact that none of the parent interviewees ever mentioned not teaching their children about giving to religious causes, even those parents who we knew from the congregation records were not actually givers themselves.

In addition, parents who described using modeling techniques for teaching their children about giving also often described not knowing whether their children actually took note of their giving behavior. For example, parents made statements such as, "I think they see me and my wife give;" "I guess [by] seeing examples from us [they may learn to give];" or "It's just kind of there for her [the chance to learn about giving] because it's always done." Statements such as these indicate that this initial modeling category is one that is often done passively and without conscious attention. Hence we separate it from the more specific and explicit approaches to giving described below. However, there were a few exceptional cases of parents who described it as a more intentional method of teaching giving. One parent explained, "They see it [giving]. Because every Sunday, they know we have envelopes," and this parent continues by saying, "They know this [giving] is an every Sunday thing."

It seems then that most parents who have not given a great deal of conscious thought to how to teach their children about giving employ an "osmosis" form of modeling, meaning they hope that children learn through absorption by being exposed to the giving behavior of parents. Some parents who took this "osmosis" form of modeling giving described it though as being intentional because they saw the regularity of the modeled behavior as an effective means of communicating its importance to their children. Nevertheless, the implicit aspect of this method distinguishes it from those that follow. In terms of prevalence, modeling occurred evenly across the congregations studied, and there were no noticeable differences in terms of gender or socioeconomic status.

3.2. Providing Money to Children to Give

The second teaching method identified here involves parents providing their children with money for the explicit purpose of donating it to the church or charity. One parent outlined the rationale behind this method, stating:

> I did it early on. This was before they had any of their own money, really. Just because they wanted to put something into the basket. And so I felt like that was a good [thing]. If the physical act of putting something in the basket were to help them understand the importance of providing that support, I thought it was a good exercise [13].

Here, the parent gives each child a dollar bill or loose change, with the aim of creating a habit that the child will eventually sustain with their own money.

A majority of respondents professed to employ this method with their children, though that is perhaps because interviewers asked directly about this method. This may have conveyed to parents that this is a desirable practice and provoked their mentioning something they would have otherwise forgotten or neglected to mention. However, the same would also be true in many forms of survey and experimental research, though the distribution of this method relative to other suggested methods may be different than what is found in this open-ended interview format.

Despite the fact that many parents mentioned this approach, few seemed to rely solely on this method for teaching their children to give. Parents who mentioned it often qualified that this was something they used to do in the past, saying, "When they were really little we did, but after that, no, we didn't" or "If they don't have it, we do give it to them." This provides evidence that parent methods for teaching about giving may be dynamic and changing over time in relation to child development stages. Parents may begin in early ages with giving their children money to donate and then move toward more explicit verbalized forms of teaching giving as their children develop the cognitive capacity for those discussions.

It is worth noting however that some parents we interviewed specifically mentioned not using this method for teaching about giving. For example, one parent explained, "My husband does that. I think it's unconscionable [for him to hand money out during church], but last week we were at church. We were at a different church on vacation, and he starts handing out money to them, like 'here's $2.' I'm like 'what are you doing!?'" Another parent articulated her dissatisfaction with this handout method:

> My husband would give each one of them a quarter. He goes, 'Ok, this is for your offering.' I'm just 'Ehhh.' It grated on me. It was just him giving them a quarter to put in the thing. There was no, there was nothing that they were doing at all [13].

Thus, a handful of parents—notably mothers in this case—specifically mentioned not liking this method for teaching about giving. This seemed to be for a variety of reasons that deserve further exploration, especially considering the gendered nature of the critique coming from wives disliking a behavior of their husbands.

While we only had a few instances of this critique, we explore each of the three critiques for indications of what in particular was seen to be a problematic aspect of the approach. In one case, it seemed to be about the visual attention on money, with the parent worried this would be seen as flaunting their money to others and having to endure embarrassment of showing their money to other congregants, even for the purpose of giving it away. In another case, it seemed that the dismay conveyed was rather that the dollar amounts were too small, that giving quarters was worse than giving nothing because it almost insulted the act of giving in amounts that were expected to be greater. In a third case it seemed that the critiquing parent desired the other parent to teach their child about giving in a way that was more explicit, akin to the approaches below.

Although given the insights from some parents regarding teaching about giving being dynamic over the life course, we wonder if the dismay over the other parent employing this method was more about a developmental mismatch, an embarrassment that one parent was employing a method perhaps more appropriate for early childhood while the other considered their children to be developmentally ready for more advanced methods.

Regardless, it was clear that some parents considered this to be an effective method of teaching giving, at least at developmentally appropriate stages. That a handful of parents critiqued the method, or perhaps the use of the method in isolation, and the gendered aspect of these critiques are areas worth investigating further in future studies. It is also notable that there was a considerable disparity between congregations with parents using this method. All but one parent at the mainline Protestant church mentioned using this method, while parents at the evangelical Protestant and black Protestant church were split evenly between those who did and those who did not provide their children with money for giving. This also indicates that a large proportion of parents across all these congregations employ this method and warrants its further study.

3.3. Handing Giving Envelopes to Children

Another method described in parent interviews seems to attempt to blend the previous two methods. When employing this method, parents hand an envelope that contains their own monetary offering to their children so that they can place it in the plate or basket for the parent. As is the case with the previous form of teaching giving, in this form of teaching the parent also models religious giving by actively bringing the giving act to the child's attention and gives the child an experience in sharing bodily in the giving act.

At the same time, parents employing this method sometimes described it as distinct from that of giving money directly to children for them to put into a collection (Section 3.2). For example, one parent's explanation of this method helps to illuminate the distinction from the previous method discussed:

> Okay, do we hand them our envelope to set in the plate? Yes. Do I give them money to put in the offering plate upstairs? No, I do not. I think that's a, because that's not the point of giving, if somebody, you need, it's first fruits. It's something that you've worked and you've labored for. So if you hand it to your child to throw in there, that's not teaching them anything [13].

Although parents rarely mentioned using this method, it is important to distinguish it from the one previously discussed because in the former method the children are performing the giving act using money they are directly holding and could perceive to be their own, especially among younger children. In distinction, this method of handing to a child an envelope containing money appeared to still bring the child in on the giving act while also making clearer that the parent was the one who labored for the money given, which appeared to be an important qualitative distinction for a handful of the interviewees as it corrected what they viewed to be problematic about the method described in Section 3.2.

3.4. Teaching to Give through Conversation

In distinction from the previous three methods, this method does not involve the giving act by either the parents or youth, and instead teaches giving by conversational means.[2] This category encompasses a wide variety of conversations that parents reported having with their children. Parents in this category may have explained the importance of giving, produced reasons for its practice, or discussed their child's own practice of financial giving. Using this coding scheme, approximately one-half of parent respondents employed this method.

Often this method is used to provide important information about giving that children might not otherwise glean from signals at church services, Sunday school, or youth group. For example, one parent stated, "[Parents] need to explain to [their children] why they are giving tithes so they have a better understanding of it. There are a lot of adults who don't know why you should tithe." Another parent agreed that while modeling may be helpful, oral training is imperative to learning how to give: "Explain to them what it is, yes. And money, period. How to be a good steward."

In a similar vein, parents also use oral communication to remind children of this part of their involvement in church and to keep these ideas at the forefront, especially as coupled with the modeling methods previously described. For example, one parent explained, "Every now and then I'll say, 'Do you realize there's $4 in this envelope this week?' Or whatever it is and I'll say, 'Doesn't that make you feel good that you're giving back?'" By periodically maintaining an explicit discussion about giving, parents use this method to verbalize lessons about giving that might not be conveyed any other way.

Teaching financial giving through conversation did not vary across denomination. However, of note is that this method appears to be a mostly upper-class phenomenon, as this method tended to be used by high-income households and by high givers. It is also notable that a gender difference was detected, with a majority of fathers reporting using this method and a minority of mothers reporting it, suggesting that fathers are more likely to teach giving orally to their children.

---

[2] That distinction being made, it is often the case that parents employing the previous methods also employ this method. The caveat regarding distinction is thus an analytical one and not of differences in lived practices.

3.5. Positive Reinforcement of Giving

Parents who used this method sought to solicit their children's continued giving by offering positive reinforcement in the form of praise or recognition on any occasion of their child's generosity. For example, one parent explained how she taught her son to tithe:

> It was really a neat moment because we went into the bank, and I showed him how to do the deposit slip, and then he got the $50 back and I told the teller "See, he is taking his tithe right off the top. And she thought that was so neat. And he didn't like [say] 'Mom would you shut up?' He just kind of smiled and was like 'Yeah that's what I'm doing.' And so he put it in his envelope the next day [13].

Given the simplicity of this method, it is notable that parents rarely reported using this method. However, it is possible that that is a method employed more often but not readily recognized by parents as one of the ways in which they teach their children to give, especially because interviewers did not specifically ask parents about this method. Alternatively, it could have been rarely reported because it requires youth having their own money to be able to give, which could be a later life developmental stage than the one at which many of these youth were in currently. Nevertheless, the fact that it was mentioned without being asked about indicates its importance as a meaningful category for at least some and warrants its investigation in future studies.

3.6. Encouraging, Expecting, or Forcing Giving

Another method employed by parents to teach giving involves parents making it known to their children that they would like them to contribute a portion of what money they receive to the church or charity. This is done with varying levels of influence, starting with parents who merely encouraged giving. For example, one parent explained, "We told him it would be nice if he would, and he did. Now is he regular about it? No. And do I sit there every week saying 'Now are you doing this?' I encourage, I don't force." Here, the outcome of whether or not the child gave is less important than the fact that the parent's wishes were explicitly made known.

An example of an elevated level of explicit expectation communication is this: "We have told him that when you get a paycheck, you need to take money out of that and set it aside to put in the church on Sunday, whether in Sunday school. That's part of what you should be doing." At further levels of encouragement, some parents ensure that their wishes are carried to fruition. One parent reported, "He gets an allowance, started an allowance at six or seven or whatever, and a portion of it went to immediate spending and a proportion of it went to the church."

Thus, while some of the parents in this category sought to encourage their children to give, others ensured their children acted upon their wishes. In terms of the proportion of parents employing this method, about half of the parents at the evangelical Protestant and black Protestant churches mentioned this method, while few parents at the mainline Protestant church mentioned using this method. Thus, it appears that strongly encouraging giving may have theological correlations. Additionally notable is this method is more prevalent among low-income parents.

3.7. Give-Save-Spend

A similar but more explicated way of teaching giving has analytical distinctions from the previous method, while also overlapping somewhat. Parents describe this method as an organized accounting system for teaching children giving. In this method a proportion of the child's money is given away, a proportion is saved, and the remaining amount is available to spend. Parents who cited this teaching style described it with notable similarity:

> They have three envelopes, when I pay them their money for the week, they have a give, a save, and a spend and they have to give ten percent and save ten percent and then they can spend the rest in the spending envelope [13].

> When they earn money, or when they receive money, you have certain jars where you have the money that you want to save; you have money that you want to spend and money that you want to give [13].

> When the kids were two [years old] they each got a bank that had different sections to it. And we started talking to them early that you give 10 percent to the Lord not because it is a magic number, not because it is a rule, but it is a good standard to live by. That you put, because they have no bills, 80 percent into savings, and they get to live off of 10 percent. We started that early with dollars and a dime goes here and a dime goes here and 80 cents goes here [13].

In terms of the prevalence of this method, there was a smaller proportion of parents utilizing this method than all those previously described. A minority of parents at the evangelical Protestant church mentioned using this method to teach giving to their children. Despite the small quantitative proportion of parents identifying this method, we find it to be substantively important because of the regularity in their descriptions of the method. This could be because of the teachings of a well-known financial advisor named Dave Ramsey, whose courses and teachings are familiar in evangelical Protestant churches. However, a similar proportion of parents at the mainline Protestant church also described using this method. Alternatively, none of the parents at the black Protestant church mentioned this method. Additionally of note in the proportional differences in the employment of this method are that it was most frequent among middle class parents and least frequent among high-income parents.

3.8. Emphasize Giving of Time

When asked about the avenues by which their children learn to give, some parents reported that they placed a greater importance on their children's giving of their time rather than their money. For example, one parent stated, "Oh, volunteering time, I push that more. Because the lack of financing, you know." One possible explanation of this method may be that some parents characterize time contributions as more valuable than financial contributions at this stage of the child's life, as they are not able to contribute substantial dollar amounts. Other parents indicated that a lesson on learning to give should address the equal contribution of both time and money. One parent stated, "But also it's not just about the money; giving is also about time. And I like to encourage that too." Another parent agrees, "I think it's important that they learn to give, and it should not only be giving of money but giving of yourself." In summary, in discussions regarding giving financially, one of the important methods that parents described was discussing money along with discussions of giving time. Two-thirds of all instances of this method occurred at the evangelical Protestant church. In addition, all but one instance of this method occurred in households with annual incomes above $60,000.

3.9. Emphasize Fiscal Responsibility

In a final but a rare method, some parents described incorporating teaching about financial giving within a broader education on fiscal responsibility. This was an outlier method that was only mentioned by four respondents, three at the evangelical Protestant church and one at the mainline Protestant church. All four of the respondents who mentioned this method had relatively high annual household incomes and had advanced degrees. For example, one parent described talking about tithing along with a discussion of tax deductions: "We talked about the tax implications too. Tax deduction. That's fine. There's nothing wrong with getting a tax deduction for donations to the church." Later, the same parent discussed another important lesson:

> Yeah, we talk a lot about living within your means, and we have a very rich uncle and it's kind of hard to be around them because sometimes it's embarrassing. I mean he's a lovely person. We love him dearly, but at Christmas we get showered with all these expensive

gifts, and we give them a picture frame or something. And so we just talk about that all the time. Things they might want at the grocery, and we don't just lavish them with anything and everything they want [13].

Despite being in relatively high income households, the parents in these money-conscious families teach their children about giving as part of a broader teaching about planning-oriented with money.

3.10. Diversified Parent Approaches

To summarize, some of the parental methods used to teach financial giving include modeling giving, providing money to children explicitly for giving, or handing children their offering envelope. Other parents talk with their children about giving to religious or charitable causes during which a variety of topics were discussed; still other parents offered positive reinforcement in the form of praise or recognition on the occasion of their child's generosity. Parents also mentioned encouraging, expecting, or even forcing their children to give a portion of their income to church or charity; some compelling their children to give by organizing a system where a set percentage of the child's income would be given away, a set percentage would be saved, and the remaining percentage would be available to spend. Other parents placed greater importance on their children giving time. Lastly, parents also mentioned incorporating a lesson on giving into a larger framework of fiscal responsibility.

Further examination of the data indicates that the methods outlined above could be further categorized into methods of modeling (Sections 3.1–3.3), methods of talking (Sections 3.4 and 3.5), or methods of directing (Sections 3.6–3.8). Parental modeling of giving at church services, provision of money to children for giving, or the giving of offertory envelopes to children all share a common thread in that they provide youth with a portrait of generosity that they may emulate. Talking to youth about giving or offering positive reinforcement on the occasion of youth generosity both teach giving through conversational means. When parents emphasize the giving of time rather than the giving of money, stress fiscal responsibility, or encourage, expect, or force their children to give through the Give-Save-Spend model, they actively direct their children toward a desired end.

3.10.1. Modeling Methods

While neither socioeconomic status nor gender were related to the prevalence of methods of modeling, the congregations varied in the use of modeling methods. All but one parent at the mainline Protestant church mentioned using at least one modeling method, and nearly one-half used two. While slightly less common at the black Protestant church, the vast majority of parents cited using at least one modeling method. Parents at the evangelical Protestant church relied on modeling the least to teach their children giving, as evidenced by the significant minority of parents who did not use a modeling method at all. Overall, modeling methods were most pervasively used across all denominations, incomes, and giving categories. Use of these methods was polarized across income, with high incidence in both low income and high-income households and reduced occurrence in middle-income households.

3.10.2. Talking Methods

The use of talking methods was uniformly spread across congregations with about half of all parents teaching giving to their children via conversational means. Fathers, however, were much more likely to mention these methods than mothers; the vast majority of fathers interviewed reported use of a talking method, while mothers were evenly split on its use. In addition, when socioeconomic status of the parent was taken into account, the data reveals a potential positive relationship between socioeconomic status and the incidence of talking methods.

3.10.3. Directing Methods

Methods that relied on an active effort of parents to encourage or enforce a certain goal were more common at the evangelical Protestant and black Protestant churches, with a significant minority of evangelical Protestant parents claiming to use more than one of these methods. These methods were uncommon at the mainline Protestant church, where the vast majority of parents did not mention that they used any of the four directing methods described above. Use of these methods was inversely related to percent of income given, with a majority of low-income households reporting use of at least one of these methods. These methods were also more popular among mothers; about half of mothers claimed to use at least one of these methods, while a minority of fathers did.

Thus, while fathers are more likely to approach the topic of giving with their children conversationally, mothers tend to make their specific wishes directly known to their children and more actively push them toward that goal. In addition, the mainline Protestant parishioners appear to have taken a more passive or indirect route to teaching their children to give, relying on modeling methods, especially providing youth with money to give, while imposing few demands or requirements on youth. The evangelical Protestant and black Protestant churches rely on these methods less, opting instead to focus on the more active methods that require parental involvement in the personal lives and finances of their children. Mainline Protestant parents also tended to implement less parental teaching methods overall, seemingly relying more on the church or other sources to teach their children.

3.10.4. A "Diversified Portfolio"

Another key finding is that parents who reported regularly teaching their children about giving employed multiple of the above methods. The most common methods employed were (a) Give-Save-Spend; (b) modeling giving for their children; (c) providing their children money for giving; and (d) talking to their children about giving. Notable is that of those parents who regularly taught giving to their children, a large majority employed three or more of the teaching methods. While all of these regular giving teaching parents employed at least one "directing" method, they also typically coupled it with modeling or talking methods, or all three forms. In fact it was only among those parents who did not mention regularly teaching about giving that we found reliance on a singular method. Thus, it seems that among these religious interviewees, the norm is to have a "diversified portfolio" of giving teaching methods.

Parents with diversified portfolios of teaching methods were commonly among the most frequent church attendees, attending church services weekly or more. Similarly, parents who employed few methods were marked by infrequent church attendance. One may expect that higher income parents would teach giving to their children with greater intensity, but analysis of the data indicates a counter-intuitive relationship with income. The highest concentration of parents who employed only one teaching method was found in the high-income category, and prevalence of "one method users" increased with rising income levels. Thus, middle-income and frequent religious attenders were those who relied most upon a diversified portfolio for giving, and these were also the same parents who reported that they regularly taught their children to give.

4. Findings from Youth Interviews

After having presented the analysis of parental giving methods, the next logical question is how these giving methods transmit to their children. To begin to assess this question, we first categorized major themes from the youth interviews in response to our asking their thoughts and feelings about religious giving. As is shown in the results below, the most evident theme in youth interviews was their general inarticulateness, seeming disinterest, and confusion on the topic of giving. It is notable that youth were articulate about other matters in the interviews, and thus the difference in their giving responses implied it was that topic in particular upon which they had not had many discussions or thoughts prior to our interview.

4.1. Limited Responses: One-Word Answers

One of the common trends that emerged in discussions with youth about religious financial giving is a tendency to respond with one-word answers, possibly to avoid or skip over the portion of the interview dedicated to religious financial giving. The following interview is an example:

I: How do you feel about giving money away? Or donating money to church or to charity? Do you think that people should do it or it doesn't matter?
R: It doesn't matter.
I: Ok. Have you ever given money away?
R: Yeah.
I: You do? Ok. Who did you give money away to?
R: Umm, to the church.
I: Ok. Like in the [offering] plate?
R: Yeah.
I: Ok, and what about your parents? Do they give money too?
R: Yep [13].

As this interview exemplifies, many of the youth we talked with about giving answered our questions with a series of monosyllabic responses. The interviewee does not appear to have substantive opinions or formalized ideas on the topic of giving. Another example of this follows:

I: Do you think giving money to charity is something we should do?
R: Yeah.
I: How about giving money to the church?
R: That's good too.
I: Do you currently give any money away to the church or charity?
R: Yep.
I: To charity or to church?
R: Church.
I: Do you know if it's something your parents do?
R: Yep.
I: They do?
R: Yeah, they give money on Sunday [13].

Approximately one third of all youth interviewed had responses that we coded under this limited response, one-word answer theme. The limited responses were numerous, and thus we also coded into a second category of responses that—while still limited—evidenced some rudimentary understanding of giving that expanded upon the one-word responses of this theme.

4.2. Limited Responses: Rudimentary Understandings

The second category of limited responses contains those that went beyond one-word responses in rudimentary understandings of giving. Following is an example of this type of response:

I: Now how do you feel about giving money away or donating money to your church or any other charity? How do you feel about that?
R: I feel good about it.
I: You feel good? You think people should do that, or no?
R: Yeah, I think people should do that.
I: Why?
R: Like, it'll help other people; it'll help the church.

I: Now what about donating money to the church? Tithing?

R: Yeah, so that they can like, help others and...[trails off].

I: So you think that's good too.

R: Yes [13].

About one third of all youth interviewed were coded into this rudimentary explanation category due to their explanations being similar to the quotes above. That is, the responses in this category shared in common that they went beyond the one-word responses of the first category but still did not evidence many thoughts, feelings, or interests in giving other than simple statements, such as: "if people need help, they should help" or "if it's for a good cause I think it's a good thing." The responses in this category also differed from a third type of limited response: confused answers.

4.3. Limited Responses: Confused Answers

In a third version of limited responses, youth talked at greater length than the one-word or rudimentary understanding responses. However, the meaning of in their more extended responses was unclear. We code this is a limited response because the meaning it conveys is limited, and our interpretation was that this limited meaning reflected limited respondent understanding. As an example of the type of responses in this category, here is one youth interview exchange:

I: How do you feel about giving money away or giving money to church or charity? What do you feel about that?

R: I feel like I'm doing something right and I need to do it because maybe I'm not in that person's situation. And I seen so much that I've gone down in the world and people need it. Well, you know, I'll give them what I think I should give. I haven't just stuck up.

I: How do you feel about giving money away or donating money to church or charity?

R: I'll think of, I'm giving money to a charity of people that they don't have any food or anything. So I would just give money to people that have charity that are charity and stuff [13].

This is an example of a limited response that is more elaborated in terms of word count, but which conveys a somewhat jumbled and limited sense of what giving is, why one does it, and what—if any—interest the respondent has in giving. These confused efforts to convey specific thoughts on financial giving suggest that this may be the first time these youth have thought about these topics, or at least that may be the first attempt to discuss giving and verbalize giving without parent input.

4.4. Feeling Responses

Another version of a somewhat limited response type is one that is differentiated in terms of an emphasis of feelings about giving, or views as it being something that feels good to do. For example, in response to our questions about giving, youth typically said something along the lines of: "I feel good about it;" "I think it's good;" "I don't have a problem with it." Here is an additional example of the type of responses in this category within their interview context:

I: How do you feel about giving money away or donating money to church or charity?

R: I feel good.

I: You feel good about it. Do you think it's something people should do?

R: Yes, because it's for a good cause its not like it is for a bad cause or anything.

I: How do you feel about giving money away or donating money to charity or the church?

R: I feel good because it goes to a special need.

I: Do you think it's something people should do or not?

R: Should [do].

I: They should do it?

R: Uh-huh [yes] [13].

Nearly a third of responses were coded as having this feeling response regarding giving as a "feel-good" activity in which to engage. Beyond these more basic categories of responses, the only response category that evidenced a greater level of interest, cognitive engagement, or articulateness about giving were the hypothetical responses described next.

4.5. Hypothetical Responses

While the trend overall in the youth interviews was one of general inarticulateness or fairly basic understanding of giving, there was a final group of responses that were comparatively articulate. In this category of respondents, youth communicate their opinions and practices concerning financial giving clearly and with substance beyond a rudimentary understanding or basic view: That giving is a good thing to do. However, these responses still do not evidence whether youth actually engage in giving with any regularity, as they discussed giving in hypothetical terms. In examples of this response type, youth discussed giving in a way that sounded like they were interested and had regular involvement in giving. Yet when they provided examples, it sounded as if their giving had only happened one time or episodically. Thus, on one level they could engage in hypothetically discussing giving, but on another level it was an activity in which they had only engage once or twice.

For example, one interviewee said, "Once I was at the store and I donated money to other groups that, like praise dancing groups, and churches." Another respondent reported giving, but when asked where he contributes money, the respondent reported that his giving consisted of buying pizza from a concession stand that donated a portion of its profits to the church:

> I: Do you currently give any money away?
> R: Yeah, I give some.
> I: Okay, what do you give it to?
> R: Like (church name), they have the bank that helps (church name) out when you buy something.
> I: Oh yeah, is it a percentage or something?
> R: No, it's like the concession stand, but.
> I: Oh, the pizza.
> R: Yeah, and all that. That helps go towards it, and you get something in return so [13].

In many other cases within this category, responses indicated that youth were imagining what they should or could do in giving, as opposed to what they actually do. This occurred when youth described their giving habits in terms of hypothetical giving situations, or used if-statements to describe situations that seemed rare but could potentially happen or had at some point in the past. Youth in this category reported, "If I'm at the store and a person asks me for a dollar, I'm like 'here you can have a dollar'" or "If I go to the movies, there's a thing to donate to a charity for cancer, and it's like two dollars. I'll donate to that." Respondents also called their responses examples:

> Like say if, for example, somebody's out on the street, and they're standing there with a sign that they want money. I wouldn't give them money; I probably would go and buy them something instead, so I know that the money is going to something good instead of to drugs or something instead [13].

This example does not sound to us as though it happened, but rather is an example of what would be an acceptable response to not wanting to give money to a homeless person in case it is not used for the giver-intended purposes. However, there is no indication that the youth describing this has engaged in buying something instead or had a dialog with this possible giving recipient.

Though there were not as many responses in this category as the above categories, the instances of this kind of response were nevertheless substantively notable. Of interest in these responses is that many youth appeared to want to respond to our questions as if they were givers, despite apparently not participating in giving with any regularity. Perhaps members of this group may have desired to present examples of rare or hypothetical giving scenarios in an effort to appear generous. In other words, the only cases in which interviewed youth displayed more thoughtful, cognitively engaged, interested responses on giving is when they appeared to be rationalizing their limited participation in it by performing hypothetically to a socially desired expectation.

4.6. Articulateness and Thoughtfulness on Other Matters

Thus far, we have reported an overall trend for youth to be relatively inarticulate about giving, not obviously evidencing thoughtfulness or interest in giving. This raises questions as to whether the youth in this study were simply too young to be articulate or thoughtful at all, with giving talk being one example of a broader trend. However, we found youth to be capable of speaking at length or in greater detail across a number of complex topics. For example, when asked about his favorite part of church services, one youth provided the following thoughtful answer:

> I think the time with children, because I think it's more personal for the kids. Like if you're three or four [years old], a sermon is not going to mean a lot to you. You're just going to be like, "Uh, why are we still here?" And you'll obviously be bored because you don't have a really long attention span, but then it makes it more personal for the pastor or the youth leader or whoever's teaching it to get to know the kids. I think the kids like it because they're like, "Wow, I'm appreciated, and I get this entire thing for me" [13].

In asking a different youth interviewee about religious beliefs, we also found thoughtful responses:

> I: Can you tell me more about your religious beliefs? What are some of the things that you believe religiously?
> R: I basically believe in the doctrine that (church name) has, which is: we believe in the three and one, that God the father, God the son, God the Holy Spirit. Everything, all the Ten Commandments, obviously. I believe that there is eternal life for those that come to know Christ, and that it's not by—we can't get to heaven by ourselves. It's through God that we can. It's grace that gets us there and what we can do.
> I: What is God like to you?
> R: God is someone that loves me and cares about me. Someone that is, people can be wrong, but God cannot be wrong.
> I: Do you feel close to God? How close do you feel to God?
> R: I feel fairly close. I mean it's sometimes difficult because we get so caught up in every other thing—everyday life. Sometimes there's problems, but through all of it I feel pretty close.
> I: And who or what is Jesus?
> R: Jesus is our Lord and Savior [13].

Additionally, there were a handful of youth interviewees who were fairly articulate about giving:

> I: How do you feel about giving money away or donating money to a church or charity? Do you think that's something people should do or not?
> R: I think it's one of those things where it depends on who it is. Like, some people are, you know, willing with their money. I think that people who aren't, it's all within their own personal journey. Like, how that applies.
> I: Do you personally donate money to church or charity, or do you know if your parents do?
> R: Whenever I have money, or a job or whatever, I do tithe. You know, like 10 percent of your wages kind of thing. And I know my parents are very strong believers in that concept [13].

Thus, combined these responses evidence that interviewed youth were able to be articulate about a range of matters, including abstract beliefs and church activities. However, when it came to talking about giving for the majority of these youth, these articulate cases were the rare exception.

5. Findings from Linking Parent and Youth Responses

In this section we consider the parent and youth responses together. We began with finding a total of nine methods that parents employ for teaching about giving, ranging from minimal engagement to high levels of direct engagement in teaching giving. However, in the youth interviews, we find five typical categories of responses. Four of these were fairly limited or confused responses, and one was that giving was generally a "feel-good" activity. That left one set of youth responses that relayed more thoughtfulness and articulation about giving, but through what sounded like hypothetical approaches they could take to giving rather than acts in which they actually regularly engage.

This identifies a disconnect between the two interview sets: the parent interviews leave the impression that these religious parents are highly involved in teaching their children about giving, but the youth interviews give the impression that they have learned little about giving, or at least are not that accustomed to talking about it. To more fully investigate this phenomenon, we here link the parent interviews with the interviews from their own children. Unlike in other studies that investigate parents or youth independently, this study enabled a direct connection between interviews. We thus here summarize the findings gleaned from parent-youth pairing, a matching of the method employed by the parent and the thoughts and feelings expressed by their child.

We began these analyses with the expectation that articulate youth responses would be more common among the children of parents who reported regular teaching about giving and using a diverse portfolio of methods for transmitting giving to their offspring. However, we find counter-intuitively that the limited, rather inarticulate youth responses were the norm across all method types, including parents who employed a diverse portfolio of methods regularly. For example, one parent interview served on the finance committee at the mainline Protestant church and reported using four of the above methods to teach giving. The following is an excerpt from this interview regarding teaching children to give:

> I: How important is it that he [your child] learns about giving to the church?
> R: Very important. I've been trying to do that for several years now to get him to understand it.
> I: So you started when he was pretty young?
> R: He gets an allowance, started an allowance at six or seven, or whatever, and a portion of it went to immediate spending and a proportion of it went to the church.
> I: So do you feel that giving to the church is important to his faith life?
> R: Yes [13].

Despite this parent describing teaching his child to give since an early age, his son displayed the same limited and inarticulate responses about giving as children of parents with less giving focus:

> I: How do you feel about donating or giving money away to church or charity?
> R: If it's going to what you give it for, sure.
> I: Sure, fine?
> R: Yeah.
> I: Do you think it's something people should do?
> R: Only for the right causes.
> I: Do you currently give any money away?
> R: Not now [13].

Thus, despite this parent employing a Give-Save-Spend method for giving and reporting regularly teaching about giving since a young age, the child of this parent was coded among the limited responses that elaborated beyond one-word answers but still evidenced limited understanding of or ability to articulate a commitment to or interest in giving. Taken at face value, this could be interpreted as indicating that nearly all interviewed parents were unsuccessful in transmitting giving to their children, despite the method employed or the regularity of giving teaching. However, others of our findings indicate that this is not necessarily the case. Next we summarize insights gained from our congregation member interviews, including those with parents, as givers reflected retrospectively upon how they had learned to give.

6. Findings from Parent Reflections on Learning to Give

In one third of both the parent and congregational involvement interviews, when asked to speak about how they learned to give money, interviewees indicated that their own habits of sustained giving did not emerge until later in life, after they had transitioned from adolescence into adulthood. Addressing how she learned to give, one woman reported "My parents [gave to the church]. I never did. When I was a teenager, you know, my money was mine and I was pretty self absorbed." Adults often referenced how they learned to give as a gradual process, something that grew along with their life course development. One adult interviewee reported:

> It was gradually over a time. My perspective on it changed, but it changed as a result of preaching. We have to be taught that as we learn about God, adults begin to talk, but God is the one that does the teaching. When we learn that God is able to provide for us in the midst of everything, then we're more apt to trust him. And it's a matter of trust. That's what giving is: it's a matter of trust [13].

This account indicates that it would be possible for this same interviewee to have sounded inarticulate and disinterested had we interviewed him when he was a youth. Yet that did not indicate that giving methods were unsuccessfully transmitting giving practices to him. Instead, he recounts that his giving practices were realizing through a gradual process that actualized across the life course.

It is also notable that many adult congregants specifically mentioned having been taught to give by their parents. One example of the kind of exchange that demonstrated this follows:

> I: How did you learn about giving to the church?
> R: I just grew up with that. I mean that was just part of growing up.
> I: So was there an age where you just realized the importance of it?
> R: I'm sure when I was young I had all those things where you learned about giving to the church and how important that was. I would probably say when you become an adult or when you start working and you start giving your actual money to the church it changes the meaning and makes it more important to you, more special. That's because it is your money, not your parents' [13].

From interview accounts such as these, we learned that giving seemed to develop gradually across the life course, upon a bedrock of parental teaching in childhood. Moreover, many regular attenders describe a gradual internalizing of their church calls to give. For example, the following exchange represents a similar explanation relayed to us by many regular attenders:

> I: How did you learn about giving to the church?
> R: Through biblical teaching. When I went to church as a kid I knew that the collection basket came around and I would put my little [offering] in there, but I didn't really understand the concept of tithing.
> I: At what age did you realize the importance of giving?

R: It wasn't a one age. It was gradual. As a young adult going to church I would give...but I really didn't understand the concept. And it gradually revealed itself to the point where it is effortless. And if I could give more I would because I understand the importance of it. But that was a process. I am 40 years old [13].

Across the range of questions we asked about giving, congregant accounts of learning to give revealed a complex interaction of factors. For many, it seemed the "recipe" was first being taught to give by parents and later having parental giving messages reinforced in other contexts. It seemed to us that hearing calls to give in religious congregations as adults seemed to activate dormant parental socialization on the importance of giving. First came the teaching, then a gradual internalization, and then a trigger or exposure to calls to give as an adult activated underlying mechanisms.

Based on these adult giving reflections, generous behavior can be understood from a life course perspective. Such a view contextualizes the youth responses as merely a snapshot of young American Christians at an early stage in their journey of religious giving. According to these giver recollections, parental teaching about giving appears to not necessarily result in immediate returns but rather lays a foundation of giving-related ideas and practices that individuals activate and draw upon later in life. As these young believers increase in age, income, faith, and understanding, it is reasonable to expect that they will grow into the giving mentalities that their parents have developed for themselves, or at least that they will learn to give more generously than those peers who were never taught by their parents. Thus, this analysis indicates that giving as an adult is frequently related to both having learned about giving from parents as a child, and having a gradual process of internalizing calls to give that is activated into giving activities as an adult, often by exposure to regular calls to give.

7. Discussion and Implications

Given that prior research found parents to be a key factor in prosocial and giving behaviors, this study examined intergenerational transmission of financial giving. We investigated parental methods for teaching their children to give, youth thoughts and feelings about giving, and then linked parental methods to youth responses. We also investigated adult reflections on how they learned to give. Examining the methods that parents use in teaching their children about giving revealed many had a "diversified portfolio." Linking the parent methods responses to youth responses, and informing these by congregant reflections on learning to give, revealed that learning to give may be a dynamic process that unfolds gradually across the life course. These interviews also indicated the importance of extra-familial transmission of giving, such as through hearing religious calls to give in religious participation during adulthood.

7.1. A Diversified Portfolio of Parental Methods

One of the primary contributions of this in-depth analysis of parental giving methods is revealing that many parents who reported that they are regular teachers of giving with their children employed three or more of the nine methods described in this study. This diverse portfolio approach to giving methods was highest among the most regular religious attenders, which indicates that there may be a relationship between participating regularly in religious practices and regularly teaching about giving practices through a range of approaches. Since this is an emergent theme that was discovered in the process of conducting this study and its analyses, it is one that is in need of further investigation. To our knowledge, no other study has revealed this and perhaps could not through typical approaches.

For instance, future studies could investigate the prevalence of multiple methods in broader samples through large sample survey research that provides respondents with a "check all that apply" option for their giving methods, rather than providing mutually exclusive response options. The number of methods employed could be a constructed measure from this question that would be available to investigate via inferential statistics controlling for correlated factors. Additionally, longitudinal studies could track the giving behaviors of children socialized in a diverse portfolio of methods to investigate whether their later life giving frequency or amounts were greater than those socialized with single-method approaches.

7.2. Learning to Give as a Life Course Process

Unless something has dramatically changed across generations among parents regularly involving their children in religious and giving activities, comparing the results of the youth-parent linked interviews to the results of the later life congregant interviews reveals something important about learning to give. Most the youth were fairly inarticulate in their accounts of giving and gave the appearance of being uninterested. However, their more senior counterparts were articulate and thoughtful about their giving. Moreover, later life congregants described learning to give as an unfolding process. Many referenced having been taught to give by their parents during their childhood as an important factor explaining why they currently give. However, many also qualified that these parental lessons did not trigger immediately but rather activated later in life as an adult. This implies that parental giving teaching in childhood is an important factor even if it is not immediately evidenced in youth articulations about or conveyed interest in giving.

In other words, an approach not taking this in-depth account could mistakenly assume that transmission of giving activities from parent to child is only evidenced if youth give within a short duration relative to their having been taught to give, or are able to articulate thoughtful reasons why they do or will give that reflect the learning they acquired. For example, an experimental study could invite parents to teach their children about giving and then study for one year whether there were increases in youth giving explanations. However, the implications of this study are that the results of that approach would not yield an accurate representation of a foundation that may have been laid for later adulthood. The in-depth approach of this study gives credit to the dynamic processes of giving across the life course and reveals that early teaching of giving may be an important condition for giving, even if it is not manifested and detectable until later in life course.

7.3. Extra-Familial Calls to Give

We would be remiss if we did not mention that parents are not the only socializing agent of religious giving. A number of extra-parental mechanisms were mentioned as to how children learn to give to church or charity, notably religious calls to give heard in congregations. These extra-parental methods may help to explain why the parents of some congregations favor some methods over others. For example, a majority of mainline Protestant parents mentioned that their child gets messages about giving at church, youth group, or Sunday school, while a minority of evangelical Protestant parents said this. However, a number of evangelical Protestant parents mentioned that people other than themselves model giving for their children. This suggests that parents at the mainline Protestant congregation may have more organizational support for giving socialization, while parents at the evangelical Protestant congregation may have more interpersonal support for giving socialization.

7.4. Limitations and Future Research

While this study reveals interesting findings not typically acquired through other methods, it also has its limitations. First, all interviewees were selected through congregation lists and are therefore regular-enough attenders to be on these lists, potentially resulting in a number of unmeasured self-selection effects. However, these same self-selection effects are present in all congregational-based studies and therefore offer comparable findings to those extant approaches. Second, the sample is drawn from one location and could be replicated in a larger and nationally representative study. Third, while these data contribute insights on life course developmental processes of giving, they are not longitudinal. There is thus no direct evidence of the gradual emergence of giving that respondents describe. Nevertheless, we here credit the respondents as being relatively accurate reporters of their life experiences and think it is a primary contribution of this study to detect such life course dynamics that may be missed in conventional approaches.

While this paper identifies and assesses the prevalence of a typology of parental methods used to teach giving, future research should measure the effects of the various teaching methods over time. Longitudinal research could effectively evaluate the implications raised through this cross-sectional research on what characterizes successful parental teaching by tracking the methods employed across generations and the success of these methods to elicit financial contributions. Thus, it will be important for future studies to examine early-life teachings and later-life triggers in further depth. Nonetheless, this analysis allowed the connection of parent and children reported thoughts and feelings about the topic of financial giving and shows that parental methods for teaching giving should be studied more thoroughly, especially by indicating that the particular method for teaching religious financial giving may not be nearly as important as teaching through a variety of methods. It also points to the idea that parental teaching of giving may be nearly a necessary, though potentially not sufficient, condition for children growing up to become givers.

Additionally, future research could investigate whether the methods of teaching described here can be investigated in broader categories of modeling, talking, and directing. For example, survey research could ask about each of these three methods in separate questions, with each of the subsection methods offered as multiple-selection response options. Intergenerational transmission of giving could also be studied among non-religious attendees in a similar approach to this study. Likewise, intergenerational transmission dynamics could be studied in terms of how they vary by gender or by family configurations. Finally, another potential approach would be to pair the explanations for giving identified in interviews with parents and youth on to social psychological motivations, such as altruism, duty and responsibility, guilt, social recognition, social shame, negative state-relief, reciprocity, and adverse arousal reduction.

8. Conclusions

In conclusion, this study investigated intergenerational transmission of religious giving. Interviews with religiously involved parents revealed their use of nine methods for teaching children about giving, with most employing a "diversified portfolio" which mixes three or more methods for teaching about giving. However, youth interviews indicated a general inarticulateness, confusion, and disinterest in giving, even among those whose parents taught regularly about giving. Yet retrospective congregant interviews from later in the life course report that learning to give was a gradual process that unfolded over time. In many cases, it seemed that giving later in life was shaped by parental teachings about giving in younger years, which were activated or supported in adulthood religious participation.

Acknowledgments: The authors are grateful to Christian Smith, Mary Ellen Konieczny, Katie Spencer, Carlos Tavares, Peter Mundey, Brandon Vaidyanathan, Robbee Wedow, and Kaitlyn Conway for their contributions to the project or for insights on prior drafts of the paper.

Author Contributions: Patricia Snell Herzog was the Principal Investigator for the project, supervised all data collection, conducted interviews, reviewed analyses, and co-authored the paper. Scott Mitchell conducted participant observations, analyzed the qualitative data in these analyses, and co-authored the paper.

Conflicts of Interest: The authors declare no conflict of interest.

Abbreviations

The following abbreviations are used in this manuscript:

NICS   Northern Indiana Congregation Study
I   Interviewer
R   Respondent

References

1.   Adam Davis, ed. *Hearing the Call Across Traditions.* Woodstock: Skylight Paths Publishing, 2009.
2.   Stephen R. Warner, and Judith G. Wittner. *Gatherings in Diaspora: Religious Communities and the New Immigration.* Philadelphia: Temple University Press, 1998.

3. Christian Smith, and Patricia Snell. *Souls in Transition: The Religious and Spiritual Lives of Emerging Adults.* New York: Oxford University Press, 2009.
4. Robert Wuthnow. *After the Baby Boomers: How Twenty- and Thirty-Somethings Are Shaping the Future of American Religion.* Princeton: Princeton University Press, 2010.
5. Tom Smith. "Generation Gaps in Attitudes and Values from the 1970s to the 1990s." In *On the Frontier of Adulthood: Theory, Research, and Public Policy.* Edited by Richard A. Settersten, Jr., Frank F. Furstenberg and Rubén G. Rumbaut. Chicago: University of Chicago Press, 2005, pp. 177–224.
6. Christian Smith, Michael O. Emerson, and Patricia Snell. *Passing the Plate: Why American Christians Don't Give Away More Money.* New York: Oxford University Press, 2008.
7. Rene Bekkers. "Intergenerational Transmission of Volunteering." *Acta Sociologica* 50 (2007): 99–114. [CrossRef]
8. Mark O. Wilhelm, Eleanor Brown, Patrick M. Rooney, and Richard Steinberg. "The Intergenerational Transmission of Generosity." *Journal of Public Economics* 92 (2008): 2146–56. [CrossRef] [PubMed]
9. Steinberg Richard, and Mark O. Wilhelm. "Giving: The Next Generation—Parental Effects on Donations." Working Paper No. CPNS 21, The Centre of Philanthropy and Nonprofit Studies, Queensland University of Technology, Brisbane, Australia, 2003.
10. Patricia Snell, Christian Smith, Carlos Tavares, and Kari Christoffersen. "Denominational Differences in Congregational Youth Ministry Programming and Empirical Evidence of Systematic Non-Response Biases in Surveys." *Review of Religious Research* 51 (2009): 21–38.
11. Brian Steensland, Jerry Z. Park, Mark D. Regnerus, Lynn D. Robinson, Brad Wilcox, and Robert D. Woodberry. "The Measure of American Religion: Toward Improving the State of the Art." *Social Forces* 79 (2000): 291–318.
12. Patricia Snell Herzog, and Brandon Vaidyanathan. "Conflict & Community: Twin Tensions in Becoming a Multiethnic Congregation." *Review of Religious Research* 57 (2015): 507–29. [CrossRef]
13. NICS interviews (Principal Investigator: Patricia Snell Herzog), interviews conducted May–August 2008.

![religions logo] **religions**

MDPI

Editorial

Multidimensional Perspectives on the Faith and Giving of Youth and Emerging Adults

Patricia Snell Herzog

Department of Sociology & Criminal Justice, University of Arkansas, 218 Old Main Building, Fayetteville, AR 72701, USA; herzog@uark.edu

Received: 6 July 2017; Accepted: 12 July 2017; Published: 15 July 2017

Keywords: youth; emerging adults; faith; generosity; giving; volunteering; organizational participation

1. Introduction

This volume includes eight studies of faith and giving for youth and emerging adults. Combined, we find organizational, cultural, institutional, educational, informal, familial, and developmental influences on the shape and contours of youth and emerging adult faith and giving. These studies provide some challenges to popular interpretations of Millennials, and to the ways researchers typically study religiosity and charitable giving. Accounting for the greater demographic and cultural diversity of Millennials may require changes to interpretations of young people by religious and spiritual leaders, parents, and scholars.

2. Youth and Emerging Adult Religiosity, Organizationally

In the first chapter of this volume, Williams, Irby, and Warner identify a paradox: "while (religious) attendance tends to decrease in adolescence and college, youth themselves often report that religious beliefs remain important and sometimes even increase during this period" (Williams et al. 2016, p. 1). To better understand youth faith and religiosity, this study investigated the characteristics of organizational participation for a group of college-age young people in Chicago, Illinois. Beneath the veneer of a millennial style that is ubiquitous, homogenous, and entirely individualized in its approach to faith and religiosity, these scholars instead find distinct styles. They focus on two subcultures: black young adults and white young adults, both within the religious context of their respective congregations. The organizational practices within the mostly white congregation in the study was to focus on the generational gap, to highlight the distinction between youth and their elders. Youth participated in youth-specific events and activities that functioned as an nearly distinct organization within the congregation. For the older congregants, there was fear about losing young people, and the idea was to provide youth with youth-specific activities as the way to minister to them, entrenching the view of youth as a different generation with separate needs. In contrast, the mostly black congregation had an integrationist approach to youth participation. Even amidst the youth-focused gatherings, the older congregants were present and engaged. Youth aided in the planning of the events but did not entirely run them on their own. Instead, the focus was on youth showing to the older congregants their mastery of religious content, as a way of displaying their growing maturity as full and equal congregants in the church.

Turning to the "organizational biographies" of participating youth, another distinction is revealed. Many of the white youth talked about religion as providing them with a needed service, gaining them useful skills and experiences. That orientation is most akin to the overall understanding of youth religiosity, that it is highly individualistic. Moreover, many of the white youth voiced skepticism of religion and sought to separate their authentic spirituality from the church as an institution, which could be viewed as irrelevant, suspect, or a hindrance to personal faith. While black youth also stressed that they had a choice in their religious participation, they instead more often referred to the church as a family, implying that being involved was not completely voluntary since youth have obligations to their relations. Viewing the church more as a community than an organization, the black youth did not highlight what they received by participating nor did they describe themselves as separated from the religious institution, which they viewed with less suspicion and as more integral to their identity than did the white youth.

Though the sample for this study is small and geographically situated within a particular Midwestern and urban context, the findings reveal patterns that could be analytically generalizable. Perhaps some of the trends attributed to Millennials as a whole are actually more characteristic of the white majority that comprises statistical patterns that are not disaggregated by race and other subcultural statuses. For a notable group of young people in this study, at least, religion does not seem to be becoming individualized. As identified in the introduction, this study indicates a non-linear pattern to religiosity that requires in-depth investigating to understand. Religiosity is not unilaterally declining in its significance for all these young people. Many white youth remain engaged as a form of organizational participation, and many black youth are growing further engaged as an expression of personal and community identity.

One implication of this study is that separating youth away from the primary congregation, or in other ways highlighting separation across generations, may be counter-productive. This study did not investigate whether implementing the style of one congregation within a different religious context would cause changes. However, the findings raise questions as to whether the segregated approach of the white congregations was undermining the ongoing relevance of the church among its youth. It would be wise for religious and spiritual leaders to give pause in considering whether a more integrated approach better facilitates the intergenerational connections that it seems many young people value (in this study at least). Thus, one implication of this study is that an answer to "how can we engage young people?" is not to engage them as young people, with distinct needs and interests, but rather to treat them as integral and equal members of the religious community.

Likewise, parents who take approaches similar to the white congregations may also want to reconsider whether stressing generational differences is effective. While it can be natural to discuss the ways technological changes in recent decades have changed social interactions, youth value intergenerational connection across these changes (Boyd 2014). For example, in my own research, I find that intergenerational understanding is facilitated by focusing on how technology affects all generations similarly, such as through pressures to be "always on" and navigating setting healthy boundaries around the ability to be connected continually online. Thus, one implication of this study is that an answer to "how can we help young people emerge into religiously and spiritually mature leaders?" is to relate with them as people sharing the same culture, the same technology changes, but with distinct skills and experiences given their generational histories in relation to cultural and technological changes. Engaging in bidirectional learning about the strategies youth and their elders employ to navigate these changes could provide a helpful approach to integration that shifts away from highlighting generational distinctions toward finding common ground.

3. Youth Religiosity, Counter-Culturally

In contrast to the American culture of religiosity as mainstream and in slow decline across generations, the religiosity in China has been increasing. Wang, in Chapter 2 of this volume, reports that the number of religious affiliates in China increased sixfold in a mere two decades, with a sizable increase among young people (Wang 2016). This study sought answers to "What propels young people to begin religious attendance or affiliation?" To investigate that question, the study focused on a university town, which has a number of Christian campus groups increasing exposure to religiosity for young Chinese students. Despite these efforts, the vast majority of students studied still report having "no faith." Many of the college students surveyed reported gaining exposure to Christianity, but this did not readily convert to knowledge of or interest in learning about religion.

In that mostly atheist cultural context, one of the greatest correlates of knowing about Christianity was having friends who were Christian, and one of the main ways these college students had friends who were Christian was by participating in campus fellowships. Particularly appealing were fellowship activities that provided opportunities to experience Christian culture, and be around people who are Christian, without requirements to participate in religious rituals. One of the implications of this finding for religious and spiritual leaders is that missionary work in this Chinese college town appears to be most effective when provided in a relaxing and inviting space that allows fellow students to congregate with each other and discuss Christianity without the high-stakes for participation being immediate involvement in religious rituals. More generally, another implication of this study is a caution against over-generalizing dramatic religious increases. Increases in religiosity are not uniform across China, nor across different age cohorts. In this case of college students in an urban area, religious exposure has increased at a significantly higher rate than religious affiliation or participation. However, it is possible that religiosity may be in its early phases, beginning first with exposure and perhaps later leading to further engagement.

4. Emerging Adult Religiosity, Subculturally

In Chapter 3, Jeung, Esaki, and Liu study the religiosity of Chinese and Japanese American young adults (Jeung et al. 2015). Rather than explaining change in religious affiliation, this study sought to understand persistence in disaffiliation. Challenging the belief and belonging paradigm, the researchers of this study question whether the terms religion and belief aptly describe the kinds of spiritual activities in which Chinese and Japanese have traditionally engaged, which focus instead on rituals and relations. The Asian Americans in this study were found not to report high levels of belief in God and other religious concepts, but they did report belief in supernatural forces, such as spiritual energy within physical objects and persistence of ancestral spirits. Likewise, while few of the Chinese and Japanese Americans reported praying regularly, many reported having shrines at home and celebrating religious holidays such as Christmas and Lunar New Year.

Thus, one implication of this study is that the rise of religious nones in the U.S. could be, at least in part, due to a misinterpretation. Some American subcultures have a long-standing tradition of disaffiliation, and the representation of these groups among millennial Americans could lead some to conclude religious decline, where in fact merely religious difference exists. For those whose ancestry is from China, religion was regulated, leaving atheism as the dominant belief system. More generally, the word religion in Asia can be associated with colonization by westerners, especially in Japan where it was through military enforcement that Christians were allowed to be missionaries. When peering beneath the surface of the superimposed categories that religious affiliation implies, spiritual rituals are evident, and these rituals are akin to the religious practices of Asian religions. Many seemingly religious "nones" then, at least in this case among young Japanese and Chinese Americans, are in fact quite spiritual in ways that could also be understood to be religious.

Considering that Millennials represent the most diverse generation alive to date, with the highest rate of foreign-born population alive in the U.S., this study indicates that part of detecting a decline in religiosity among this younger cohort may rather be an indication of the way religiosity is expressed. As identified in the introduction, it seems that for the subcultural groups of this study that religiosity is expressed in less formal ways, with an emphasis on spiritual rituals rather than affiliation with a particular religious denomination. Yet the contours of this finding would likely still be missed by a dichotomous understanding of "spiritual but not religious," as in fact many of these rituals are akin to practices for traditional non-western religions. One implication then is that studying the religiosity and spirituality of Millennials may require more nuanced understandings of what "counts" as religious ritual, spiritual practice, belief and belonging. Perhaps a move from religion to faith may better tap the real beliefs and practices of the disaffiliated—who seem to be religious "nones," but who may not be entirely disaffiliated when properly understood.

For religious and spiritual leaders, one implication is the need to attend to the hybridized rituals and belief systems in which youth engage. Beginning from a Western and Christo-centric understanding of what counts as religion may miss the more nuanced ways that young people engage in religiosity and spirituality. Rather than assuming that disaffiliated means "unchurched," it is best with this diverse generation to ask and understand first. The questions need to cover more of a range than service attendance and prayer and can begin from inquiry into what holds meaning, what rituals are practiced because they are valued as transcending routine and everyday experiences. Then one can ask why these rituals hold meaning, from where those beliefs come from, and ultimately can gain a sense of a richer faith life than many typical religious categories convey.

5. Youth and Emerging Adult Religiosity, Institutionally

The fourth chapter of this volume presents results of a study that McCallion, Ligas, and Seroka conducted on youth ministry within the Archdiocese of Detroit. After documenting the history of decline in investment within the Catholic Church for youth ministry, these scholars state that: "one major issue confronting religious institutions is who will fill future leadership roles" (McCallion et al. 2016, p. 3). This can become a confounding effect, as many current church leaders report that they became interested in ministry because a religious leader affected and invited them. Moreover, youth and emerging adulthood are key developmental time periods in which to establish vocational commitment, yet youth and college ministry are under-supported. This raises numerous concerns for the continuation of religious institutions among younger generations.

In response, the Archdiocese of Detroit prioritized youth and young adult ministry as a top objective. However, the institutional analysis of this study reveals problems with the actualization of this goal. For one, the number of youth ministers has not grown substantially, and many remain employed only as part-time employees. Two, the salaries paid to youth ministers are the lowest of all the ministry employees. Three, interviews with youth ministers indicate that they do not feel supported institutionally in their mission to form youth and young adults. This lack of support extends beyond meager salaries to other infrastructural issues, such as not having access to up-to-date technology to engage youth. Youth ministers also reported feeling marginalized.

When interviewed, pastors spoke about the major obstacles preventing further engagement with youth and young adults. The number one response given was money, and not enough of it. Pastors also described how the sexual abuse scandals of the Church have diminished their connections with youth, and entered distrust into their relationships, especially from parents. Another primary issue, which mirrors what was found in the white congregations of the first study, is that pastors sometimes cited feeling disconnected from youth, viewing them as having different and relativistic views of life and morality. Some were also disheartened by the declines in participation among teens, reporting that youth prefer to be engaged in other, non-church activities.

More generally, this study provides an example of the decoupling between policy and practice, showing how declaring an objective to be a priority does not mean that institutional infrastructure necessarily changes to support the implementation of this goal. Instead, the support for youth and young adult ministry remains weak in this religious institution, despite the discourse. One implication of this study for religious and spiritual leaders, then, is to implement more than "lip service" to the challenges and opportunities for engaging younger generations in religious institutions. An objective to support youth and young adult ministry requires more than simply stating it is a priority. Cultural change to organizations is challenging, but it is also possible. The key is working through formal policies to informal rules for how things are done. The linchpin between the formal and informal is infrastructural support, and investing in youth ministers who are hired full-time, paid reasonably well, and provided with opportunities to engage with and/or train from other youth minsters is key to success. This ensures that youth ministers are equipped to perform the "one the ground" work to connect with and better engage youth and young adults.

Other implications for religious and spiritual leaders derive from the findings regarding the marginalization of youth ministers. Beyond economic resources alone, most people desire a degree of social status and honor in their work. Especially if pay has to be low, it is important to ensure youth ministers feel valued and esteemed for the services they provide to young people. Moreover, youth ministry has no clear occupational trajectory, no reward system for advancement and promotion. In contemporary society, professionalization is the norm, but the occupation of youth ministry often runs counter to this norm by providing few or no ways in which youth ministers are provided with professionalization opportunities. Thus, it is important for religious and spiritual leaders to recognize the muted career trajectory of youth ministers and to provide professionalization experiences whenever possible. Options include forming a local network of youth ministers who share best practices, sending youth ministers to national conferences and events designed to enhance youth engagement, and lead pastors meeting regularly with youth ministers to mentor them toward career development and fulfillment.

6. Emerging Adult Faith & Morality, Educationally

In Chapter 5, myself, Beadle, Harris, Hood, and Venugopal investigate a college course designed to facilitate moral maturity among emerging adults (Herzog et al. 2016). The class was instructed by Daniel Harris, as the Director of the Tyson Center for Faith and Spirituality in the University of Arkansas Sam M. Walton College of Business. Serving as a mentor to participating students, Harris stimulated emerging adult development through several techniques. One was to describe the changing contexts surrounding youth and emerging adult development, including how a deeper understanding of faith and moral maturity is necessary but not typically supported by cultural contexts. The instructor described examples of how working in religiously and culturally diverse organizational settings can be enriching and also present challenges to workforce dynamics. Rather than placating these cultural and religious diversities, by not acknowledging their existence or participating in the veneer that religious distinctions do not matter in a similar fashion to how being color blind whitewashes real differences, the emerging adults were invited to reflect on real distinctions among cultural beliefs.

In addition, guest speakers visited the class and represented different major faith traditions, including Christian, Hindu, Muslim, and Atheism (also referred to as secular humanism). These guest speakers described the ways their faith undergirded their moral actions at work. For example, a Muslim landlord described how he put his faith before profit in deciding to allow tenants to remain during the economic downturn, despite their being behind in paying rent. Likewise, a Christian described how her faith supported getting through a difficult family challenge that could have otherwise more significantly affected her work life. Emerging adults participating in the class were also asked to read several texts reflecting on the ways faith (in any form) provides meaning and guides moral decision-making. Then students were required to write their top values and to later refine these into a personal mission statement, which they revised in multiple drafts. The culminating assignment was an essay in which students reflected on which aspects of the course impacted them, and about how they think these impacts will affect their future work.

The results of this study—comparing outcomes for participating students to emerging adults who instead completed a traditional ethics course—indicate that this pedagogical approach was effective in raising cultural awareness among students who were otherwise fairly religiously and culturally homogenous. Participating emerging adults gained greater clarity regarding their moral values and how to articulate these in the workforce in ways that would avert conflict, not by avoiding it but by respecting diverse approaches. The implications are that college educators are able to intervene in facilitating moral maturity, even within the relatively late life stage of emerging adulthood. The approach of this course is one that can be replicated in other universities, and also in different social contexts. Religious and spiritual leaders could implement a similar approach within youth ministry approaches, especially those designed to engage college students. Moreover, the implications for parents are that adult role models can impact emerging adults and may be important for their cognitive and moral development. Perhaps these mentors could be parents themselves, and this study indicates that mentors outside the family can also be important.

7. Youth and Emerging Adult Generosity, Informally

In the sixth chapter of this volume, Fernandez, Schnitker, and Houltberg investigate charitable sporting events. The researchers state that information on *how* "adolescents make meaning of their spiritual and religious convictions in real-world contexts affect the development of generosity is an important line of research. This is especially true as changing social norms and ever-developing technology and social media continue to shape upcoming generations in new ways" (Fernandez et al. 2016, p. 1). The scholars theorize that motivations for engaging in generous activities can be religious and moral. The theory is that this occurs through a process of sanctification, in which aspects of life are viewed as having a spiritual significance. Sanctified goals can invoke more effort and satisfaction, and thus participating in an activity, such as a charitable sporting event, which is viewed as sanctified can be more compelling than alternative options. Sanctification and religiosity are not synonymous, as sanctification has to do with deriving meaning and purpose from aspects of life, which is not the same as attending services or praying regularly.

Meaning derives from having a narrative sense of one's identity as fitting together the disparate behaviors, preferences, and desires of one's life into a relatively coherent sense of self. Well-being is associated with meaning, especially when one views one's trajectory in life as growing in positive directions. This generativity is higher when one views their life as achieving a degree of self-transcendence, in contributing to the wellbeing of others. The idea, then, is that participating in charitable sporting events is a way to actualize, to visualize and represent to oneself, that meaningful generativity is achieved. Moreover, participating in such an activity can strengthen sense of belonging to a group and result in positive emotions (such as enjoyment).

Though the model proposed in this chapter is yet untested, there are implications worthy of consideration for religious and spiritual leaders. One is that participation in informal activities could be a way to express religious and spiritual inclinations. Especially for youth and emerging adults who have limited exposure or who are skeptical of organized religion, charitable events that allow for engagement with religious communities outside the context of a congregation can be a way for those interested to explore religiosity with a low initial bar for membership. Rather than investing high effort initially in membership, high effort is instead invested in something deemed to be spiritually worthy, a way of actualizing a willingness to de-prioritize personal benefit (through sacrificing physical exertion) in the service of a generous cause. Having made that initial service contribution, participants may then be more willing to engage within traditionally religious spaces, especially if invited by people with whom they formed a bond during the informal activity.

Hosting charitable sporting events on college campuses could be an especially effective way of engaging emerging adults, who are typically fairly disconnected from religious communities, either during college or throughout the multiple moves instead of college, or after, to find jobs. Moreover, this chapter has implications for the study of faith and spirituality. Would emerging adults who participate in a charitable sporting event due to religious motivations answer yes to having attended a religious service? Likely not. Would they answer yes to having volunteered time not for pay? Also likely not. Would any of the typical religiosity and spirituality questions count this form of engagement? Perhaps, maybe a participant would still rate their faith as important in their daily life. However, rating personal faith as important without social religious events is the recipe for what many scholars have called an individualized form of religiosity, which is purportedly higher among younger generations. The thought behind this chapter raises questions as to whether faith is truly becoming individualized or whether younger generations may be evolving the way that expressions of religiosity occur in social settings. In Christian theology, the Bible says in Matthew 18:20, "For where two or three gather in my name, there I am with them." Perhaps then it is time to broaden the scope of what congregating is deemed to be and consider ways that younger generations can mobilize communities with shared religiosity or spirituality outside a building.

8. Emerging Adult Volunteering, Developmentally

In Chapter 7, DeAngelis, Acevedo, and Xu study secular volunteering among college attending emerging adults in Texas. The researchers state: "Young adults in higher educational settings are often faced with a series of competing interests that motivate and modify behavioral choices in the absence of direct parental supervision. Moreover, it is at this stage of the life course that young adults can go through a process of re-centering wherein they explore their religious identity and formulate and solidify their own religious beliefs in addition to or independent of their familial religious traditions" (DeAngelis et al. 2016, p. 9). The study indicates that childhood religiosity is linked across the life course to volunteering as an emerging adult. The key ingredient for volunteering as an emerging adult is religious participation as a child that is sustained as an emerging adult. Some psychological accounts view internalization of childhood socialization as the primary mechanism by which childhood forms of social participation continue to matter once children transition to adulthood. This study both supports and challenges the notion of recentering by showing that early religious socialization does relate to later volunteering, but only when emerging adults continue to participate in religious activities.

Central to this study is an understanding of private and public forms of religiosity. Private forms of religiosity include beliefs and faith dispositions. Public forms of religiosity include social events, such as participating in religious services or praying in small groups. The psychological notion of recentering theorizes that public forms of religious participation during childhood will matter in adulthood insofar as they are internalized to private forms of religiosity during emerging adulthood. However, sociological accounts theorize that social participation is central to the link between religiosity and volunteering persisting during emerging adulthood. This study indicates the latter account best explains that ongoing social participation in public forms of religiosity is more strongly linked to volunteering as an emerging adult than is private religiosity alone.

More generally, there are implications of this study for both religious leaders and parents. Social learning early in childhood appears to have a lasting effect later in life. Parents and religious leaders can take comfort (or be cautioned) in knowing that their efforts toward socialization appear to "work." However, key to children volunteering as emerging adults is continuing to sustain public forms of religiosity into emerging adulthood. It appears that attending while a child is not enough for sustaining long-term commitment to values, such as contributing time to improve the wellbeing of others. This finding runs counter to thinking of church as the "elementary school of morals," which many emerging adults (and their parents) have reported in my own research.

Often times the cultural perception of religiosity is that it is good to be exposed while young, but once the message is understood it is to many unclear why continued and regular religious engagement is necessary. "I got it" is the sense that many emerging adults in the National Study of Youth and Religion relayed in interviews. Akin to ongoing lessons in multiplication, the idea is that seems unnecessary once the lesson is learned. However, this study reveals a contour to religiosity that highlights its distinction from other lessons learned in childhood. Unlike multiplication, it takes concerted effort to maintain a commitment to contributing to the wellbeing of others, especially in the midst of the many and competing time commitments of college life. Exposure during childhood seems to be necessary but not sufficient in the recipe of ongoing volunteering, with the remainder of the ingredients including continued engagement in religious communities.

These findings could be good news or bad news for parents. Some parents like the idea of dropping their child off to Sunday school for several years during childhood and then shifting attention to sports and other activities as children age. I have heard that reported in multiple interviews with emerging adults thinking about what their future religious socialization of their children will be, and I have also heard it reported by the parents of youth participating in youth ministry activities in religious congregations of many denominations. In that case, this study presents some bad news, as the implications are that more effort may need to be exerted beyond those early years to continue commitment to religiosity and to its values, such as volunteering, beyond elementary school years.

The good news is that there seems to be a relatively simple and practical outcome of this study. This is unlike the many studies investigating religiosity, which describe and explain the puzzle of declines in public forms of religiosity with persistence in private religiosity, leaving concerned readers with no sense of what can be done. For parents who want children to continue religious values into emerging adulthood and beyond, and for religious and spiritual leaders who work tirelessly to socialize youth into their religion, it can be disconcerting (at best) to know that many of the religious and generous activities socialized in childhood diminish over time. As an alternative, this study provides some hope to those interested in sustaining commitment to religious values, that there are some lasting effects for participating in generous activities such as volunteering. Many parents could take heed and advise their emerging adults to make the effort to get to service.

9. Youth Faith & Giving, Developmentally

In the eighth and final chapter of this volume, myself and Mitchell investigate the intergenerational transmission of religious giving among parents and youth who participate in religious youth groups (Herzog and Mitchell 2016). We asked: How do religious youth learn to give? Informed by prior studies, we viewed parents to be an integral part of learning to give to religious organizations, which we know from other studies is also associated with giving to non-religious charitable causes. From our in-depth interviews with parents, we identified nine approaches to teaching giving: (1) modeling giving by donating in children's presence; (2) providing money to children to give; (3) handing giving envelopes to children to place in donation baskets and plates; (4) teaching children to give through conversations about the importance of giving; (5) providing positive reinforcement to children for giving; (6) encouraging, expecting, or forcing giving; (7) a method called give, save, spend which explicitly categorizes a portion of children's money (such as allowances) for spending, a portion for saving, and a portion for giving; (8) describing giving of time as an alternative to donating money; and (9) emphasizing fiscal responsibility generally, in which giving was one part of a broader attention to finance discussions.

Viewing several of these methods as sharing in common their basic approach, we categorize these teaching styles into those that (a) model giving; (b) talk about the importance of giving; and (c) direct children to give. Of these, modeling methods were the most common across the different religious traditions included in this study, which consisted of a mainline Protestant church, an evangelical Protestant church, and a black Protestant church. Talking about giving did not differ across religious traditions but did differ in the gender of the parent, with fathers more often describing talking about giving than mothers. Directing methods for teaching giving were more common at the evangelical and black Protestant churches than they were at the mainline Protestant church. That was also a method employed more by mothers than fathers, and it was more common among those with lower incomes than those with higher incomes. Perhaps the most relevant finding of this study for parents and religious leaders is that the most common way to teach giving was to have a "diversified portfolio" of approaches, combining multiple methods.

In a rather unique study design, we also interviewed the youth of these parents and were able to analyze youth responses in relation to parent responses. Thus, unlike studies focusing on one or the other group, or which aggregate responses across groups, this study allowed us to see what the effect of different parental approaches appeared to be. Most studies employing this approach study youth and parents in laboratory experiments, which provide a greater ability to tease apart other explanations for cause and effect relationships. However, it is often unclear in those studies what, if any, bearing those findings have in the real world, once research participants leave the laboratory and resume everyday experiences. The approach of our study instead has greater strength in applying to everyday life, but readers should keep in mind that it is not possible in this approach to isolate the many other factors that could be related to the causes and effect patterns. In other words, the outcomes for youth could be due to other factors beyond the parent teaching approaches, such as socialization within religious settings or by religious friends. But that was not too concerning for us, since other studies indicate that those forms of religious socialization are also influenced by parents. We thus view those to be an extension of parental teaching methods and, in research terms, do not understand them to be spurious to the findings of this study.

In interviewing youth, it was apparent that many youth do not regularly talk about giving. While they were articulate about other topics, giving discussions often consisted of one-word responses that treated giving as a fairly obvious and simple topic. Some youth were somewhat confused about how to talk about giving, described it as a feeling (such as "I feel good about giving"), or positioned the discussion about giving in the hypothetical (such as "If I were to give."). Overall, we did not find a high degree of articulateness about giving and were generally surprised by the low degree of alignment between the thoughtfulness of the parent interviewees and the seeming inattentiveness of the youth interviewees. However, upon further inspection we discovered something else unexpected, which we called a "delayed onset of giving." When we interviewed the parents about how they learned to give, many of them described having been taught by their parents to give but then had that essentially lay dormant until some later point in their adulthood when their inclination to give was personally triggered.

As with the study in the seventh chapter, then, we also see implications that the recentering process of emerging adulthood is important, understanding that social learning becomes internalized and activated for adults. It seems that adult religious givers were taught to give during childhood, but did not form their own understanding of or personal motivation for giving until some later point in their life course when the inclination to give was triggered. Taking a developmental approach to giving means viewing socialization into generous activities as situated within a dynamic process of changes across the life course. We do not have sophisticated longitudinal data in this study, which track changes over time and follow the same group of parents and youth as they age. That limits what we can know conclusively. Yet, if we take people mostly at their word and as relatively decent reporters of what is actually true in their cases, then it seems that giving as an adult is linked to (a) being taught to give as a child and (b) having some trigger that internalizes giving as an adult. Combining that with findings of the previous chapter, the implication is also that experiences during childhood continue to have lasting effects and that ongoing religious participation into adulthood appears to be key in activating childhood learning.

One implication of this study for parents is that it is important to teach youth about giving. Parents often express that youth do not listen to them and generally tend to undervalue the effect they have on their children. This study provides parents with a way to think more critically about that perspective, and to consider the ways that parenting does not always result in an immediate and visible indication of effects in youth, but can lay important foundation for later activity. For religious and spiritual leaders, an implication of this study is that parents are an important part of laying the foundation for religious giving and may need encouragement and teaching about how to transmit their values for generosity to their children. Another implication for both parents and religious leaders is that it appears having a diversified portfolio of parental teaching methods is a common, and potentially effective, way to teach youth to give. In essence, there does not seem to be a "one size fits all" approach that is the panacea for teaching giving. Rather, parents can model giving, talk about giving, and direct youth to give, knowing that these efforts are likely to pay off later in their life course. Yet, another implication is that it is important to support ongoing religious participation as a way to later trigger that childhood socialization.

10. Conclusions

In summary, the scholars in this volume find youth and emerging adults to be socially influenced by their organizational, institutional, and developmental contexts. Religiosity and spirituality are in part socially constructed processes. This is not be overstated, to the detriment of recognizing the personal agency that youth and emerging adults have in navigating their faith and giving activities. Yet, given that American culture heavily emphasizes the role of individuals in shaping life outcomes, it is important to balance this with a counter cultural understanding that highlights the ways in which youth and emerging adults are affected by social participation.

Collectively, we find organizational differences in youth religious socialization, and we find ongoing development in response to religious stimuli as emerging adults. In addition, several of these studies complicate popular conceptions of Millennials as generally uninterested in religious participation. Instead, we find many non-traditional, but still social, ways of expressing religiosity. For example, participating in a charitable sporting event, having a shrine visible in households to venerate ancestors, or volunteering while in college. Perhaps the rise of religiously disaffiliated among Millennials may be an artifact of greater diversity in religious expressions, a caution to employing Western notions of what "counts" as religiosity, such as service attendance alone.

We also find that understanding youth disengagement from religion requires turning an eye toward the agents of socialization, revealing that weak infrastructural support for youth ministry may be part of the cause, as could be an orientation to youth that pits them as distinct from adults, such that their ministry is segregated from the broader religious community. Taken together, these studies indicate a need to study life course effects on adult outcomes, by investigating longitudinal data. This is a task I turn to in a forthcoming book that studies inequalities in the ways youth transition into adulthood and investigates the roles that religiosity and spirituality relate to these adulthood pathways (Herzog 2017). In addition, more studies are needed. Having listened to the practice-based knowledge of laypeople, with innovative ways of theorizing and studying faith and giving, and taken an inclusive approach, we contribute new insights worthy of further study.

Acknowledgments: The author thanks numerous youth and emerging adults for informing the research in this volume, including: Nick Bloom, Scott Mitchell, Robbee Wedow, Kaitlyn Conway, Molly Kiernan, Jessica Technow, Marie Sanchez, Josh Cook, Chris Gonzales, Scott Hurley, Molly Kring, Michelle Saucedo, Michael Thompson, Allsion VanderBroek, Janice James, Jennifer Jesse, Caitlin Smith, Zanaib Shipchandler, Xiannan Lu, Gabriel David, and Mark Trainer, Christina Williams, DeAndre' Beadle, Tiffany Miller, Tatianna Balis, Sanjana Vengupal, Bryn Smernoff, Tasmiah Amreen, Elizabeth Word, Jada Holmes, Camille Wildburger, Emma Thompson, April Moore, Grant King, Connor Thompson, Seth Washispack, Randi Combs, Carrie Nelms, Angela Cox, James Brown, Stephanie Collier, Chao Liu, Ashley Wagner, and Josh Cafferty.

Conflicts of Interest: The author declares no conflict of interest.

References

Boyd, Danah. 2014. *It's Complicated: The Social Lives of Networked Teens*. New Haven: Yale University Press.

DeAngelis, Reed T., Gabriel A. Acevedo, and Xiaohe Xu. 2016. Secular Volunteerism among Texan Emerging Adults: Exploring Pathways of Childhood and Adulthood Religiosity. *Religions* 7: article 74. [CrossRef]

Fernandez, Nathaniel A., Sarah A. Schnitker, and Benjamin J. Houltberg. 2016. Charitable Sporting Events as a Context for Building Adolescent Generosity: Examining the Role of Religiousness and Spirituality. *Religions* 7: 1–13. [CrossRef]

Herzog, Patricia Snell. 2017. *Pathways to Adulthood: Emerging Adults in Contemporary Society*. Oxford: Oxford University Press, forthcoming.

Herzog, Patricia Snell, and Scott Mitchell. 2016. Intergenerational Transmission of Religious Giving: Instilling Giving Habits across the Life Course. *Religions* 7: article 93. [CrossRef]

Herzog, Patricia Snell, De Andre' T. Beadle, Daniel E. Harris, Tiffany E. Hood, and Sanjana Venugopal. 2016. Moral and Cultural Awareness in Emerging Adulthood: Preparing for Multi-Faith Workplaces. *Religions* 7: article 40. [CrossRef]

Jeung, Russell, Brett Essaki, and Alice Liu. 2015. Redefining Religious Nones: Lessons from Chinese and Japanese American Young Adults. *Religions* 6: 891–911. [CrossRef]

McCallion, Michael, John Ligas, and George Seroka. 2016. An Institutional and Status Analysis of Youth Ministry in the Archdiocese of Detroit. *Religions* 7: article 48. [CrossRef]

Wang, Chao. 2016. College Students' Attitudes toward Christianity in Xi'an, China. *Religions* 7: article 58. [CrossRef]

Williams, Rhys H., Courtney A. Irby, and R. Stephen Warner. 2016. 'Church' in Black and White: The Organizational Lives of Young Adults. *Religions* 7: article 90. [CrossRef]

MDPI

St. Alban-Anlage 66

4052 Basel, Switzerland

Tel. +41 61 683 77 34

Fax +41 61 302 89 18

http://www.mdpi.com

Religions Editorial Office

E-mail: religions@mdpi.com

http://www.mdpi.com/journal/religions

www.ingramcontent.com/pod-product-compliance
Lightning Source LLC
Chambersburg PA
CBHW051315020426
42333CB00028B/3343